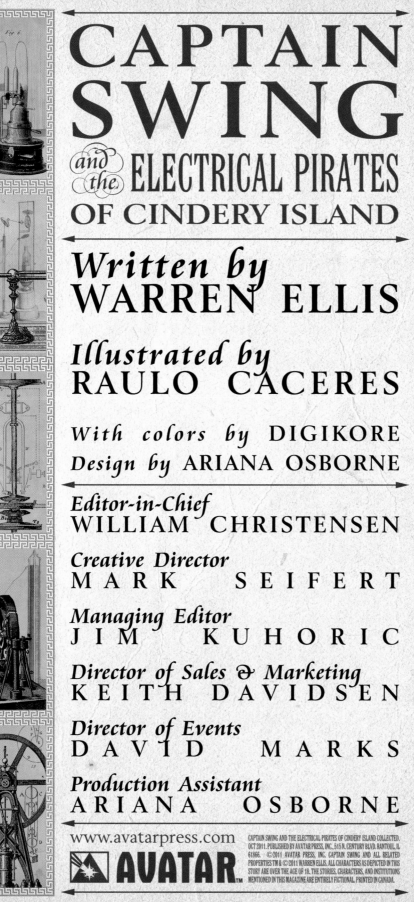
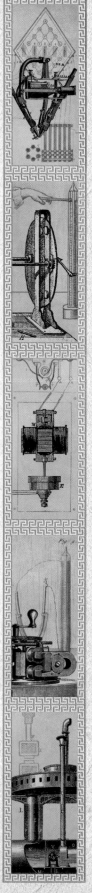

CAPTAIN SWING
and the ELECTRICAL PIRATES
OF CINDERY ISLAND

Written by
WARREN ELLIS

Illustrated by
RAULO CACERES

With colors by DIGIKORE
Design by ARIANA OSBORNE

Editor-in-Chief
WILLIAM CHRISTENSEN

Creative Director
MARK SEIFERT

Managing Editor
JIM KUHORIC

Director of Sales & Marketing
KEITH DAVIDSEN

Director of Events
DAVID MARKS

Production Assistant
ARIANA OSBORNE

www.avatarpress.com

AVATAR™

CAPTAIN SWING AND THE ELECTRICAL PIRATES OF CINDERY ISLAND COLLECTED.
OCT 2011. PUBLISHED BY AVATAR PRESS, INC., 515 N. CENTURY BLVD. RANTOUL, IL
61866. ©2011 AVATAR PRESS, INC. CAPTAIN SWING AND ALL RELATED
PROPERTIES TM & ©2011 WARREN ELLIS. ALL CHARACTERS AS DEPICTED IN THIS
STORY ARE OVER THE AGE OF 18. THE STORIES, CHARACTERS, AND INSTITUTIONS
MENTIONED IN THIS MAGAZINE ARE ENTIRELY FICTIONAL. PRINTED IN CANADA.

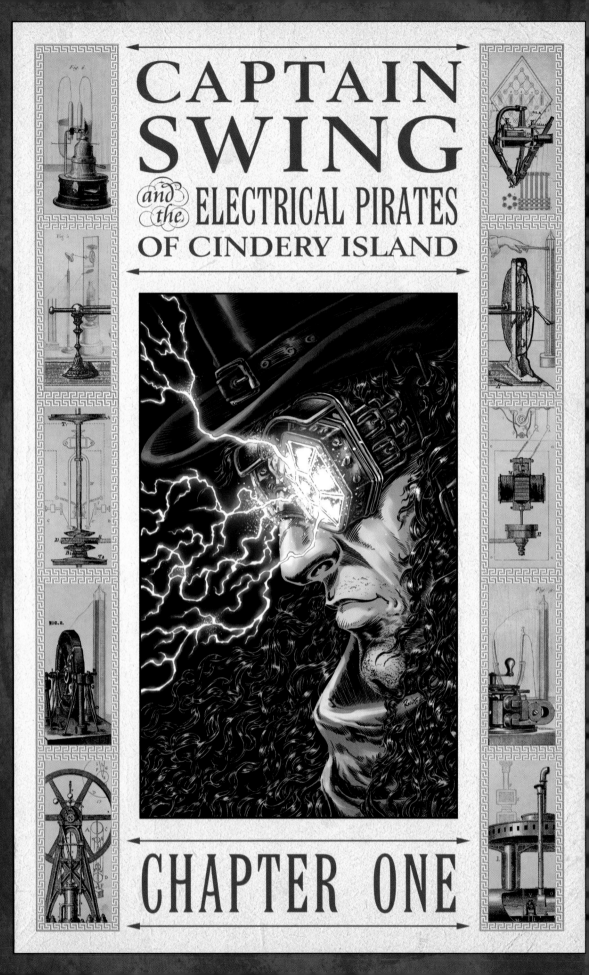

CAPTAIN SWING

and the ELECTRICAL PIRATES OF CINDERY ISLAND

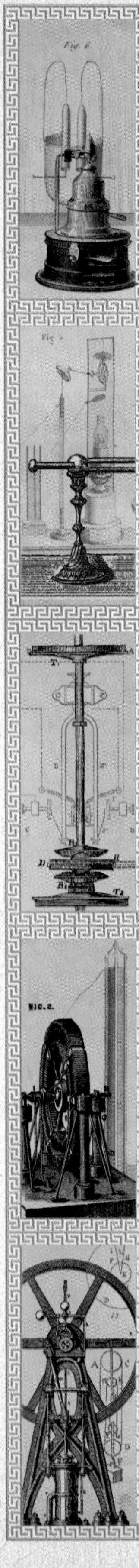

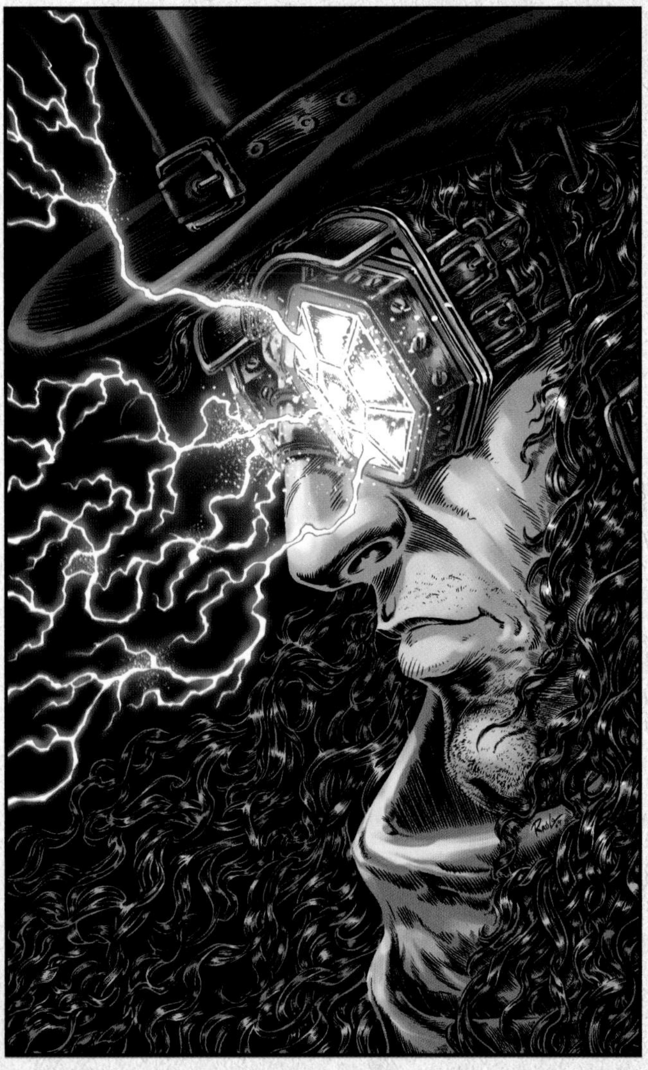

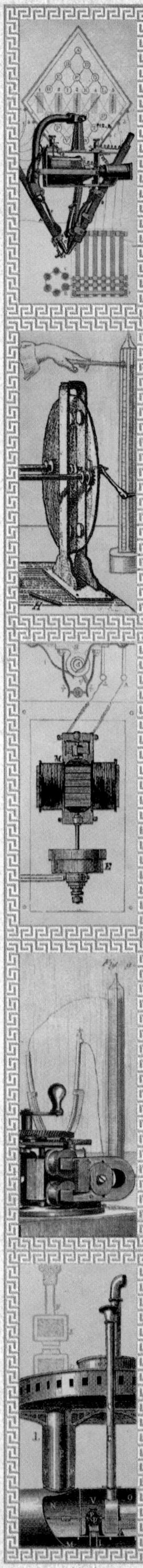

CHAPTER ONE

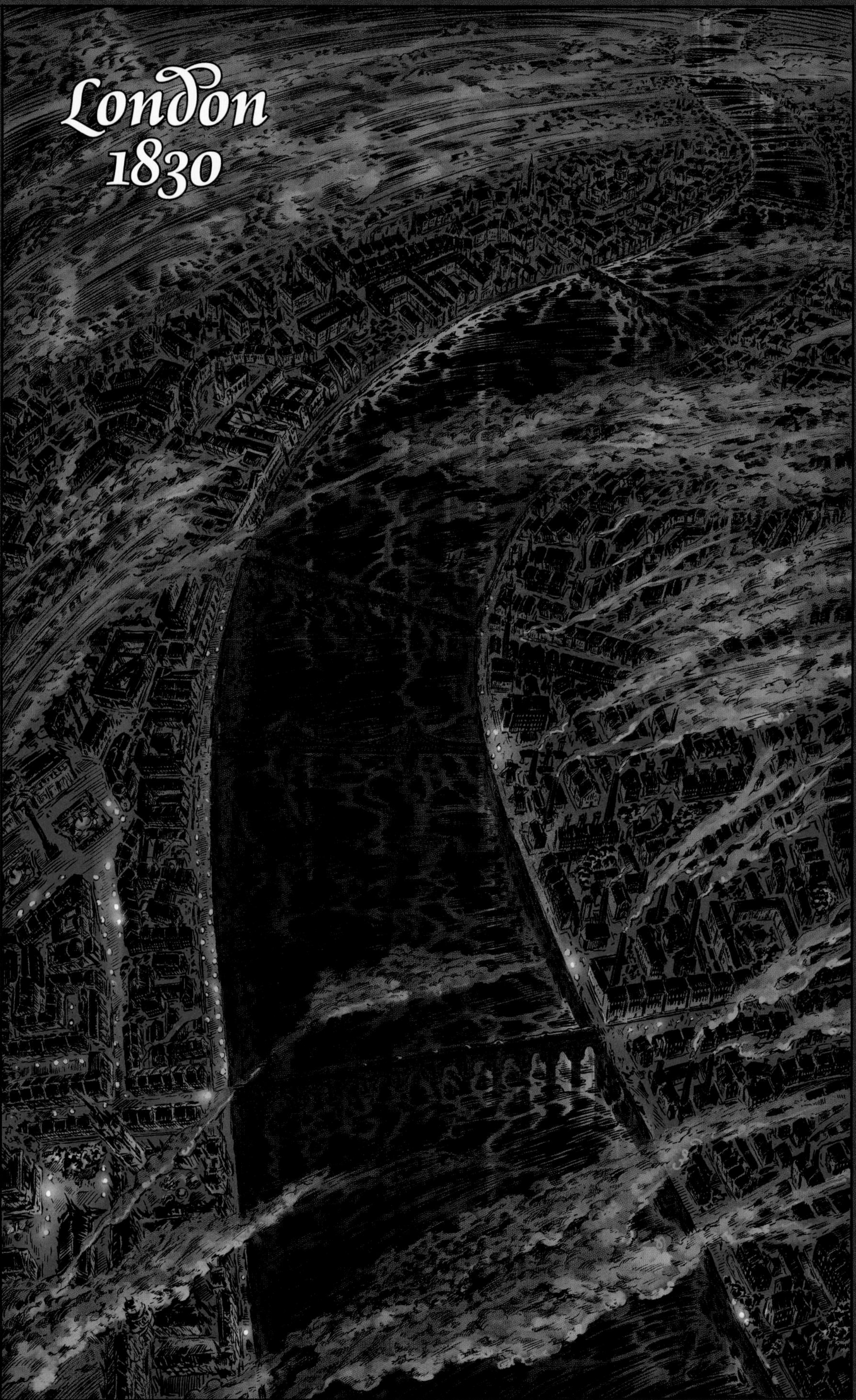
London
1830

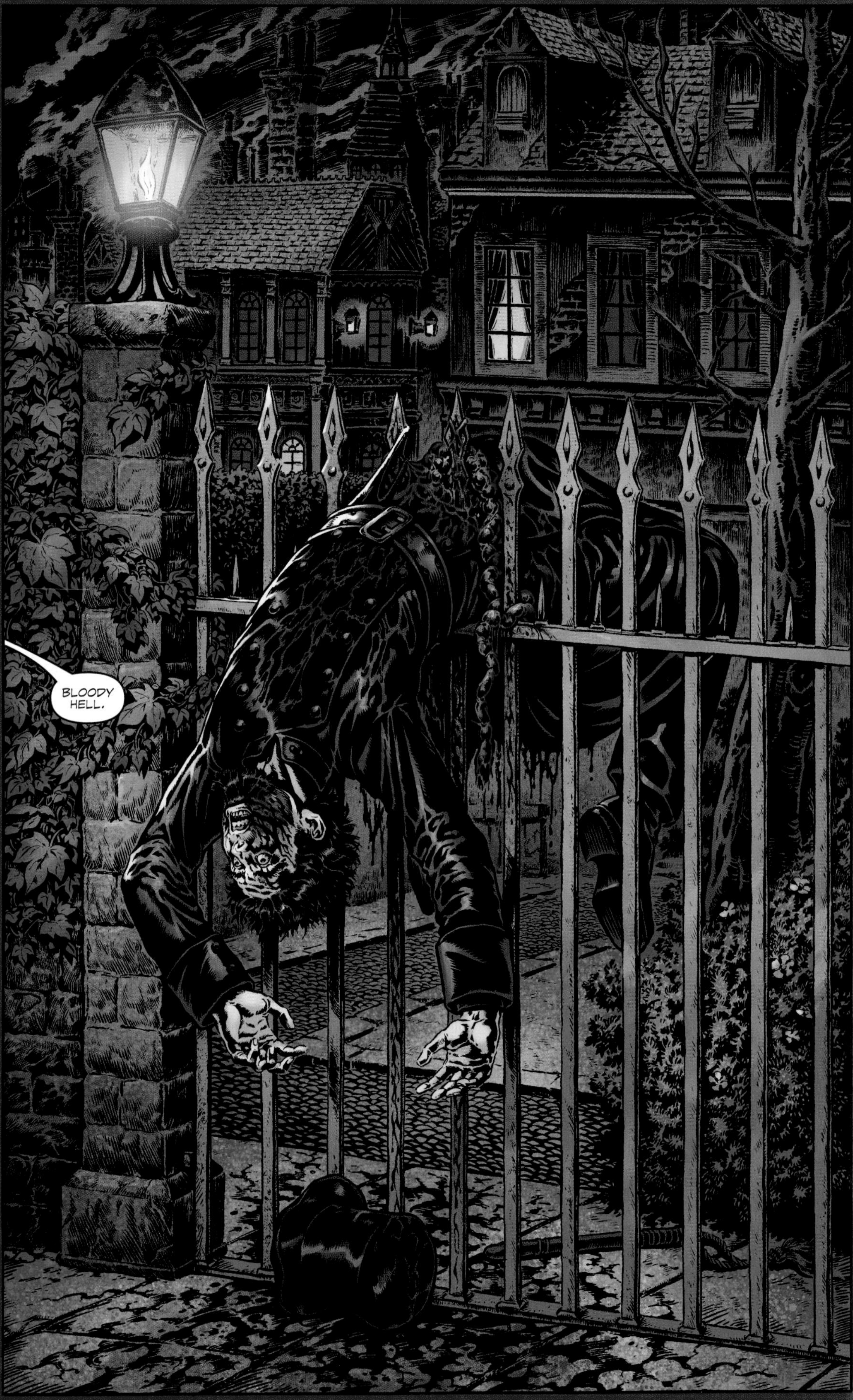
BLOODY HELL.

In 1830, there are three thousand three hundred men on the strength of the London Metropolitan Police. However, "that notwithstanding the police was said to be so good, the people would not in many cases give up their private watchmen." (HANSARD, 1830.) Known as Peelers or Bobbies after the founder of the force, Sir Robert Peel. Peel may well have said they were good, but the Met in 1830 was a shambolic outfit, containing so many wasters and drunks that the very first man on the force was sacked after four hours for being so pissed that he couldn't walk.

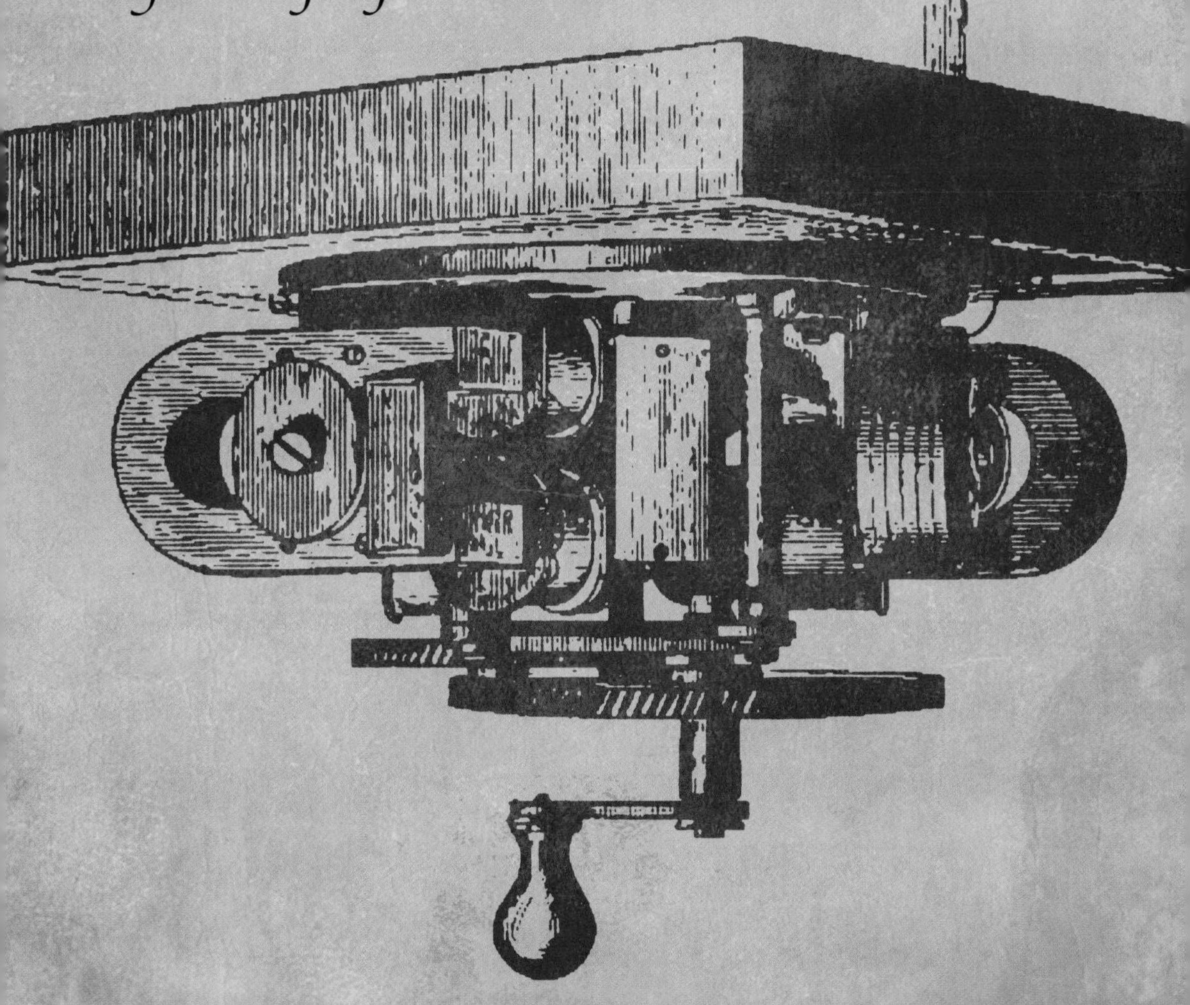

Three years from now, PC Bob Culley will be stabbed during a riot, and his murderer acquitted on a justifiable homicide defense: because the victim was a Peeler.

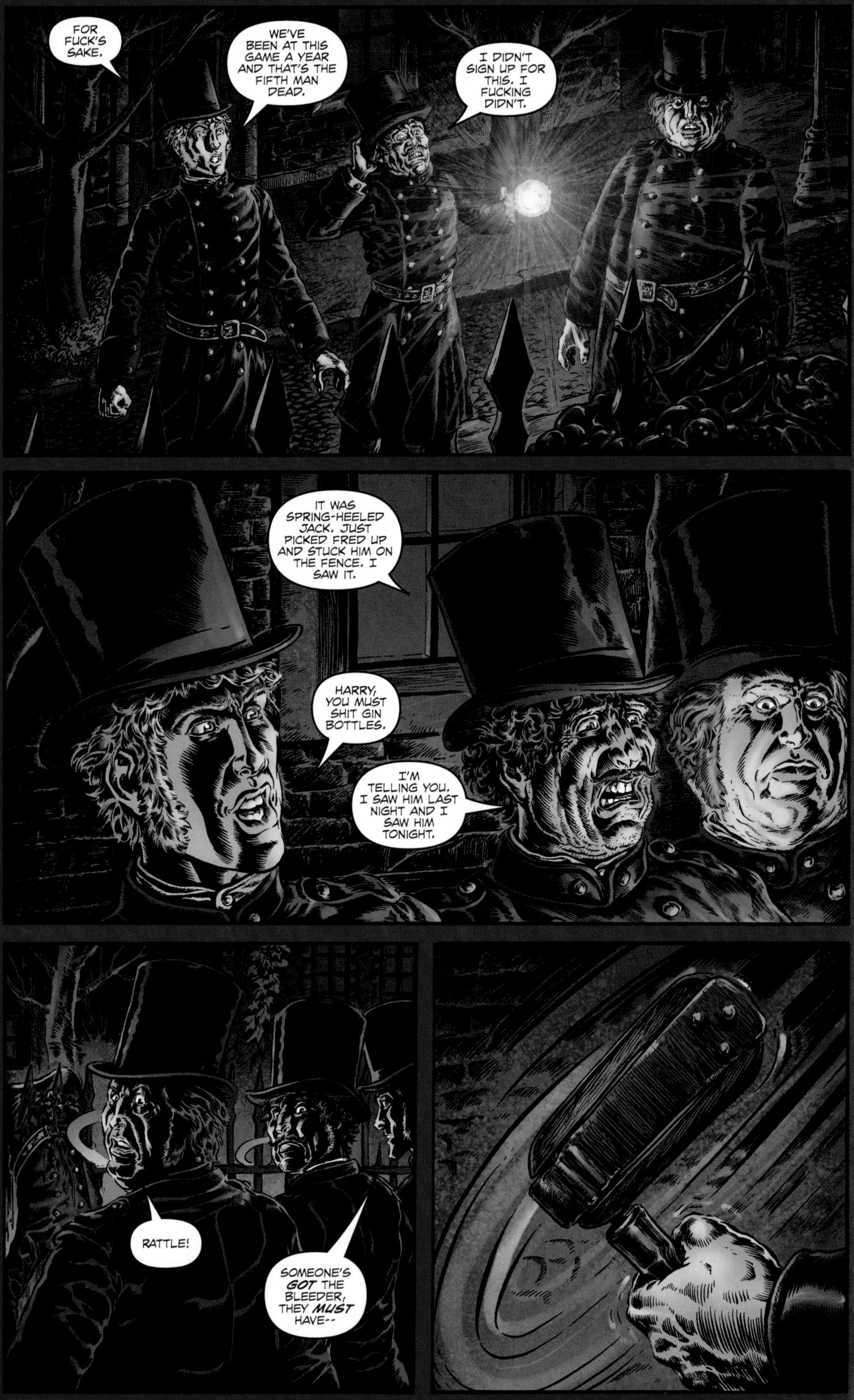
FOR FUCK'S SAKE.
WE'VE BEEN AT THIS GAME A YEAR AND THAT'S THE FIFTH MAN DEAD.
I DIDN'T SIGN UP FOR THIS. I FUCKING DIDN'T.
IT WAS SPRING-HEELED JACK. JUST PICKED FRED UP AND STUCK HIM ON THE FENCE. I SAW IT.
HARRY, YOU MUST SHIT GIN BOTTLES.
I'M TELLING YOU. I SAW HIM LAST NIGHT AND I SAW HIM TONIGHT.
RATTLE!
SOMEONE'S *GOT* THE BLEEDER, THEY *MUST* HAVE--

The equipment of a Metropolitan policeman was primitive. This is in the year that Mars was first mapped and the first intercity rail line opened, you understand: a hard top hat that could be used as a step, a long coat with stiff high collars to fend off a garotte, a wooden truncheon, and a rattle to raise an alarm and summon assistance. No guns. If you were a mounted officer, you might get a sword.

The Bow Street Runners, the precursor to London police who were run by magistrates (who hated the Peelers because the Peelers didn't answer to magistrates), were under no such restrictions. But their time was fading.

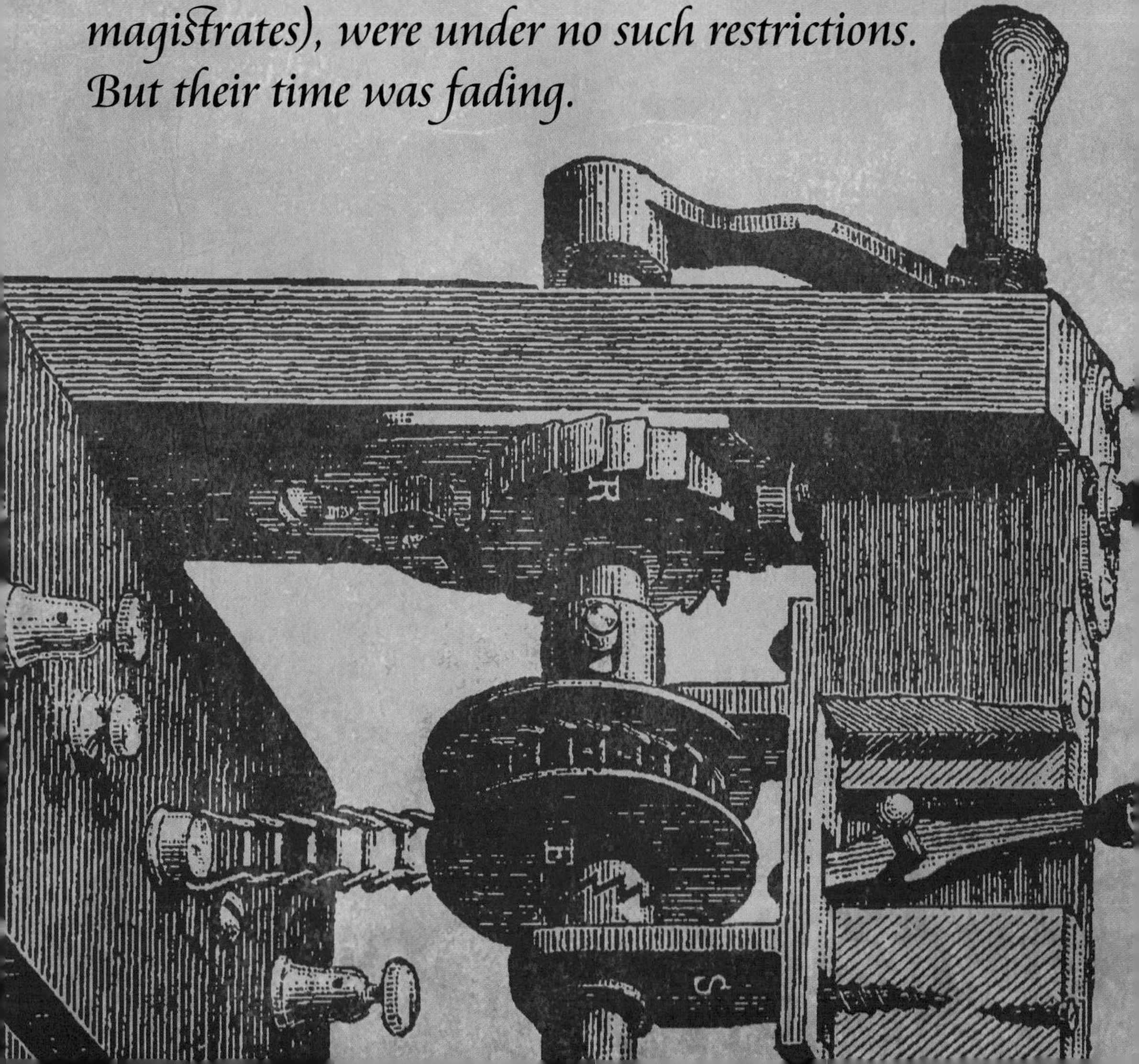

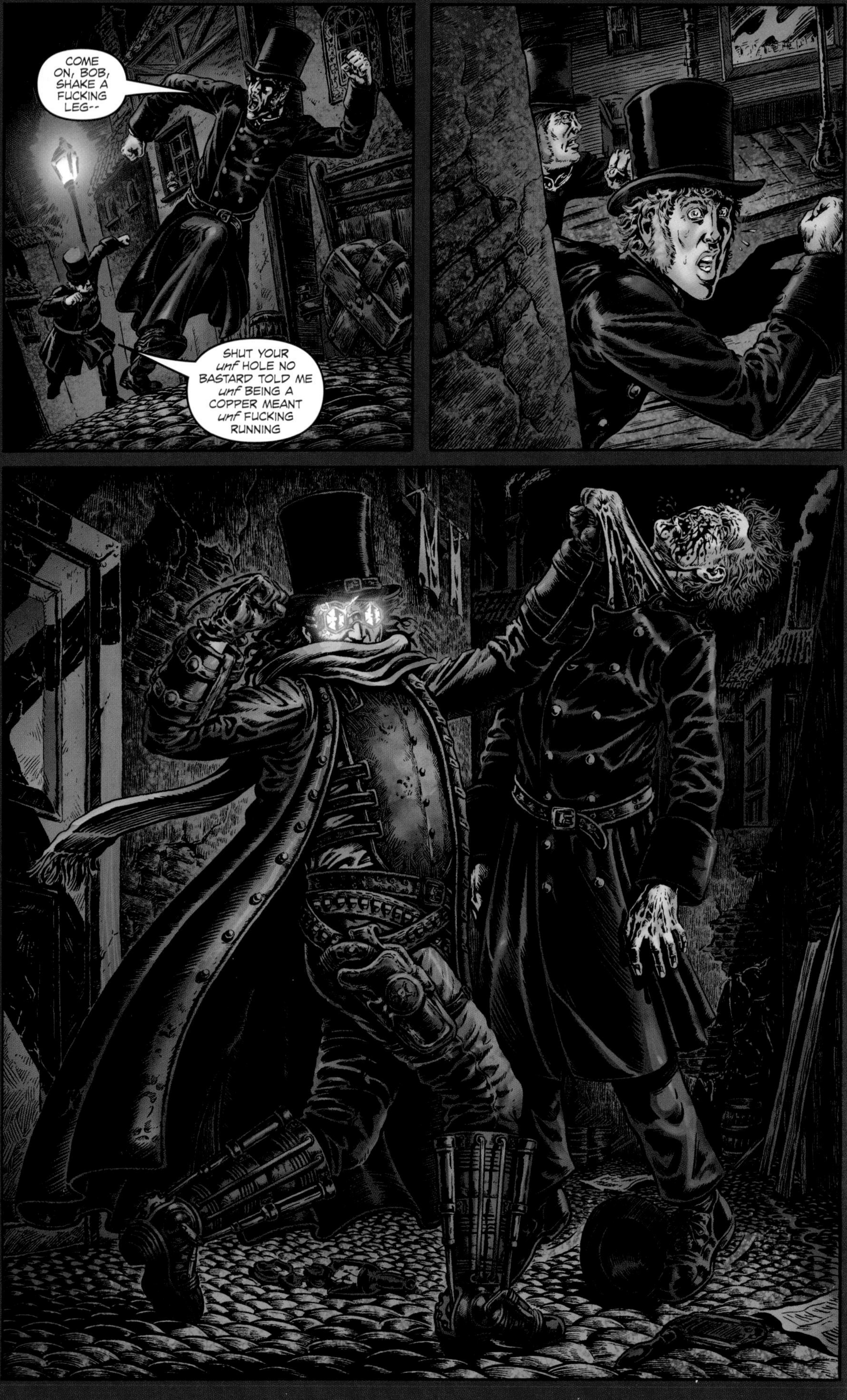
COME ON, BOB, SHAKE A FUCKING LEG--
SHUT YOUR *unf* HOLE NO BASTARD TOLD ME *unf* BEING A COPPER MEANT *unf* FUCKING RUNNING

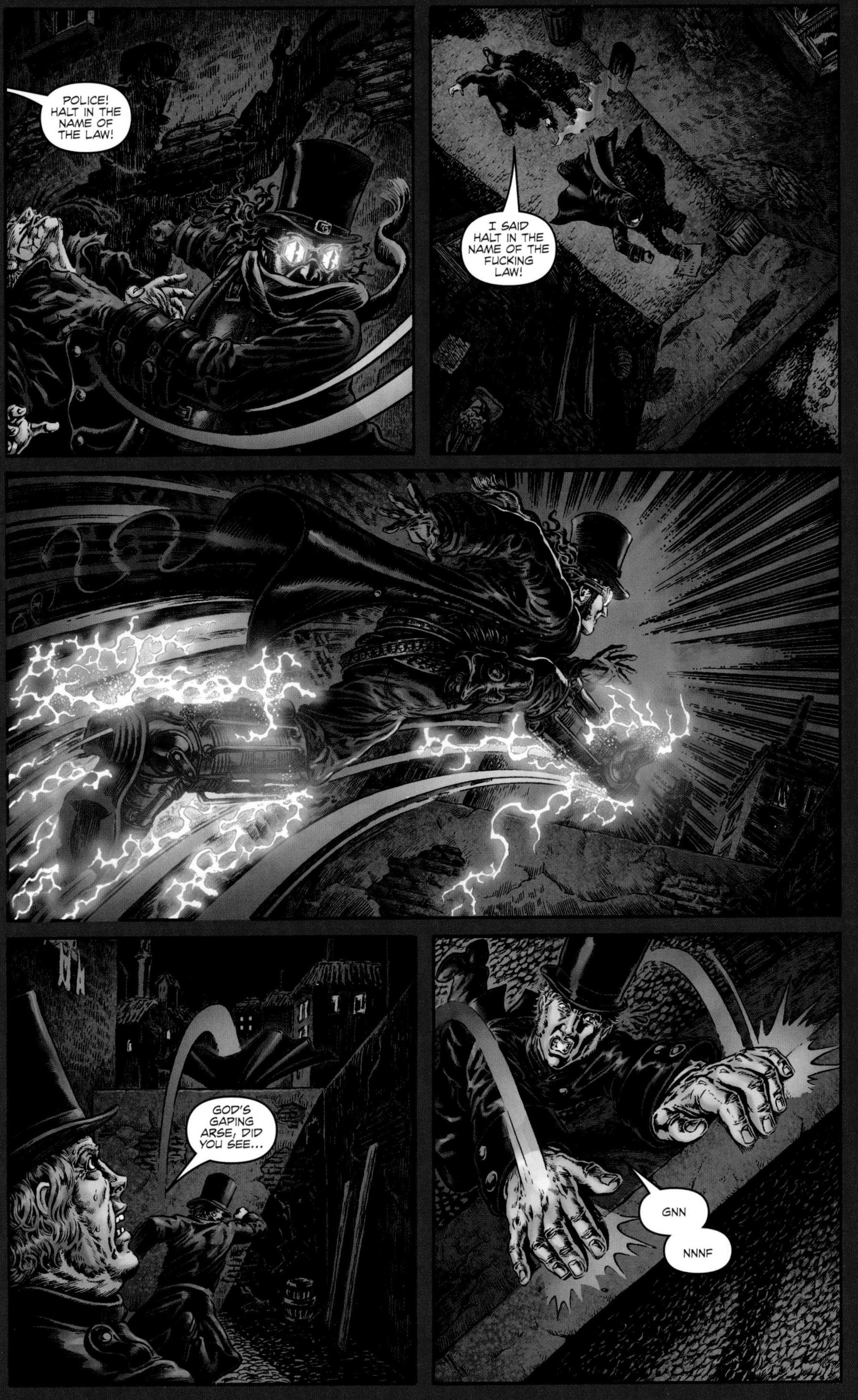
POLICE! HALT IN THE NAME OF THE LAW!
I SAID HALT IN THE NAME OF THE FUCKING LAW!
GOD'S GAPING ARSE, DID YOU SEE...
GNN
NNNF

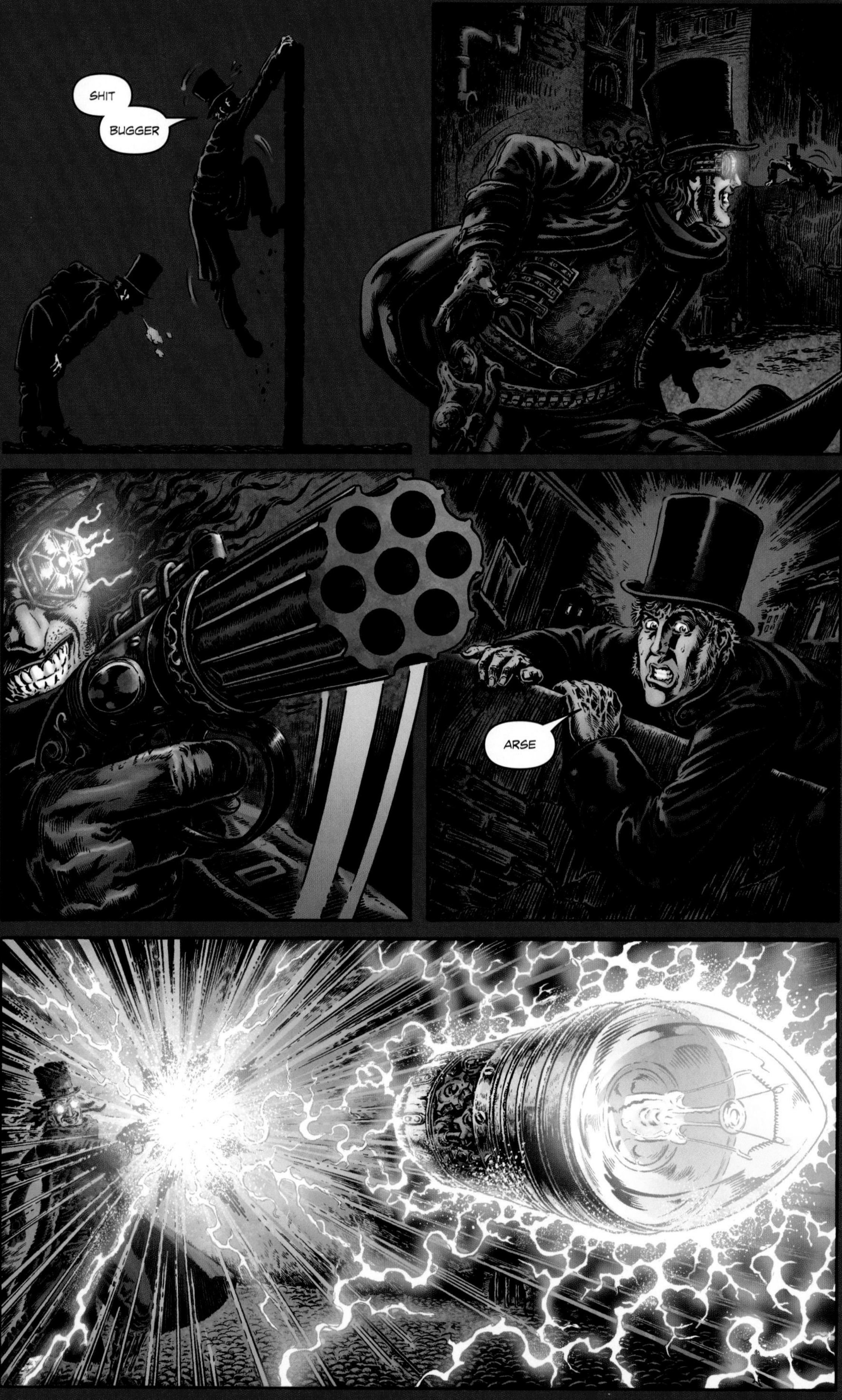
SHIT
BUGGER
ARSE

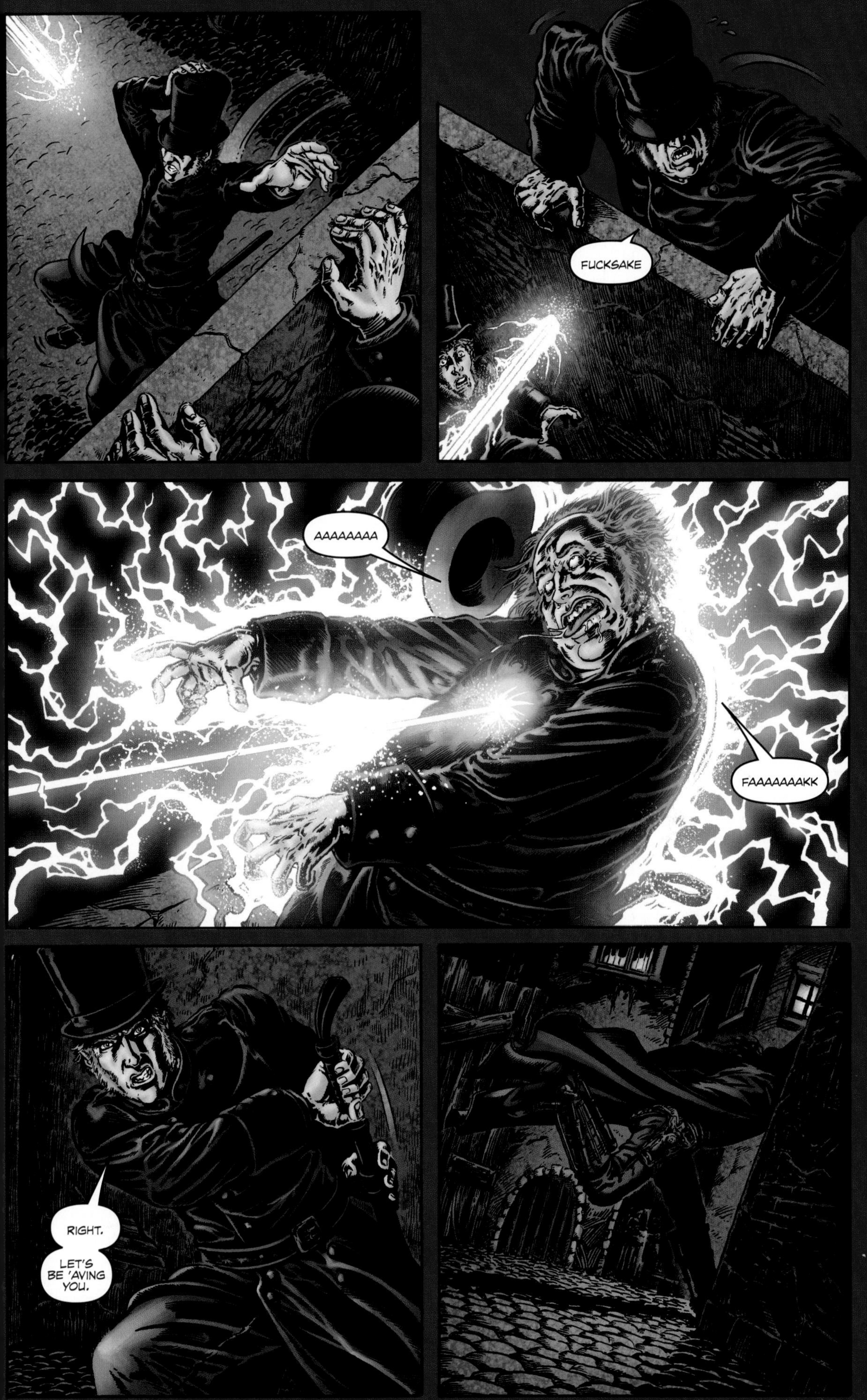
FUCKSAKE
AAAAAAAA
FAAAAAAAKK
RIGHT.
LET'S BE 'AVING YOU.

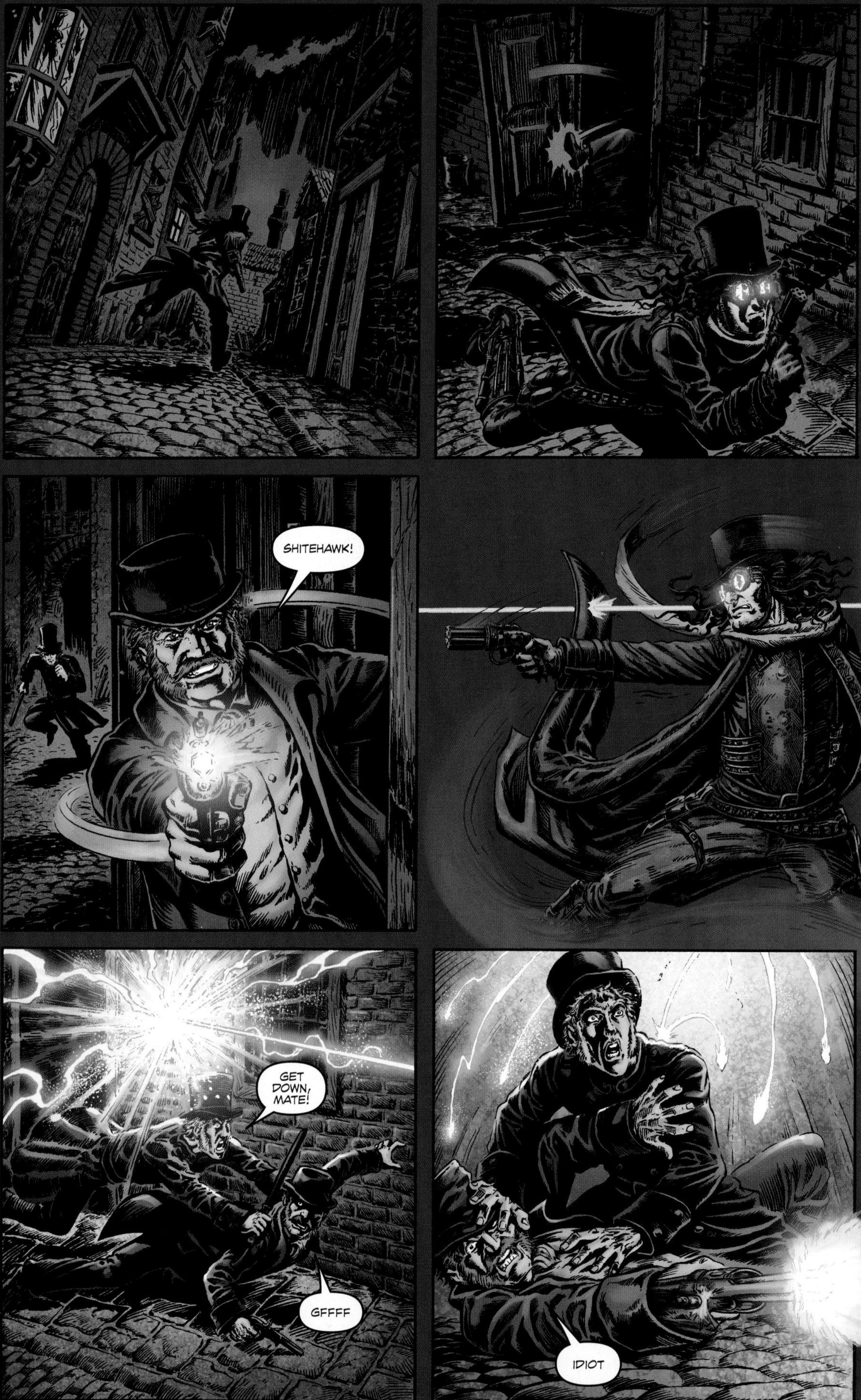
SHITEHAWK!
GET DOWN, MATE!
GFFFF
IDIOT

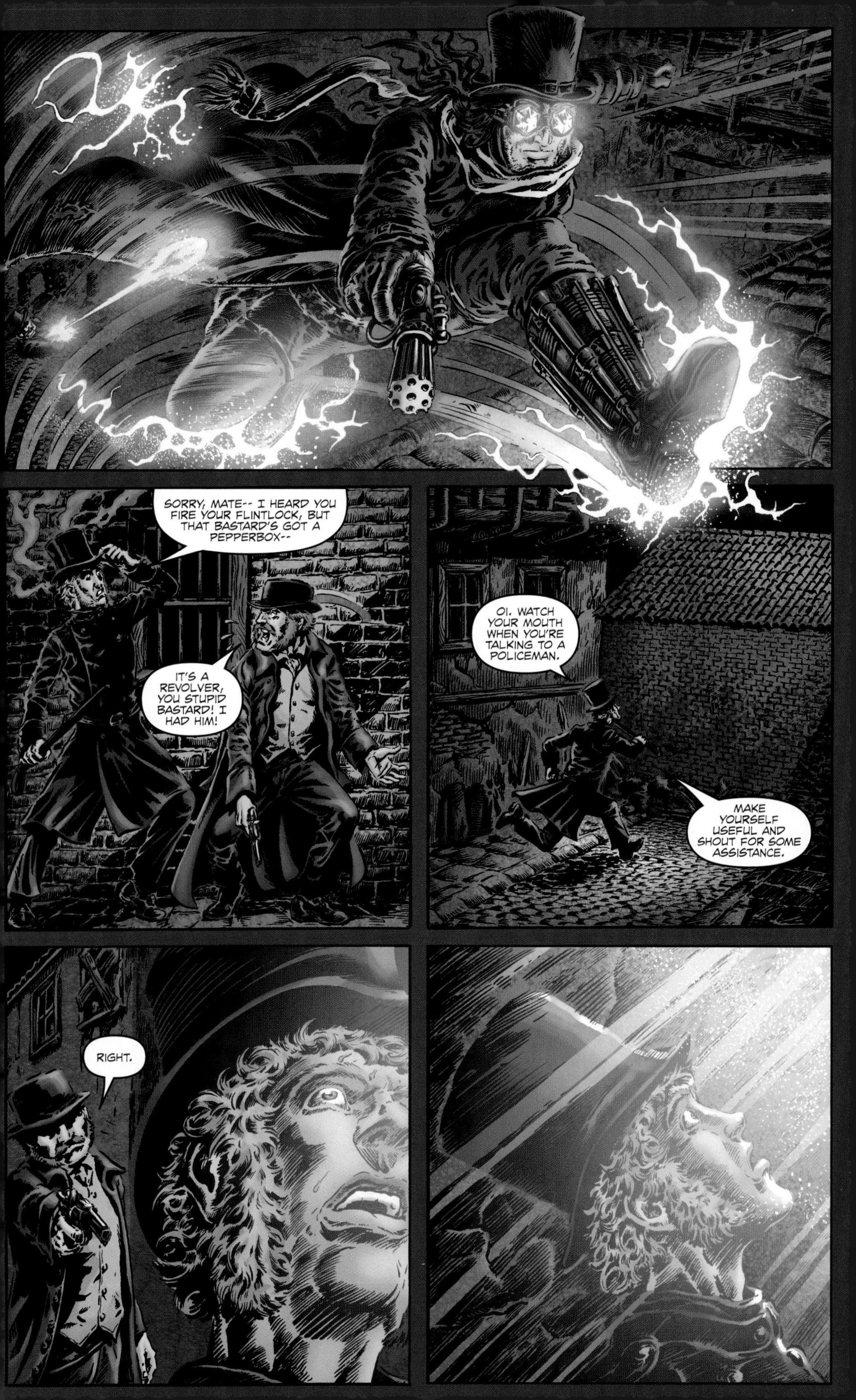
SORRY, MATE-- I HEARD YOU FIRE YOUR FLINTLOCK, BUT THAT BASTARD'S GOT A PEPPERBOX--
IT'S A REVOLVER, YOU STUPID BASTARD! I HAD HIM!
OI. WATCH YOUR MOUTH WHEN YOU'RE TALKING TO A POLICEMAN.
MAKE YOURSELF USEFUL AND SHOUT FOR SOME ASSISTANCE.
RIGHT.

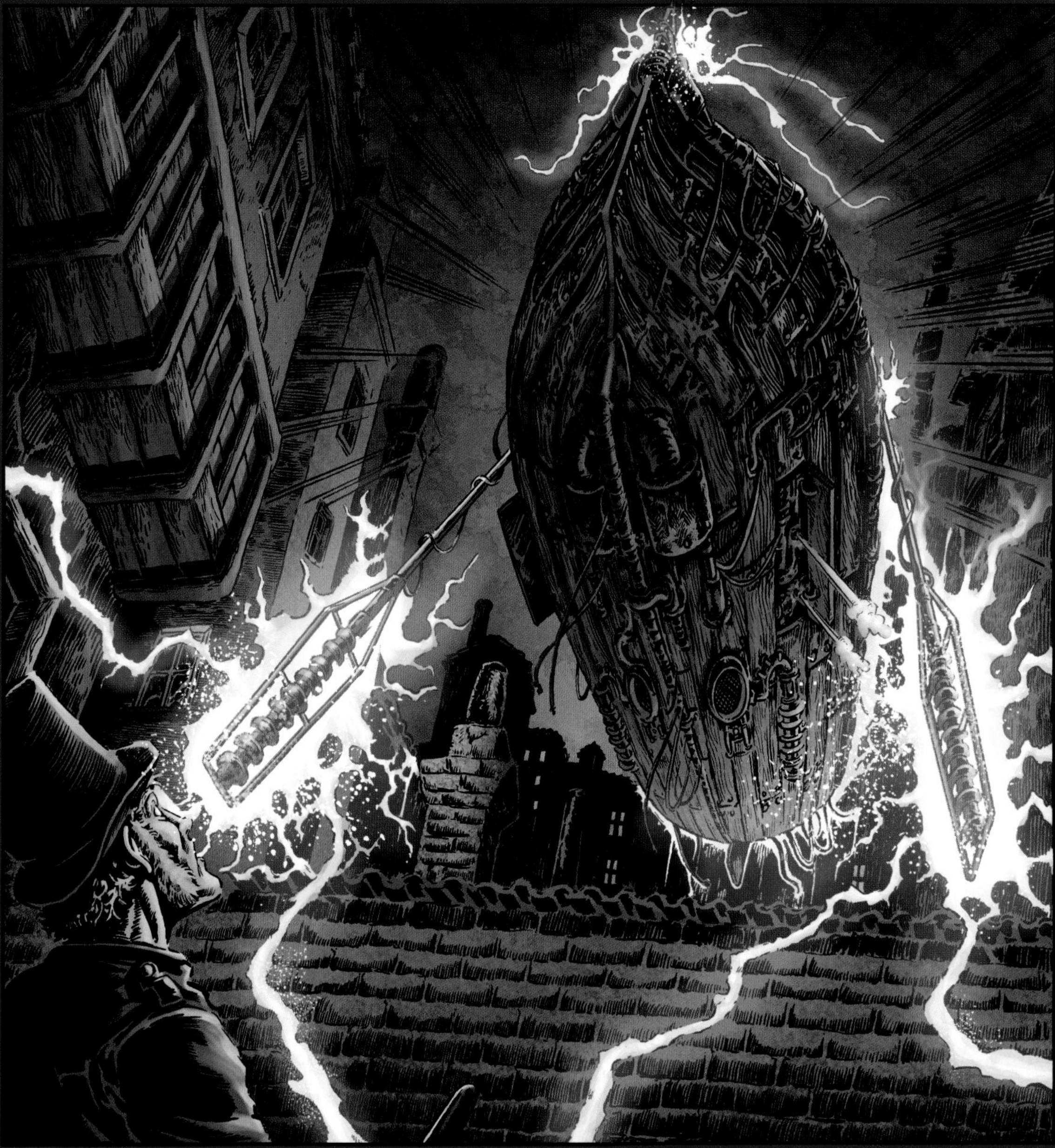

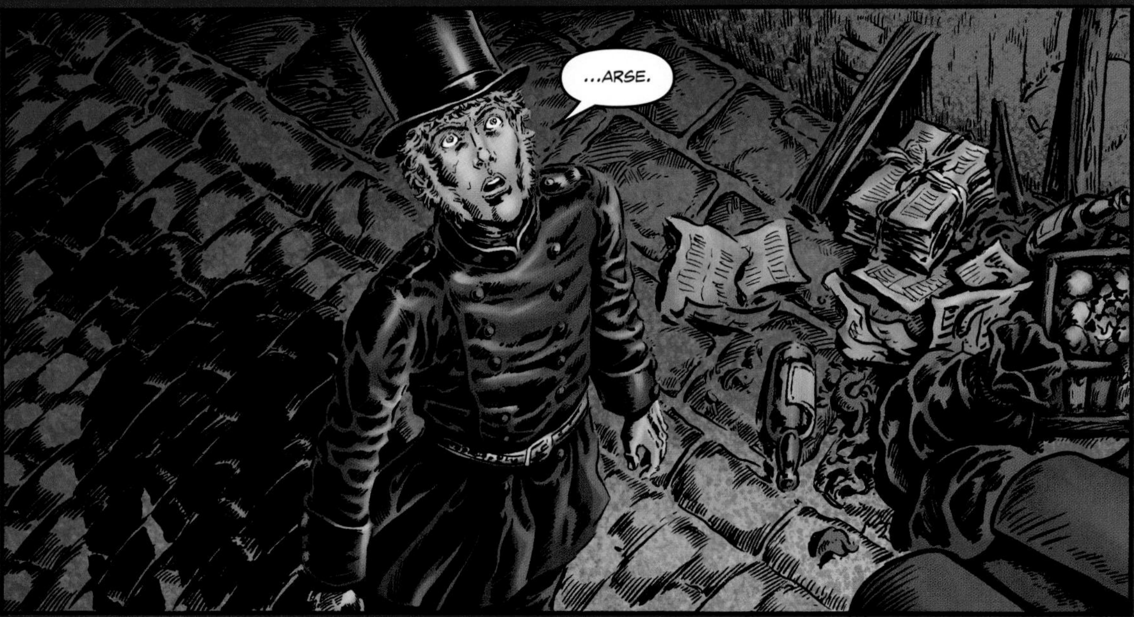
...ARSE.

Ah, electricity. Thales first transcribed the induction of static electricity in 600 BC. Otto von Guericke built friction-machines for the accumulation of static electrical charge around 1650 AD. Upon the founding date of the Metropolitan Police, Francesco Zantedeschi discovered electromagnetic induction (although, in this slow world, Michael Faraday would have been unaware of this when he published his more famous discovery of same, a year from now).

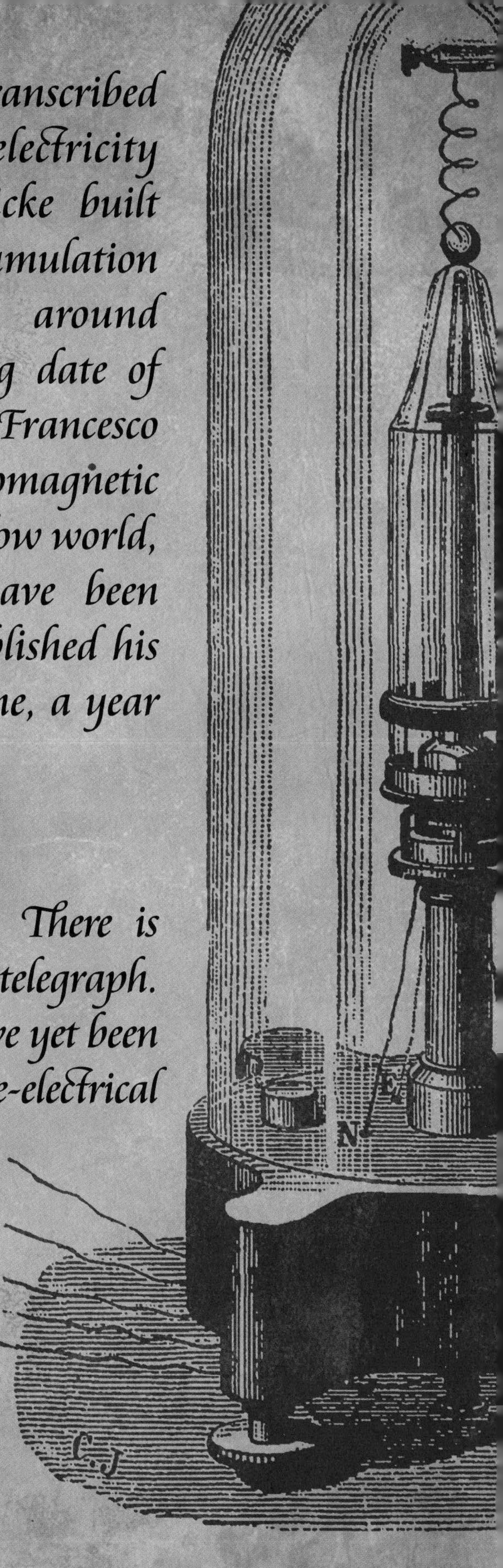

Electricity, in a slow world. There is not yet an electromagnetic telegraph. Neither Tesla nor Marconi have yet been born. It is, in large part, a pre-electrical world.

And no-one has yet found the galvanic cell that fell into the sands of Baghdad in 250 BC.

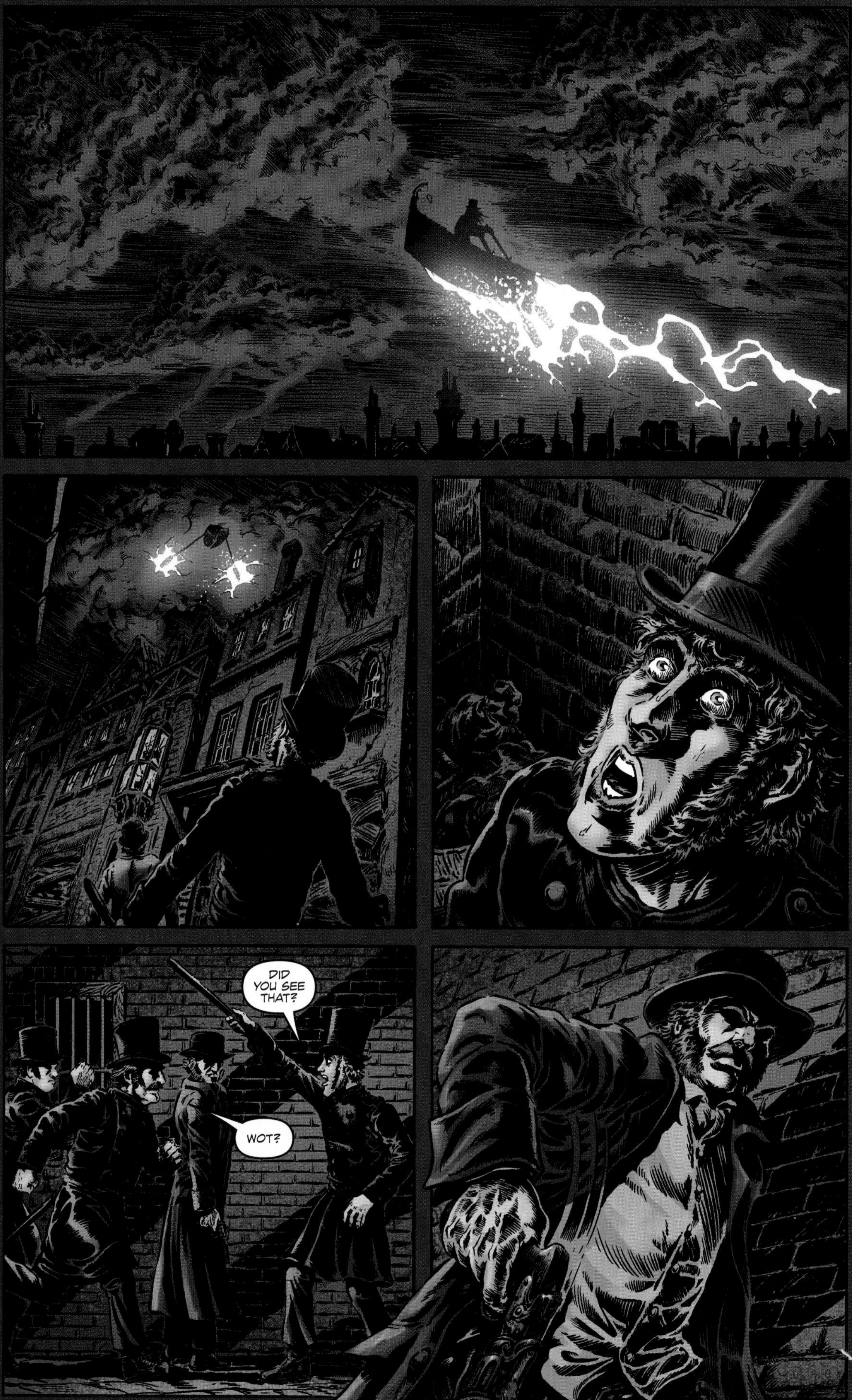
DID YOU SEE THAT?
WOT?

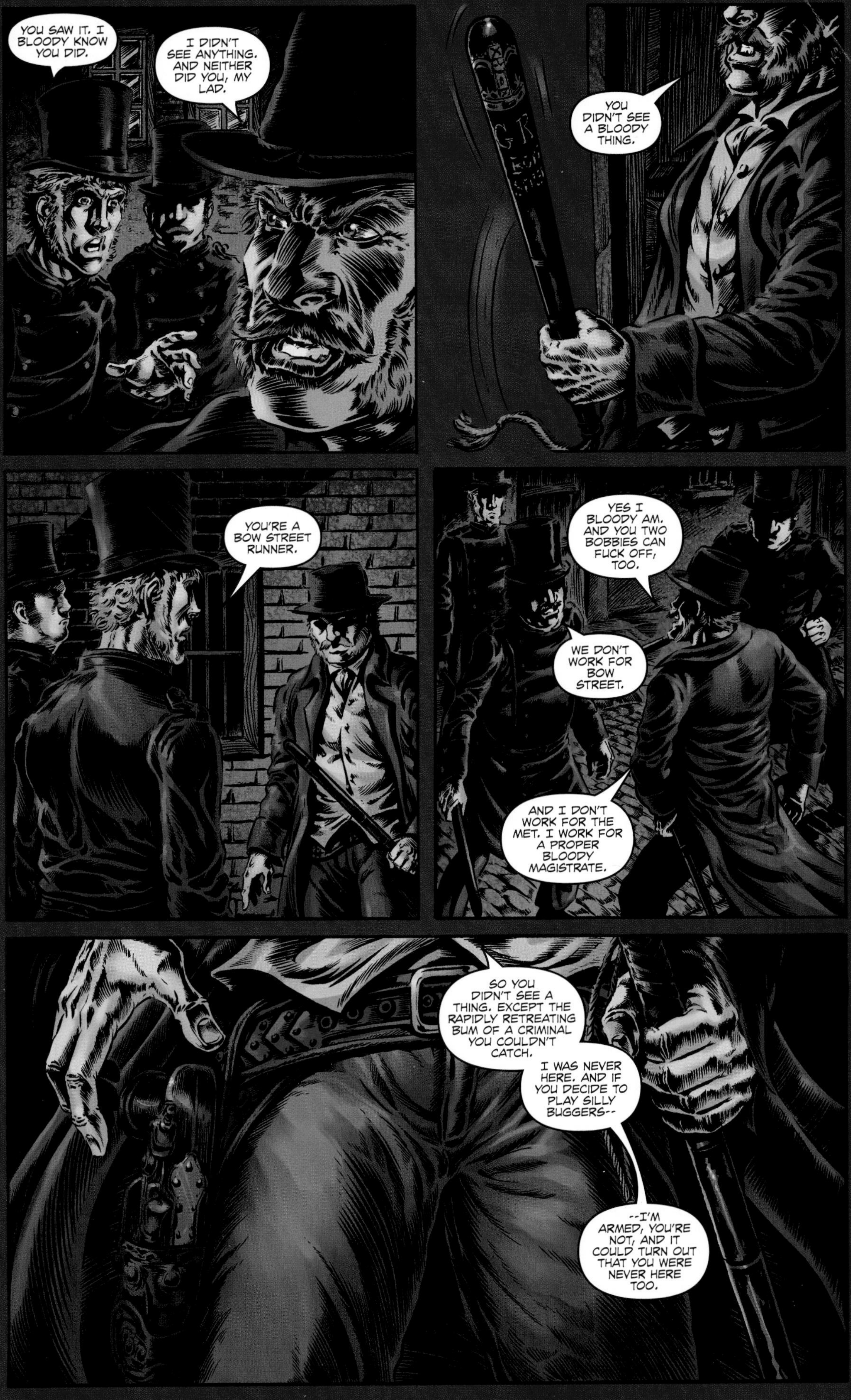
YOU SAW IT. I BLOODY KNOW YOU DID.
I DIDN'T SEE ANYTHING. AND NEITHER DID YOU, MY LAD.
YOU DIDN'T SEE A BLOODY THING.
YOU'RE A BOW STREET RUNNER.
YES I BLOODY AM. AND YOU TWO BOBBIES CAN FUCK OFF, TOO.
WE DON'T WORK FOR BOW STREET.
AND I DON'T WORK FOR THE MET. I WORK FOR A PROPER BLOODY MAGISTRATE.
SO YOU DIDN'T SEE A THING. EXCEPT THE RAPIDLY RETREATING BUM OF A CRIMINAL YOU COULDN'T CATCH.
I WAS NEVER HERE. AND IF YOU DECIDE TO PLAY SILLY BUGGERS--
--I'M ARMED, YOU'RE NOT, AND IT COULD TURN OUT THAT YOU WERE NEVER HERE TOO.

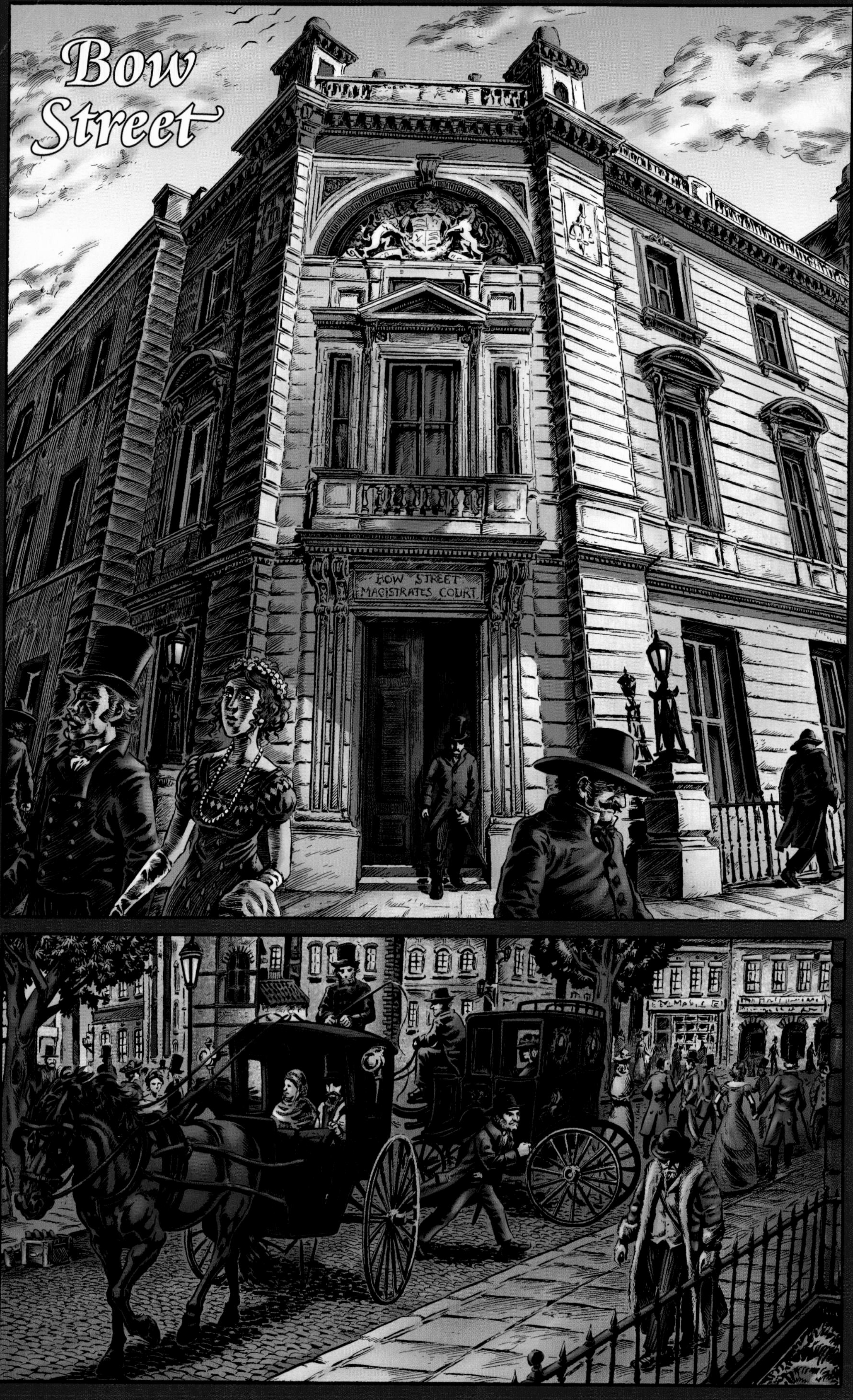
Bow Street
BOW STREET
MAGISTRATES COURT

Bow Street is the home of the Magistrates' Court, as founded by Colonel Sir Thomas de Veil: and the magistrates, the Justices Of The Peace who heard and ruled upon trials of law, operated the Bow Street Runners in its pursuit of law. Many Runners had previously been "thief-takers," freelancers hired with cash by ad hoc clubs of the aggrieved to hunt down the light-fingered and return stolen goods. Most thief-takers were, of course, thieves, extorters and murderers themselves. Thief-taker Jonathan Wild ran such an army of burglars that, upon his execution for same, Daniel Defoe reported that the biggest crowd he'd ever seen came out to cheer the hanging "as if it had been upon a triumph." The Bow Street Runners, therefore, could not have been as pure as the magisttrates would have people believe.

And neither were the magistrates.

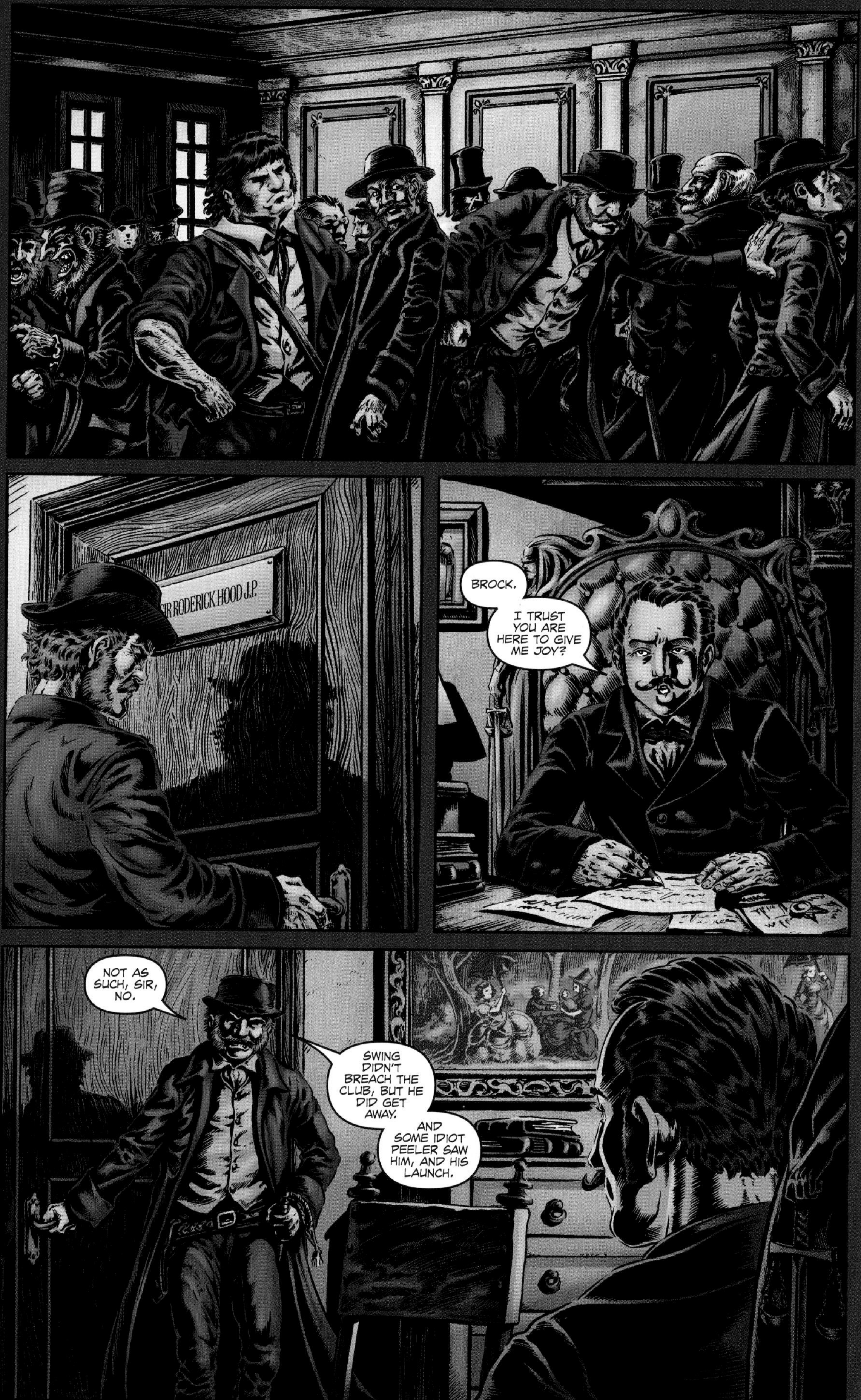
SIR RODERICK HOOD J.P.
BROCK.
I TRUST YOU ARE HERE TO GIVE ME JOY?
NOT AS SUCH, SIR, NO.
SWING DIDN'T BREACH THE CLUB, BUT HE DID GET AWAY.
AND SOME IDIOT PEELER SAW HIM, AND HIS LAUNCH.

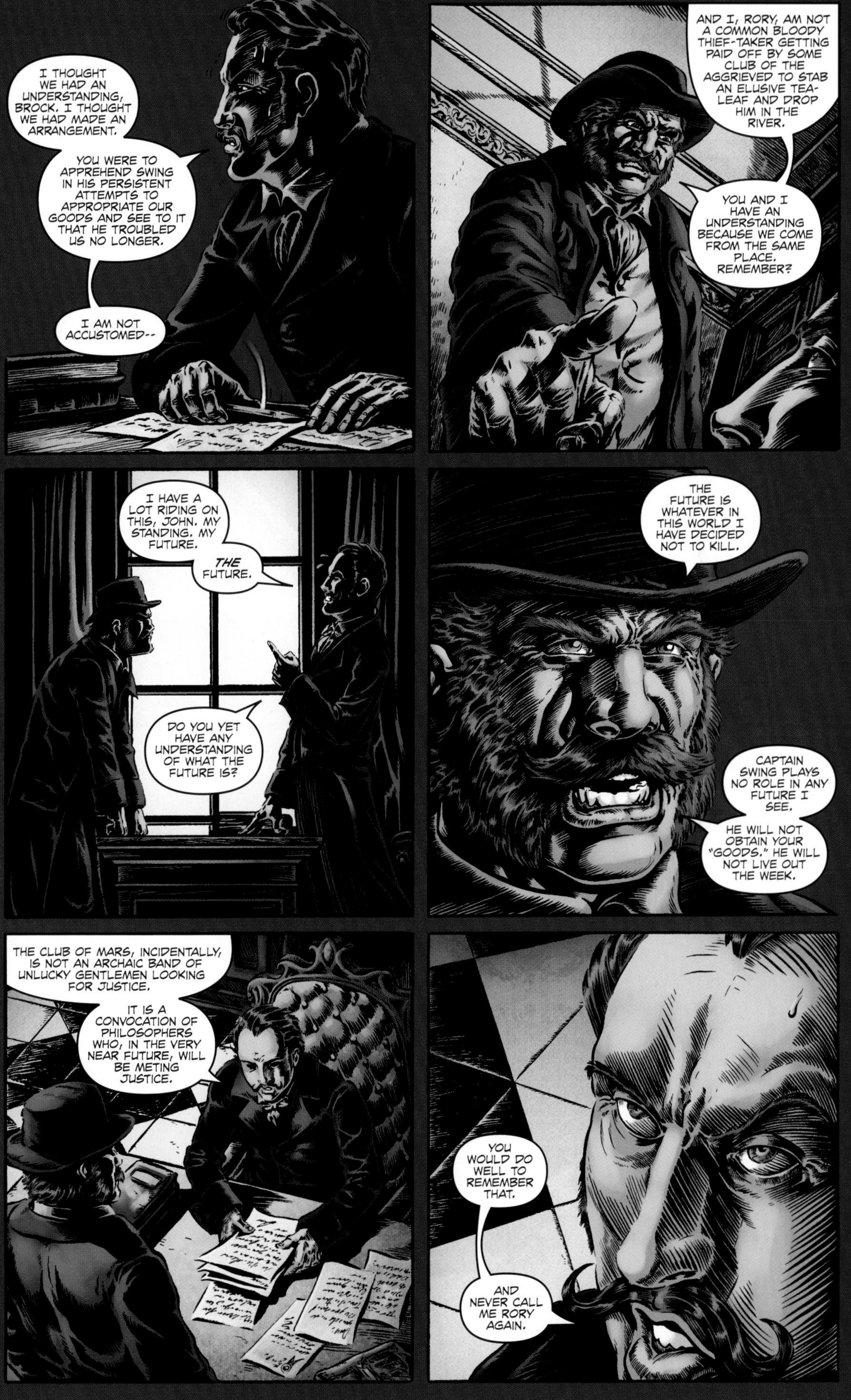
I THOUGHT WE HAD AN UNDERSTANDING, BROCK. I THOUGHT WE HAD MADE AN ARRANGEMENT.
YOU WERE TO APPREHEND SWING IN HIS PERSISTENT ATTEMPTS TO APPROPRIATE OUR GOODS AND SEE TO IT THAT HE TROUBLED US NO LONGER.
I AM NOT ACCUSTOMED--
AND I, RORY, AM NOT A COMMON BLOODY THIEF-TAKER GETTING PAID OFF BY SOME CLUB OF THE AGGRIEVED TO STAB AN ELUSIVE TEA-LEAF AND DROP HIM IN THE RIVER.
YOU AND I HAVE AN UNDERSTANDING BECAUSE WE COME FROM THE SAME PLACE. REMEMBER?
I HAVE A LOT RIDING ON THIS, JOHN. MY STANDING. MY FUTURE.
THE FUTURE.
DO YOU YET HAVE ANY UNDERSTANDING OF WHAT THE FUTURE IS?
THE FUTURE IS WHATEVER IN THIS WORLD I HAVE DECIDED NOT TO KILL.
CAPTAIN SWING PLAYS NO ROLE IN ANY FUTURE I SEE.
HE WILL NOT OBTAIN YOUR "GOODS." HE WILL NOT LIVE OUT THE WEEK.
THE CLUB OF MARS, INCIDENTALLY, IS NOT AN ARCHAIC BAND OF UNLUCKY GENTLEMEN LOOKING FOR JUSTICE.
IT IS A CONVOCATION OF PHILOSOPHERS WHO, IN THE VERY NEAR FUTURE, WILL BE METING JUSTICE.
YOU WOULD DO WELL TO REMEMBER THAT.
AND NEVER CALL ME RORY AGAIN.

The first reported sighting of Spring-Heeled
Jack is actually in 1837.

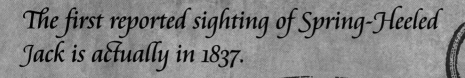

      Captain Swing was the name signed to the
communications issued by the organisers of the Swing
Riots of 1830. But the first of those letters will not be sent
until the October of the year, and this is not October.

This is a secret history.

Everything I tell you is true.

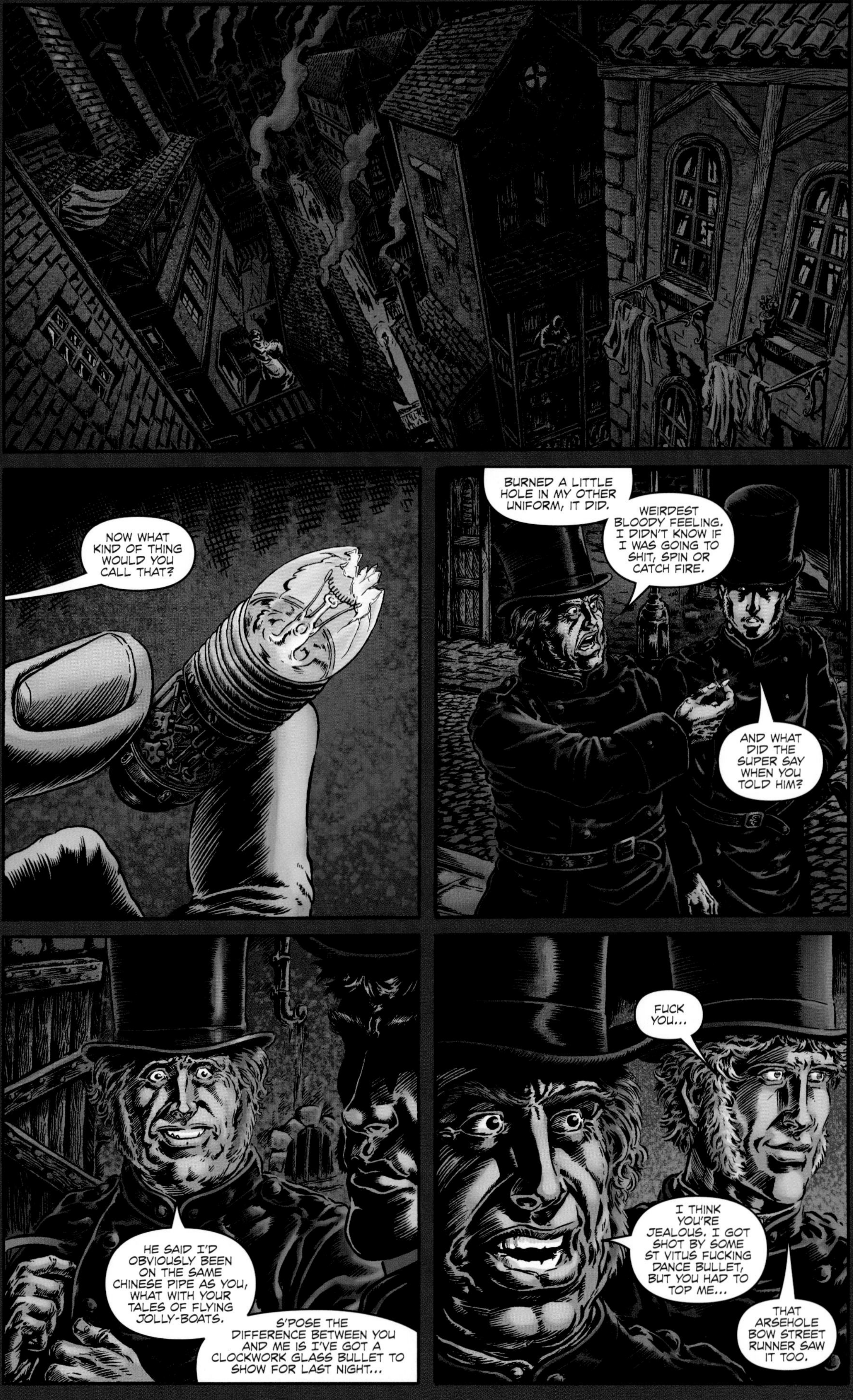
NOW WHAT KIND OF THING WOULD YOU CALL THAT?
BURNED A LITTLE HOLE IN MY OTHER UNIFORM, IT DID.
WEIRDEST BLOODY FEELING. I DIDN'T KNOW IF I WAS GOING TO SHIT, SPIN OR CATCH FIRE.
AND WHAT DID THE SUPER SAY WHEN YOU TOLD HIM?
HE SAID I'D OBVIOUSLY BEEN ON THE SAME CHINESE PIPE AS YOU, WHAT WITH YOUR TALES OF FLYING JOLLY-BOATS.
S'POSE THE DIFFERENCE BETWEEN YOU AND ME IS I'VE GOT A CLOCKWORK GLASS BULLET TO SHOW FOR LAST NIGHT...
FUCK YOU...
I THINK YOU'RE JEALOUS. I GOT SHOT BY SOME ST VITUS FUCKING DANCE BULLET, BUT YOU HAD TO TOP ME...
THAT ARSEHOLE BOW STREET RUNNER SAW IT TOO.

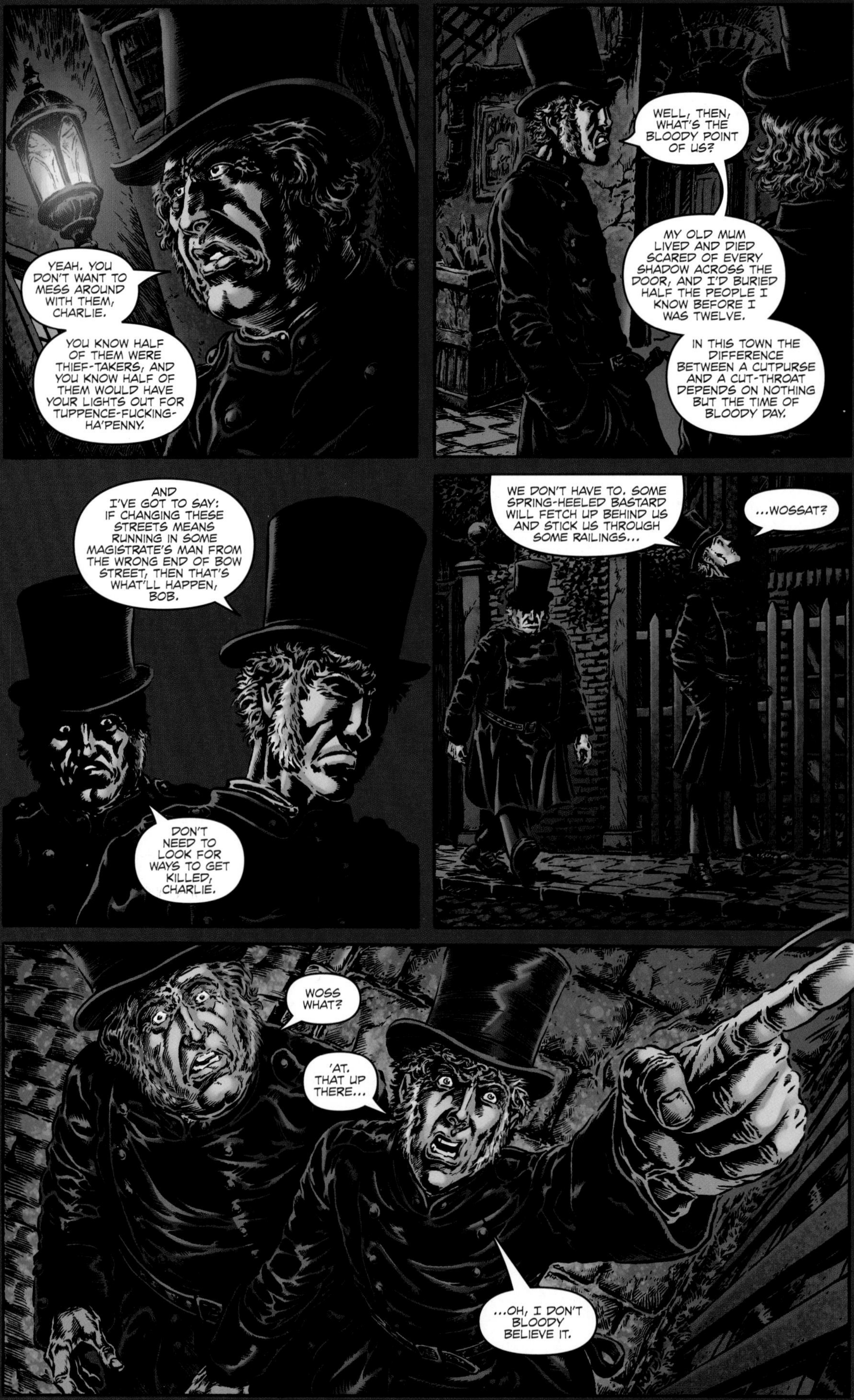
YEAH. YOU DON'T WANT TO MESS AROUND WITH THEM, CHARLIE.
YOU KNOW HALF OF THEM WERE THIEF-TAKERS, AND YOU KNOW HALF OF THEM WOULD HAVE YOUR LIGHTS OUT FOR TUPPENCE-FUCKING-HA'PENNY.
WELL, THEN, WHAT'S THE BLOODY POINT OF US?
MY OLD MUM LIVED AND DIED SCARED OF EVERY SHADOW ACROSS THE DOOR, AND I'D BURIED HALF THE PEOPLE I KNOW BEFORE I WAS TWELVE.
IN THIS TOWN THE DIFFERENCE BETWEEN A CUTPURSE AND A CUT-THROAT DEPENDS ON NOTHING BUT THE TIME OF BLOODY DAY.
AND I'VE GOT TO SAY: IF CHANGING THESE STREETS MEANS RUNNING IN SOME MAGISTRATE'S MAN FROM THE WRONG END OF BOW STREET, THEN THAT'S WHAT'LL HAPPEN, BOB.
DON'T NEED TO LOOK FOR WAYS TO GET KILLED, CHARLIE.
WE DON'T HAVE TO. SOME SPRING-HEELED BASTARD WILL FETCH UP BEHIND US AND STICK US THROUGH SOME RAILINGS...
...WOSSAT?
WOSS WHAT?
'AT. THAT UP THERE...
...OH, I DON'T BLOODY BELIEVE IT.

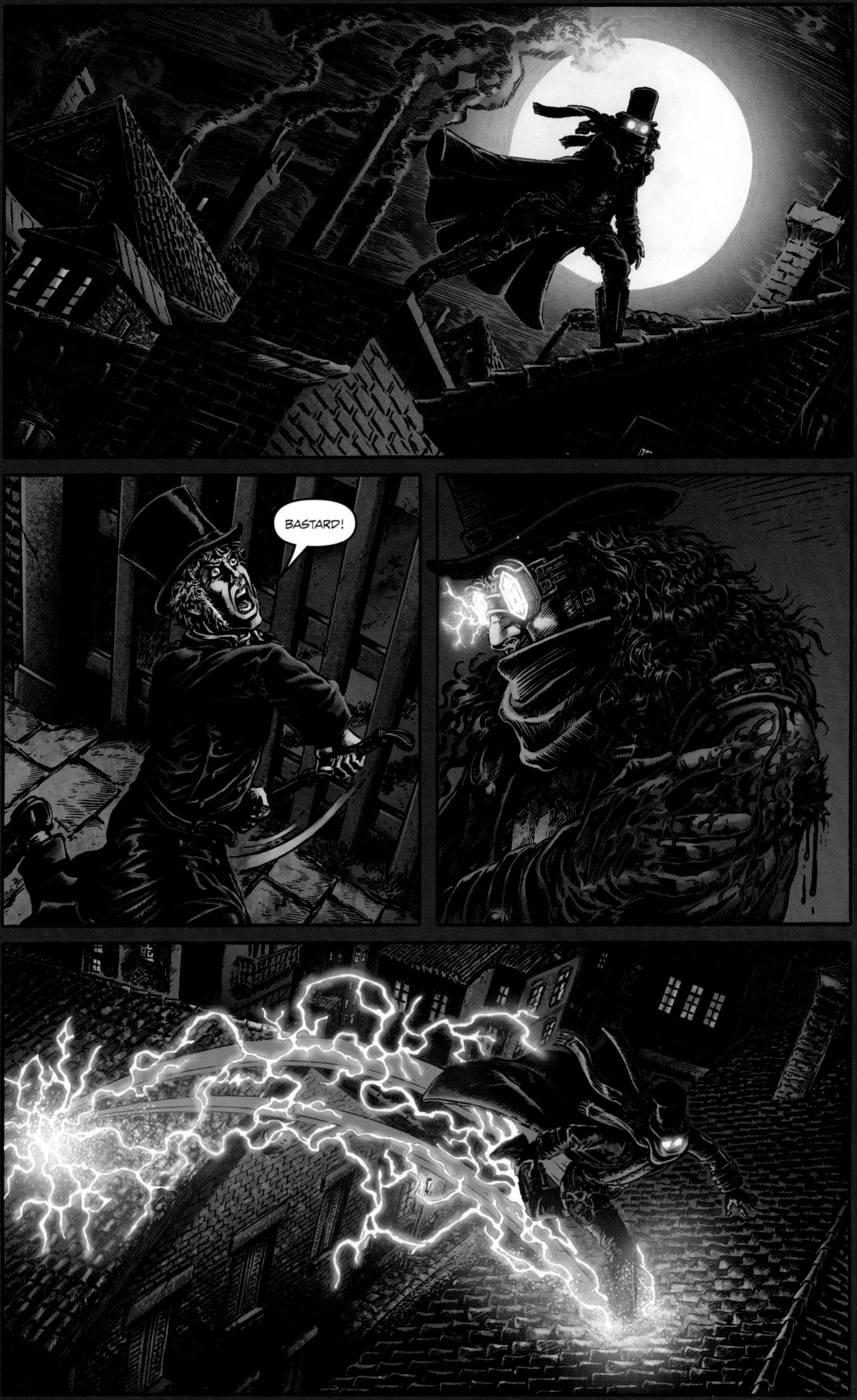
BASTARD!

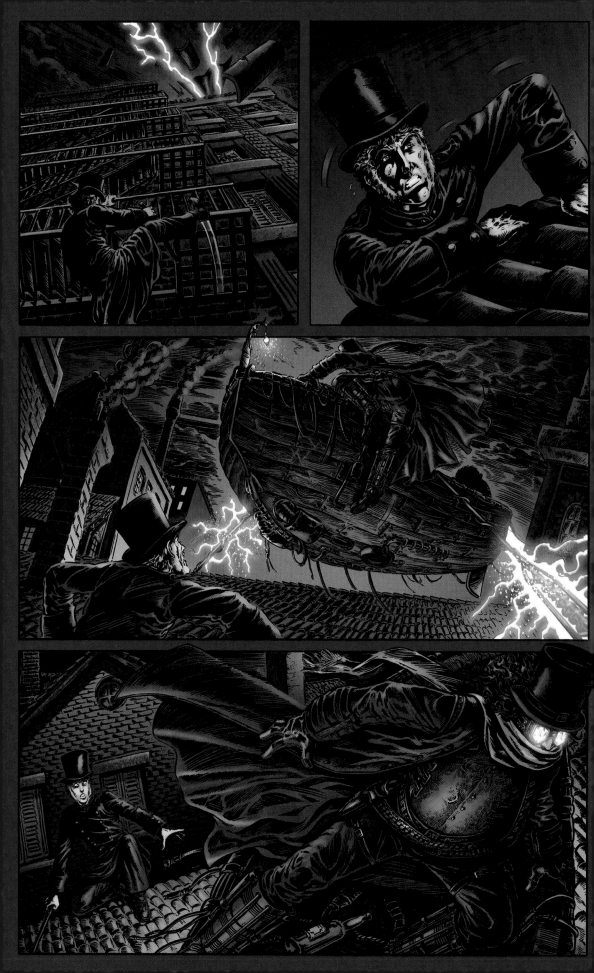

Ionic air propulsion. Electrostatic levitation. Electrogravitics. The Biefeld-Brown Effect and electro-fluid-dynamics. Nothing here is invented. It simply appears to be uchronic, counterfactual, sitting in the break of a time out of joint.

Everything I tell you is true.

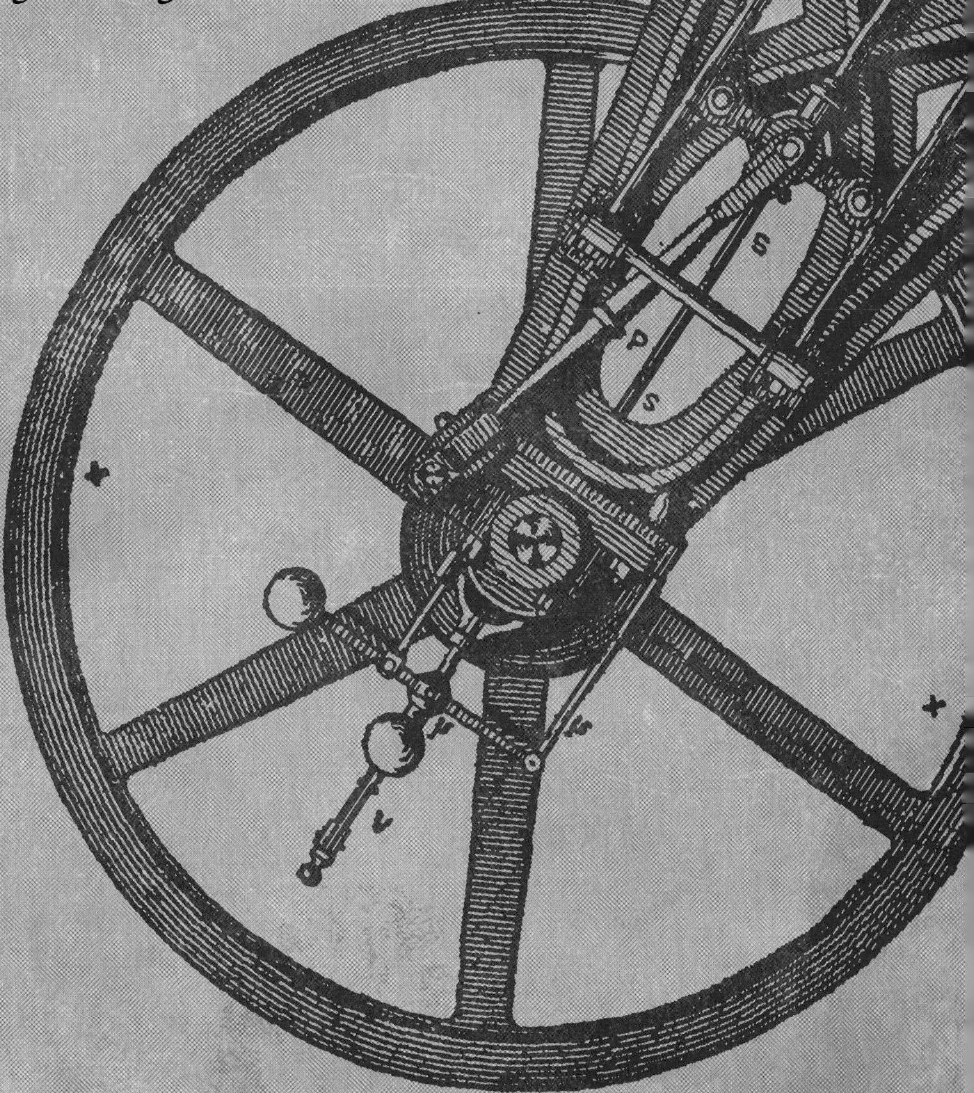

It is everyone else who's been lying to you.

I am Captain Swing.

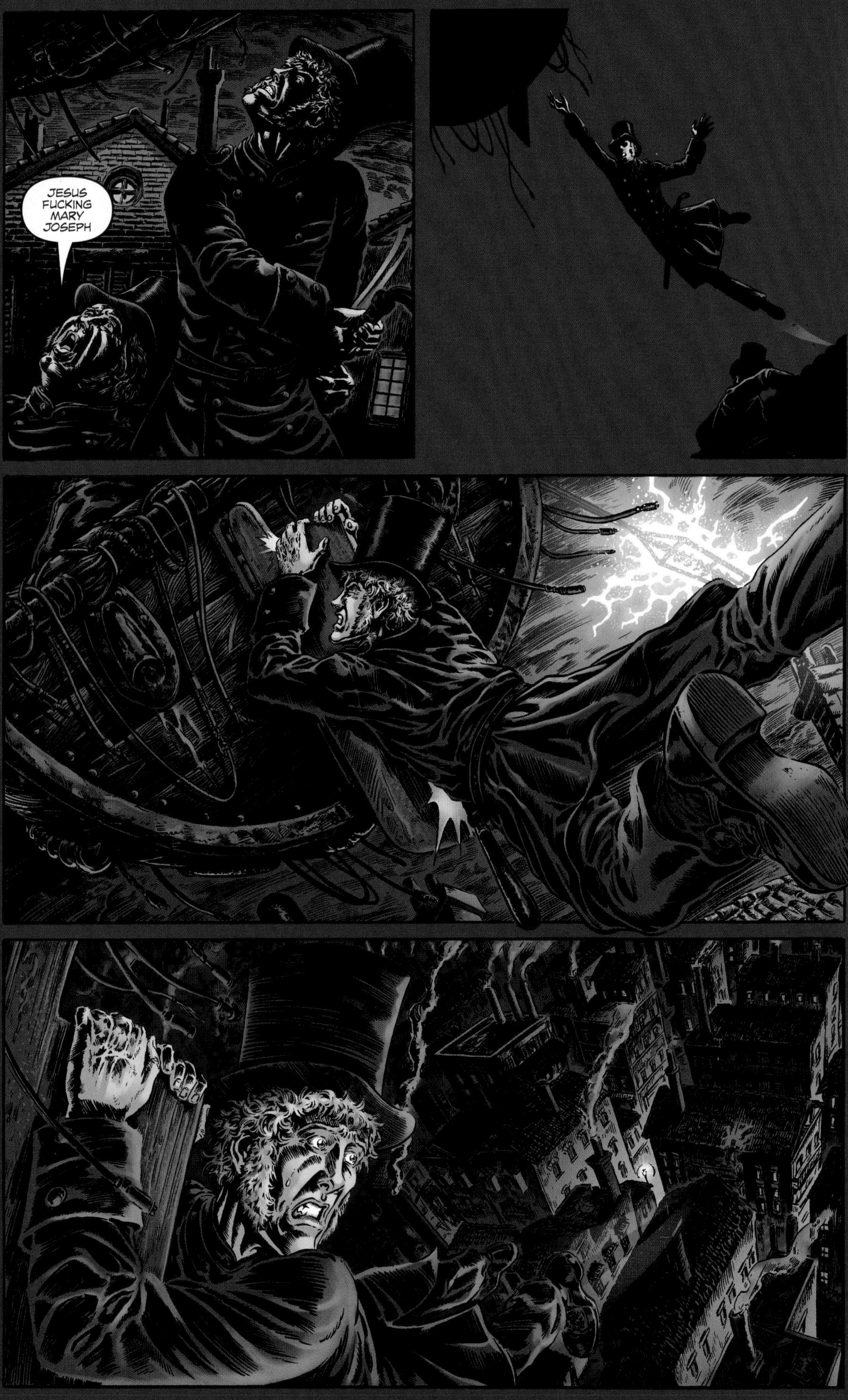
JESUS FUCKING MARY JOSEPH

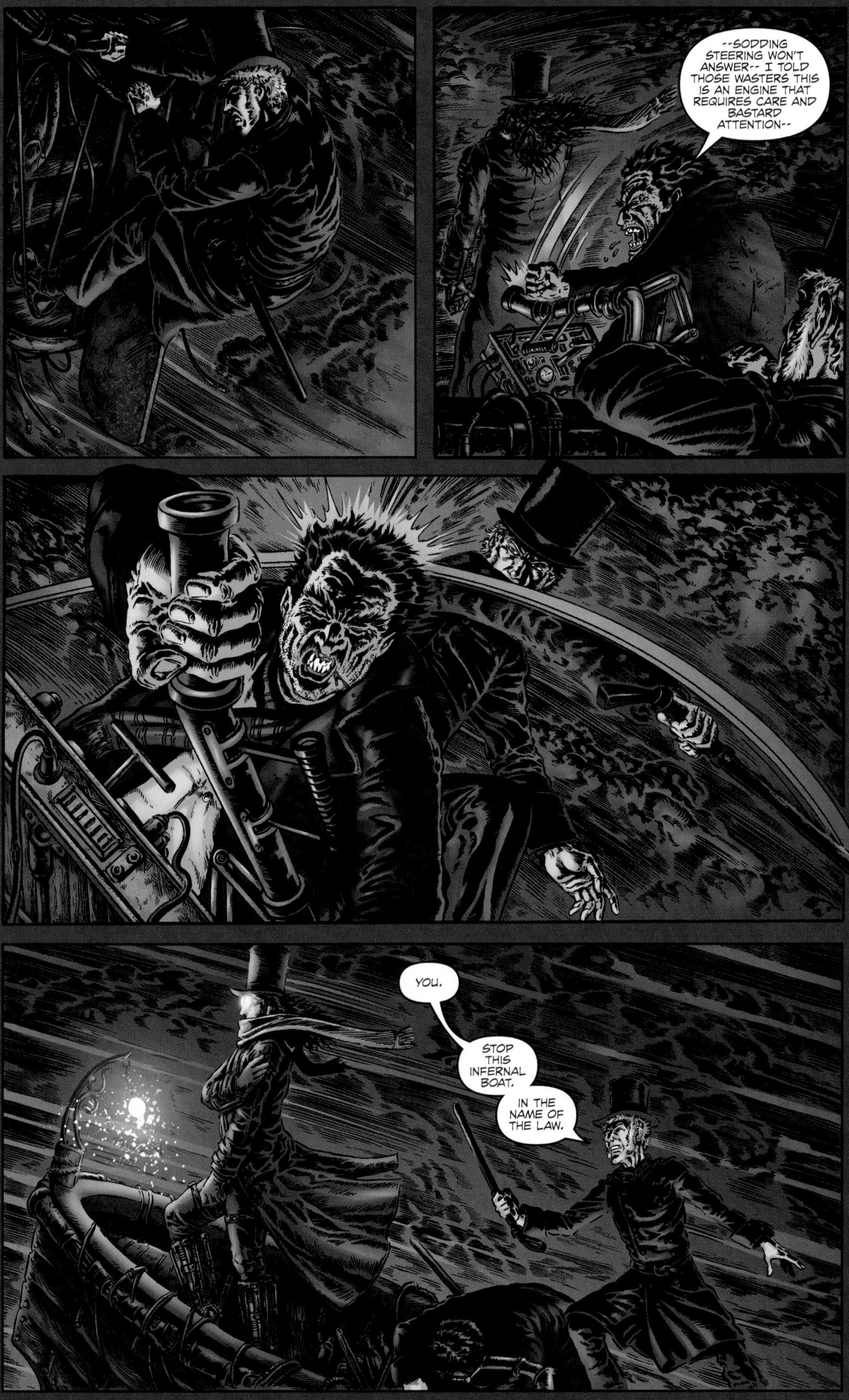
--SODDING STEERING WON'T ANSWER-- I TOLD THOSE WASTERS THIS IS AN ENGINE THAT REQUIRES CARE AND BASTARD ATTENTION--
YOU.
STOP THIS INFERNAL BOAT.
IN THE NAME OF THE LAW.

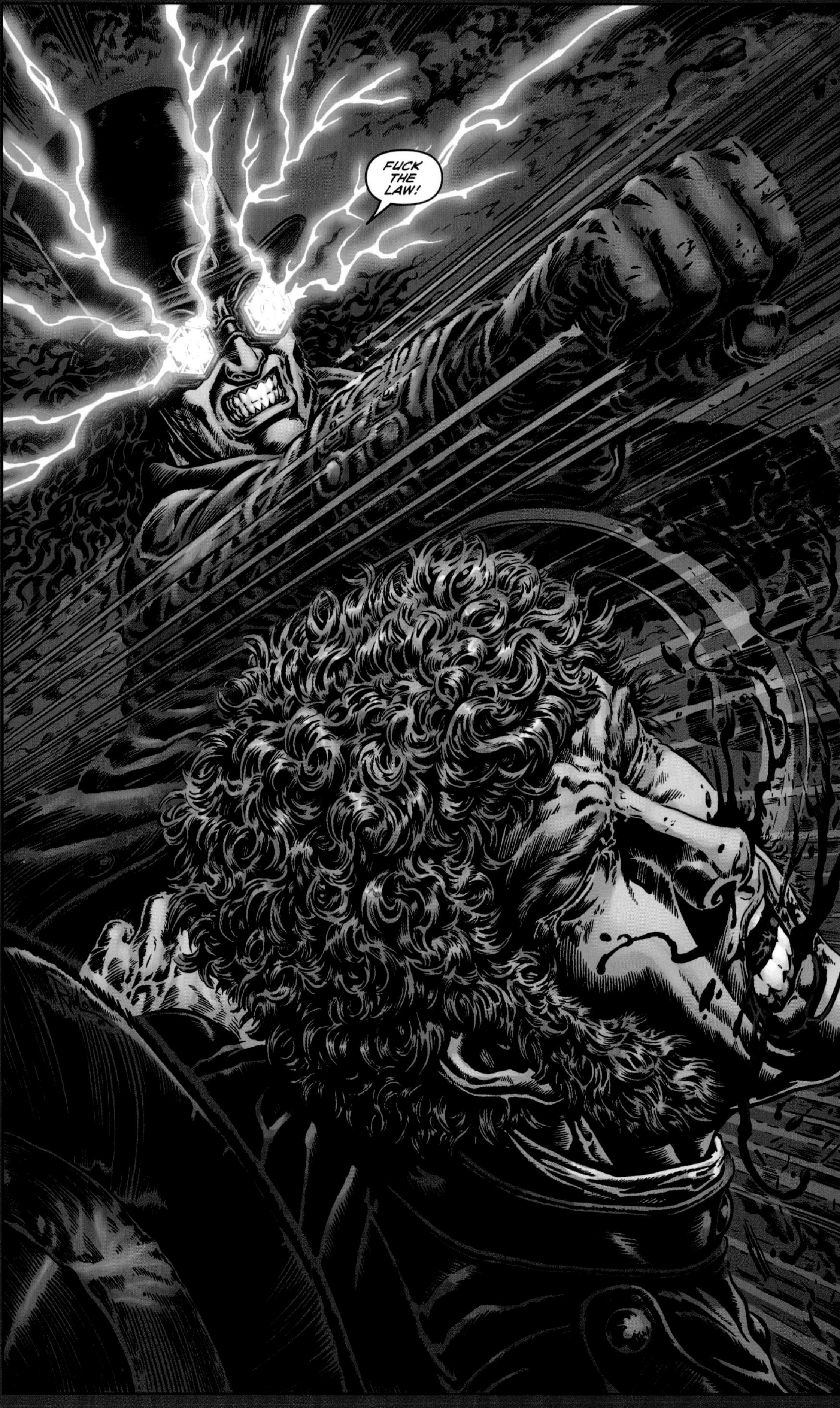
FUCK THE LAW!

CAPTAIN SWING

and the ELECTRICAL PIRATES OF CINDERY ISLAND

CHAPTER TWO

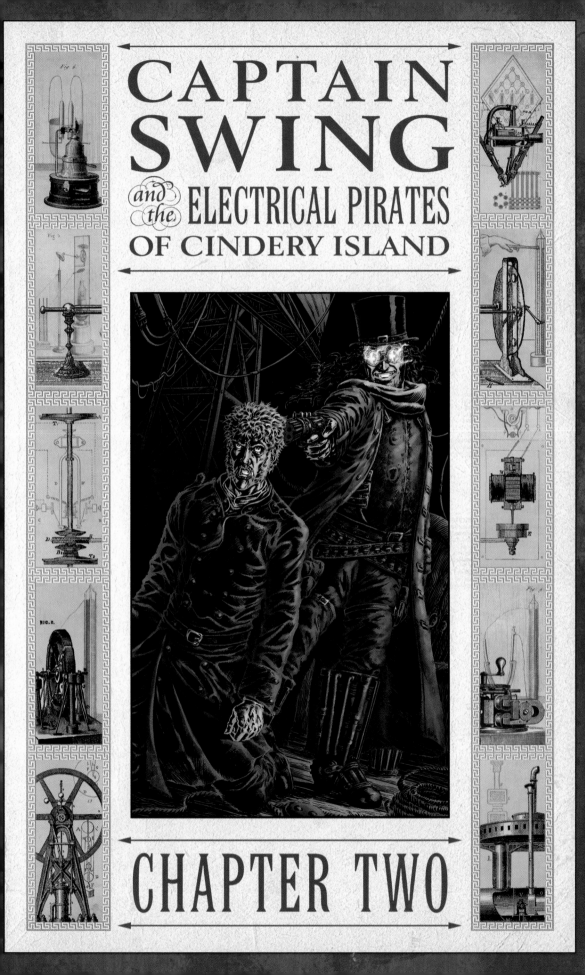

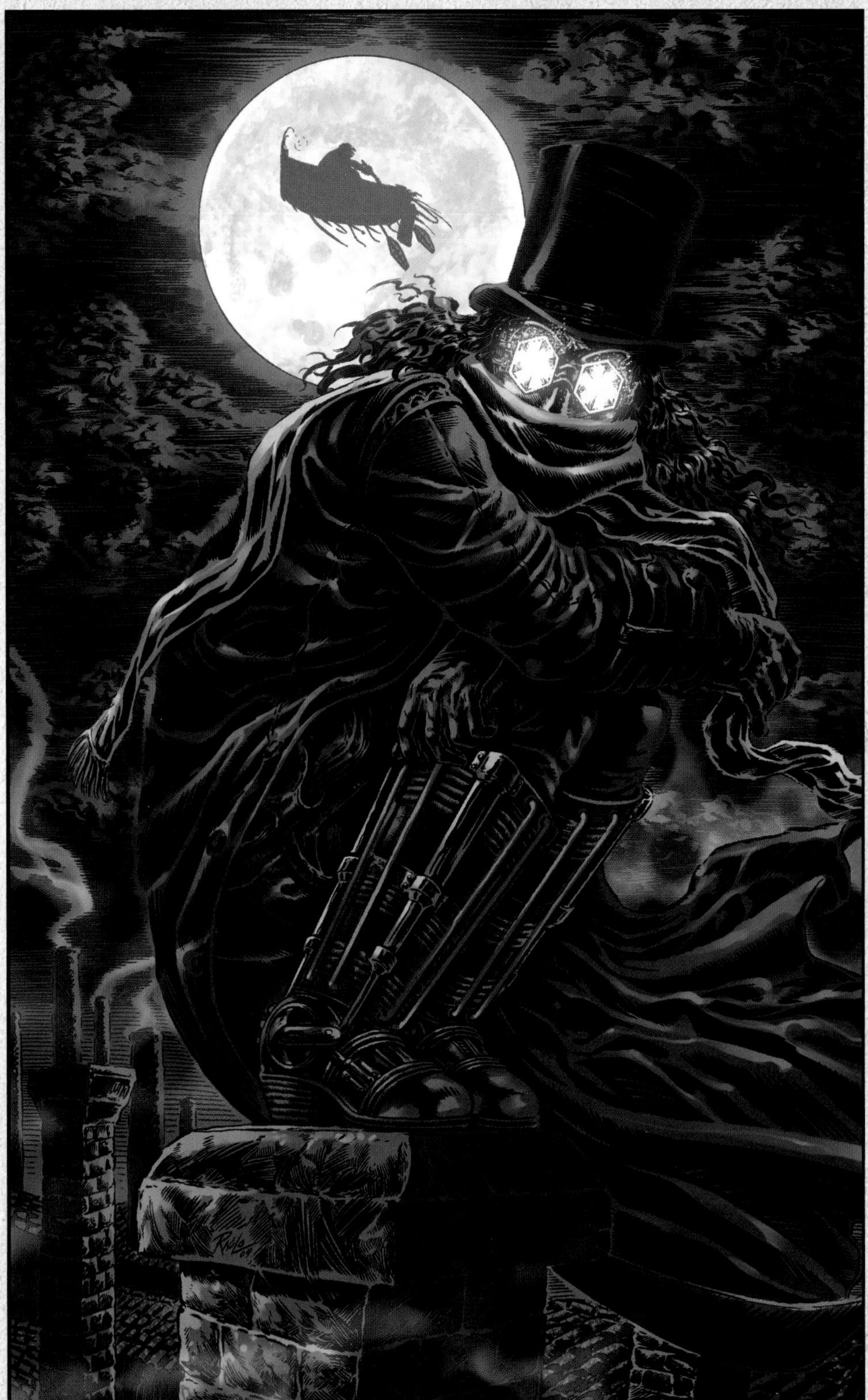

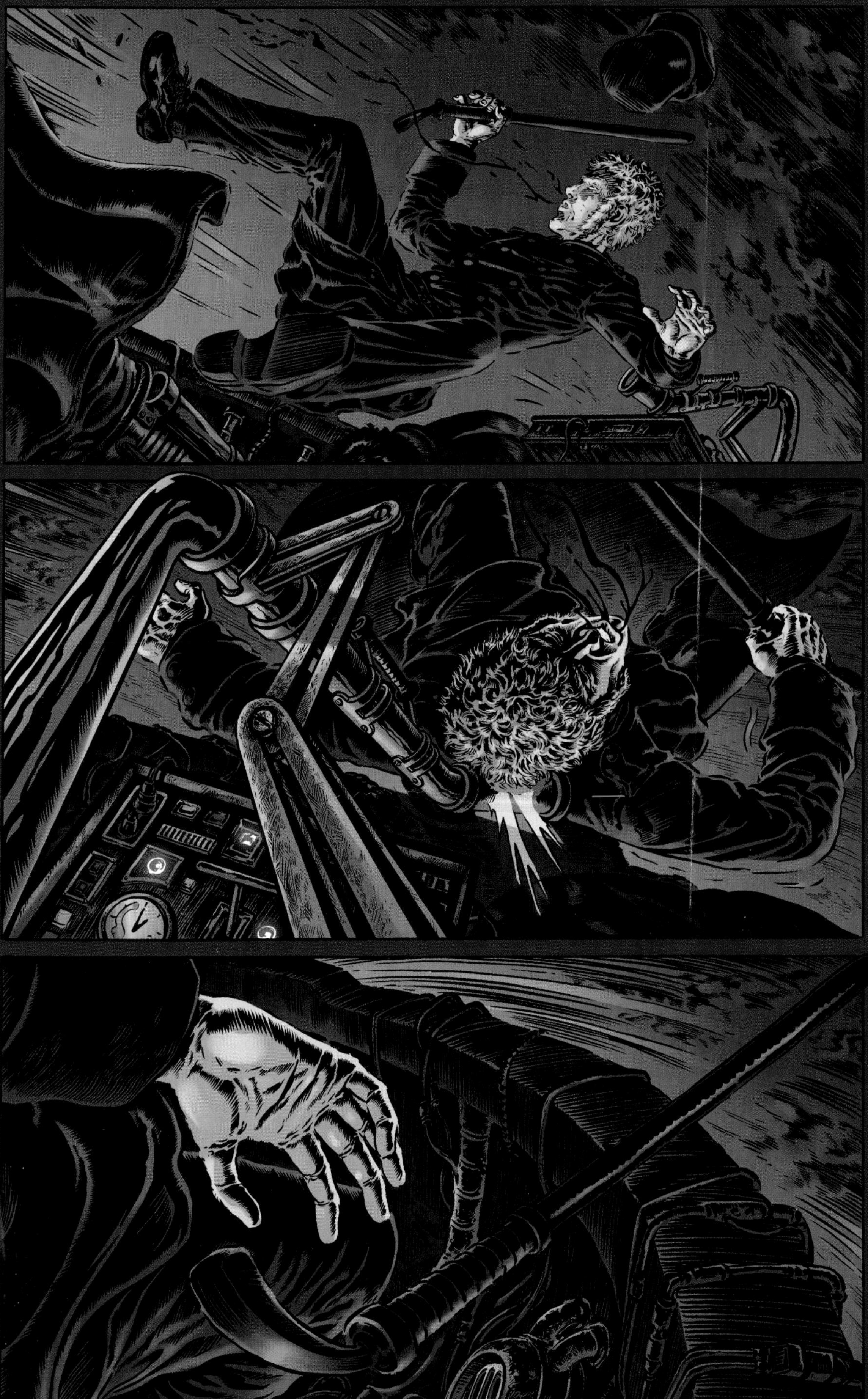

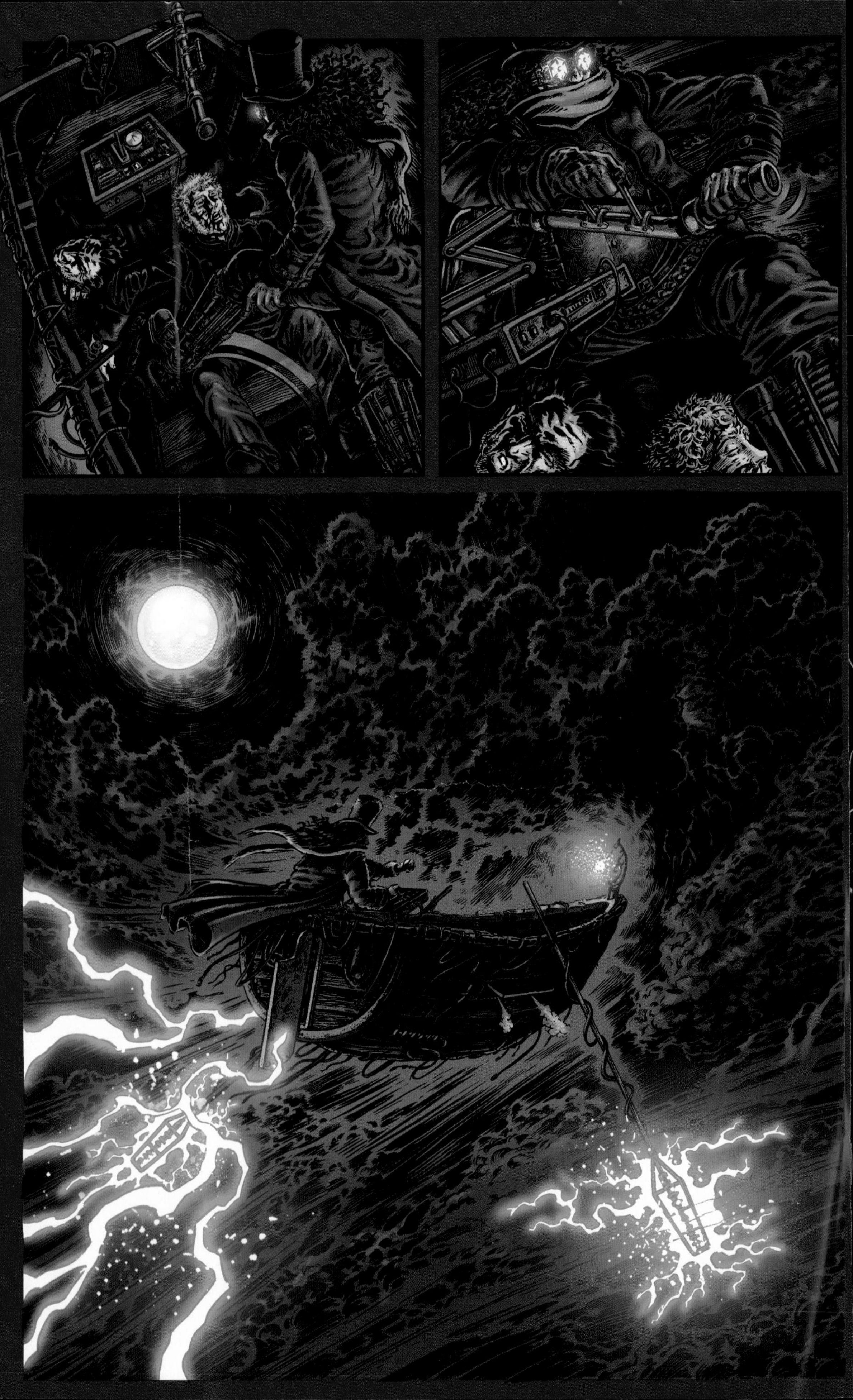

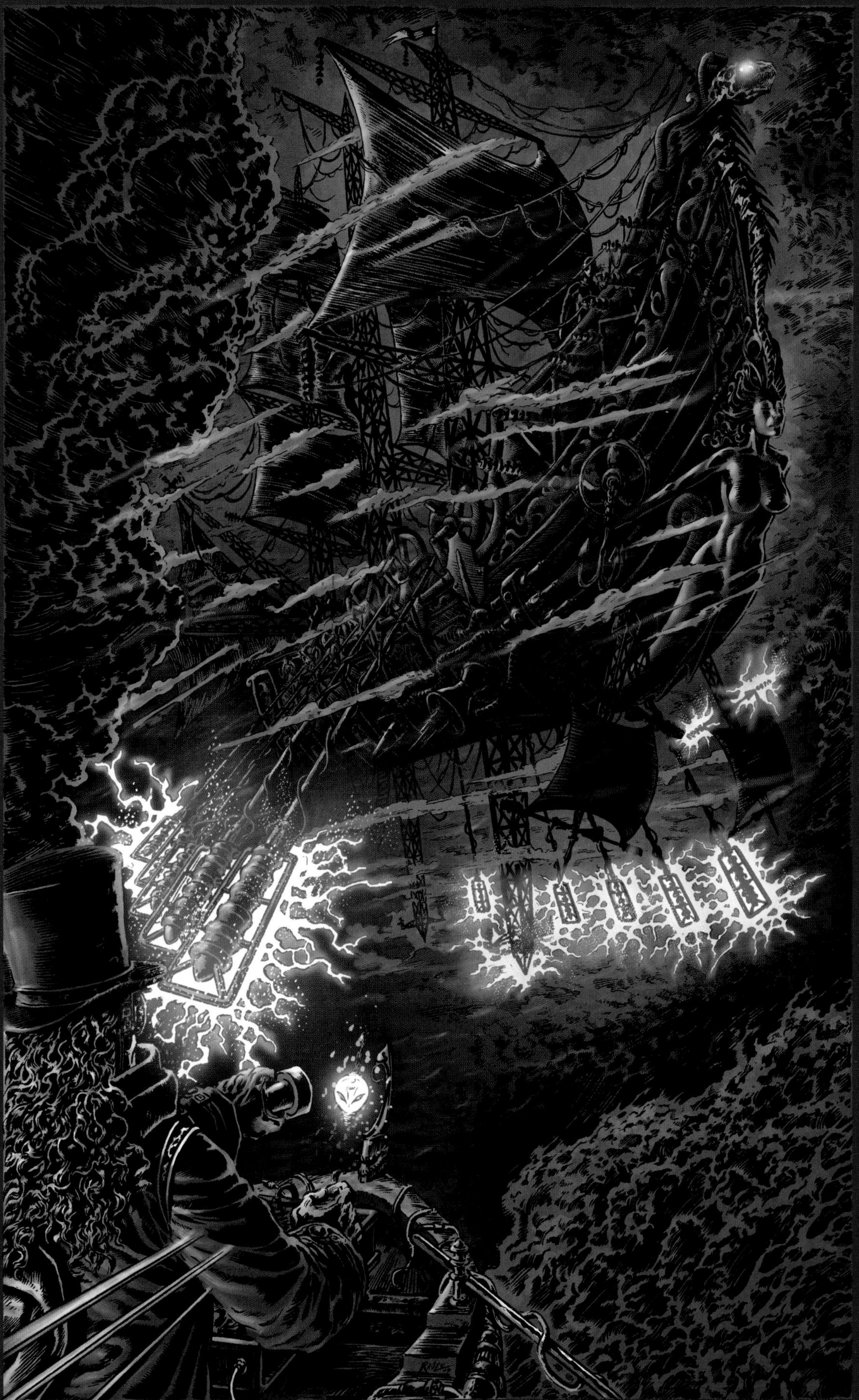

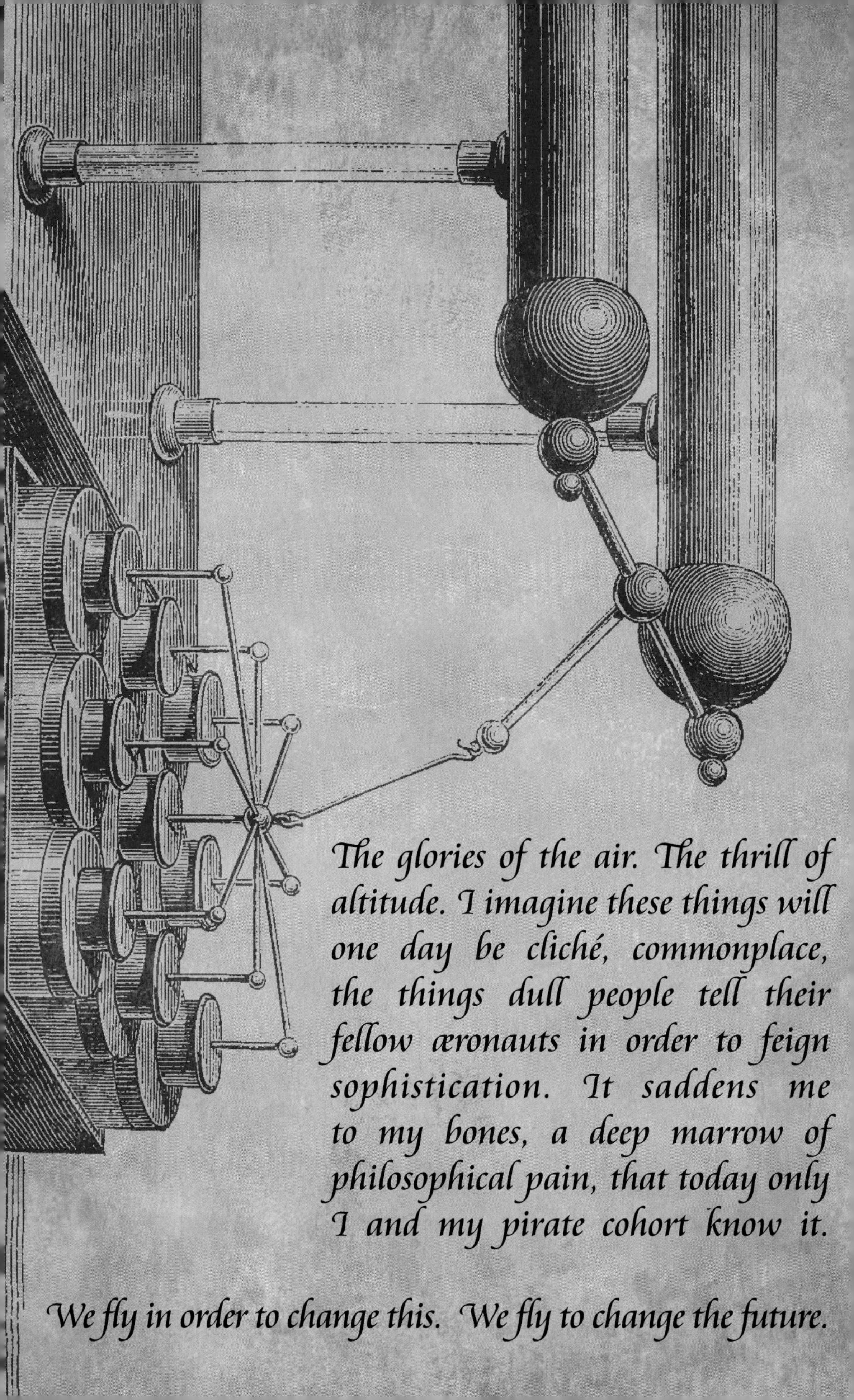

The glories of the air. The thrill of altitude. I imagine these things will one day be cliché, commonplace, the things dull people tell their fellow æronauts in order to feign sophistication. It saddens me to my bones, a deep marrow of philosophical pain, that today only I and my pirate cohort know it.

We fly in order to change this. We fly to change the future.

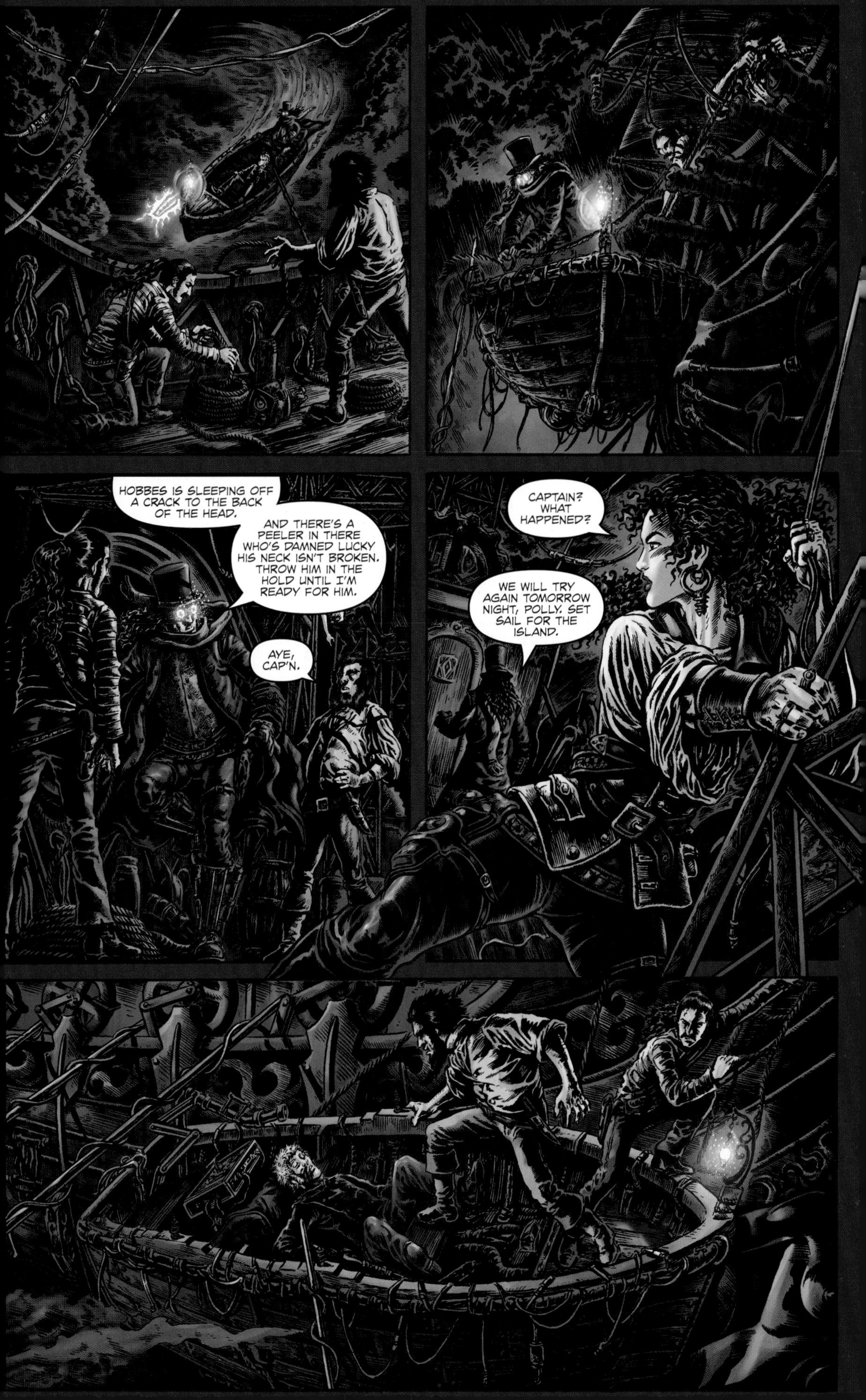
HOBBES IS SLEEPING OFF A CRACK TO THE BACK OF THE HEAD.
AND THERE'S A PEELER IN THERE WHO'S DAMNED LUCKY HIS NECK ISN'T BROKEN. THROW HIM IN THE HOLD UNTIL I'M READY FOR HIM.
AYE, CAP'N.
CAPTAIN? WHAT HAPPENED?
WE WILL TRY AGAIN TOMORROW NIGHT, POLLY. SET SAIL FOR THE ISLAND.

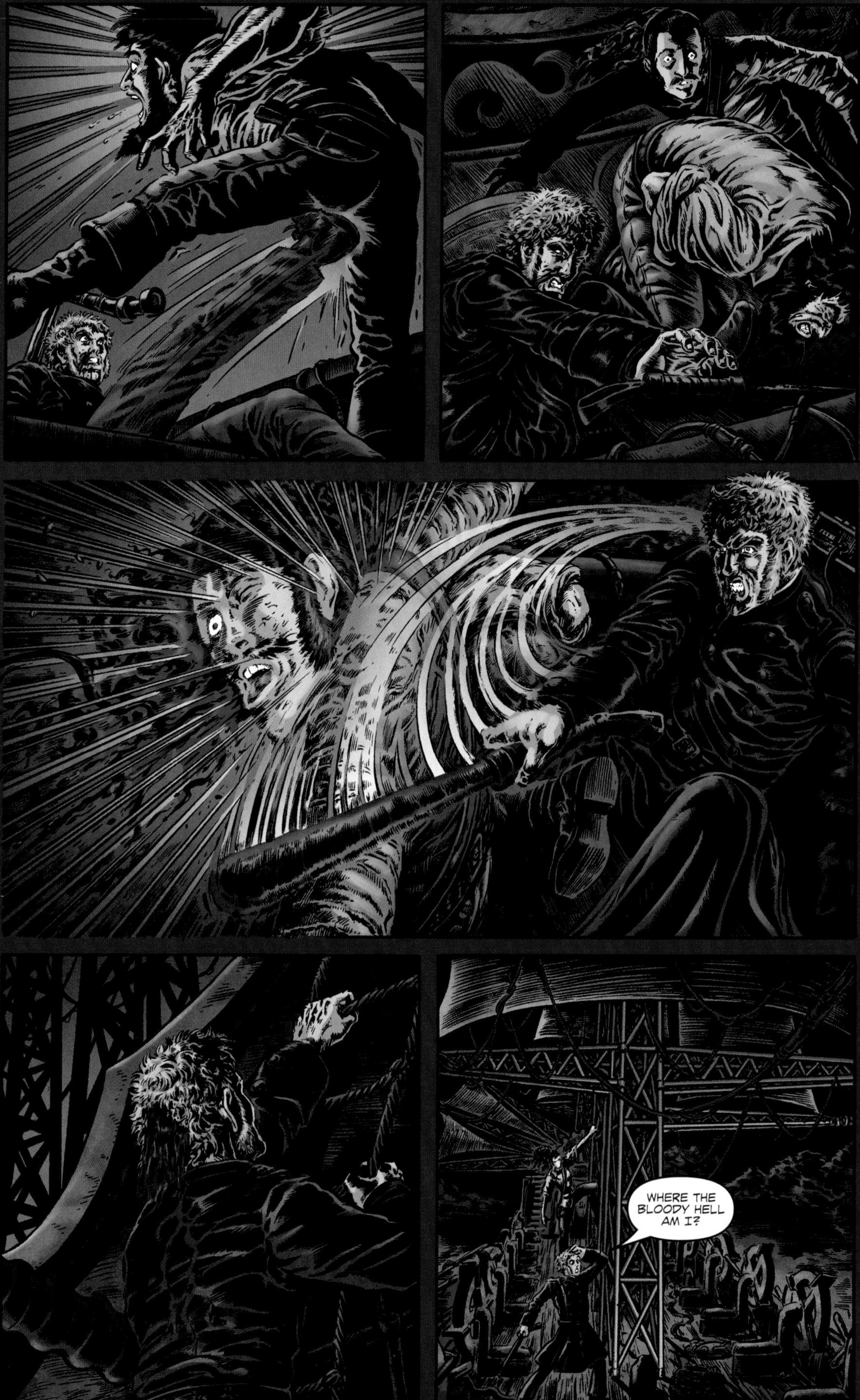
WHERE THE BLOODY HELL AM I?

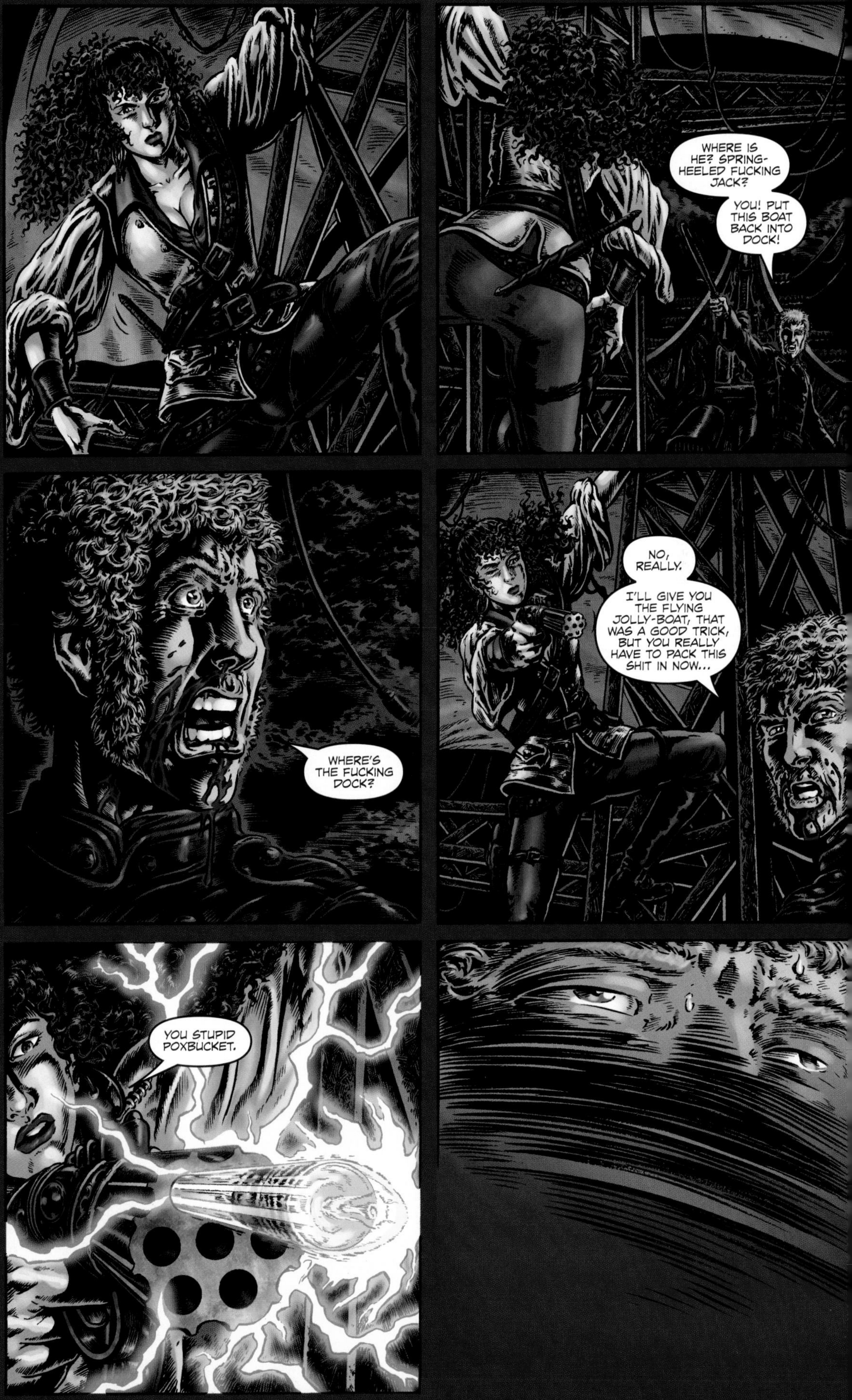
WHERE IS HE? SPRING-HEELED FUCKING JACK?
YOU! PUT THIS BOAT BACK INTO DOCK!
WHERE'S THE FUCKING DOCK?
NO, REALLY.
I'LL GIVE YOU THE FLYING JOLLY-BOAT, THAT WAS A GOOD TRICK, BUT YOU REALLY HAVE TO PACK THIS SHIT IN NOW...
YOU STUPID POXBUCKET.

It was only later that I realised how many mistakes I made, that awful night. More errors than a man of science should ever have countenanced.

The worst of which was allowing the crew to turn all their energies on the policeman, instead of to their sailing.

We dipped lower than we ought, on a night clearer than we made allowance for.

Despite our great mental exertions and attendance to the most complex of constructions, it is always the simple stupid things that see us undone.

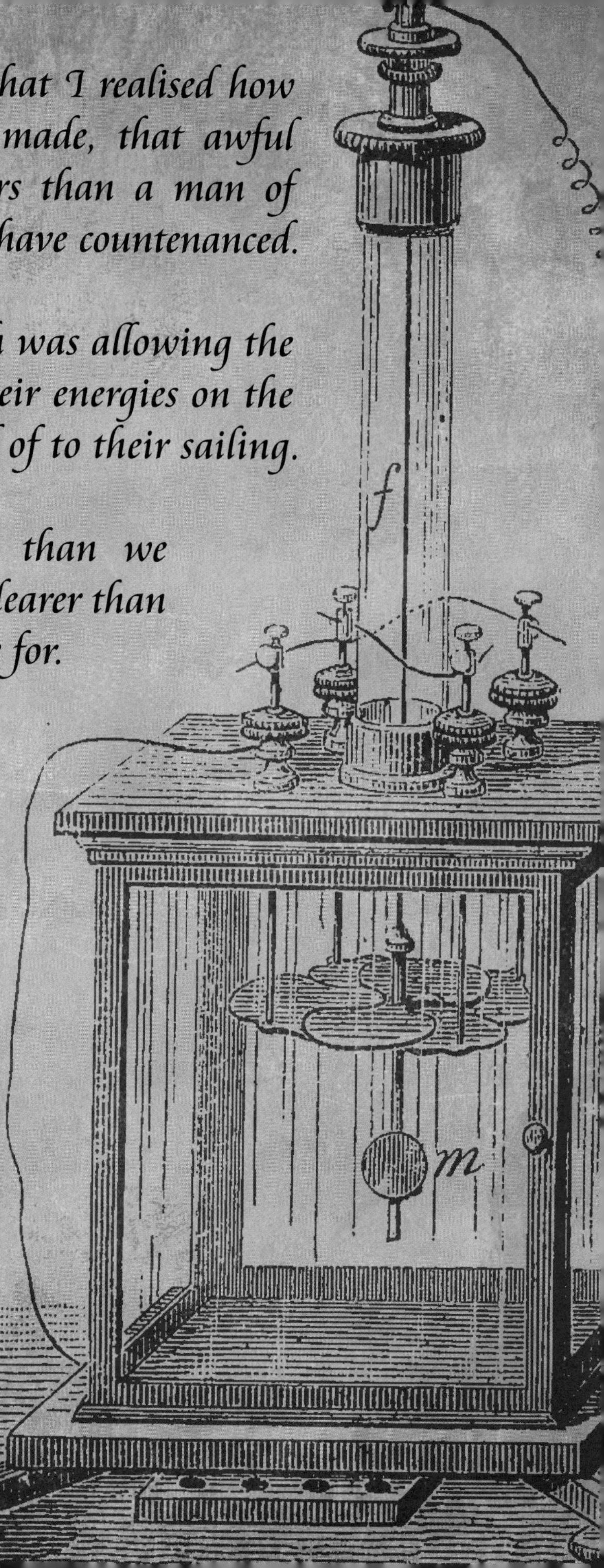
f
m

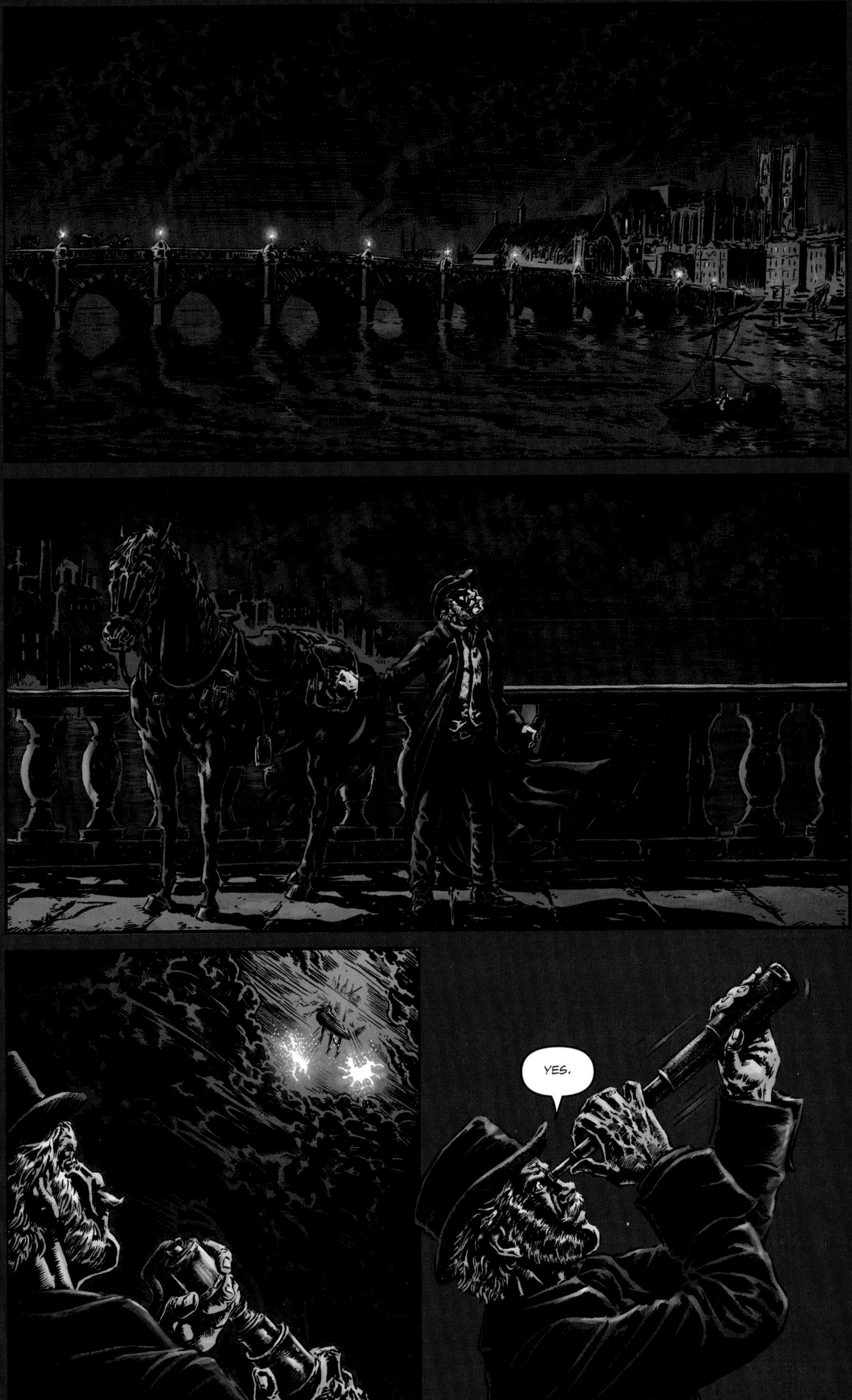
YES.

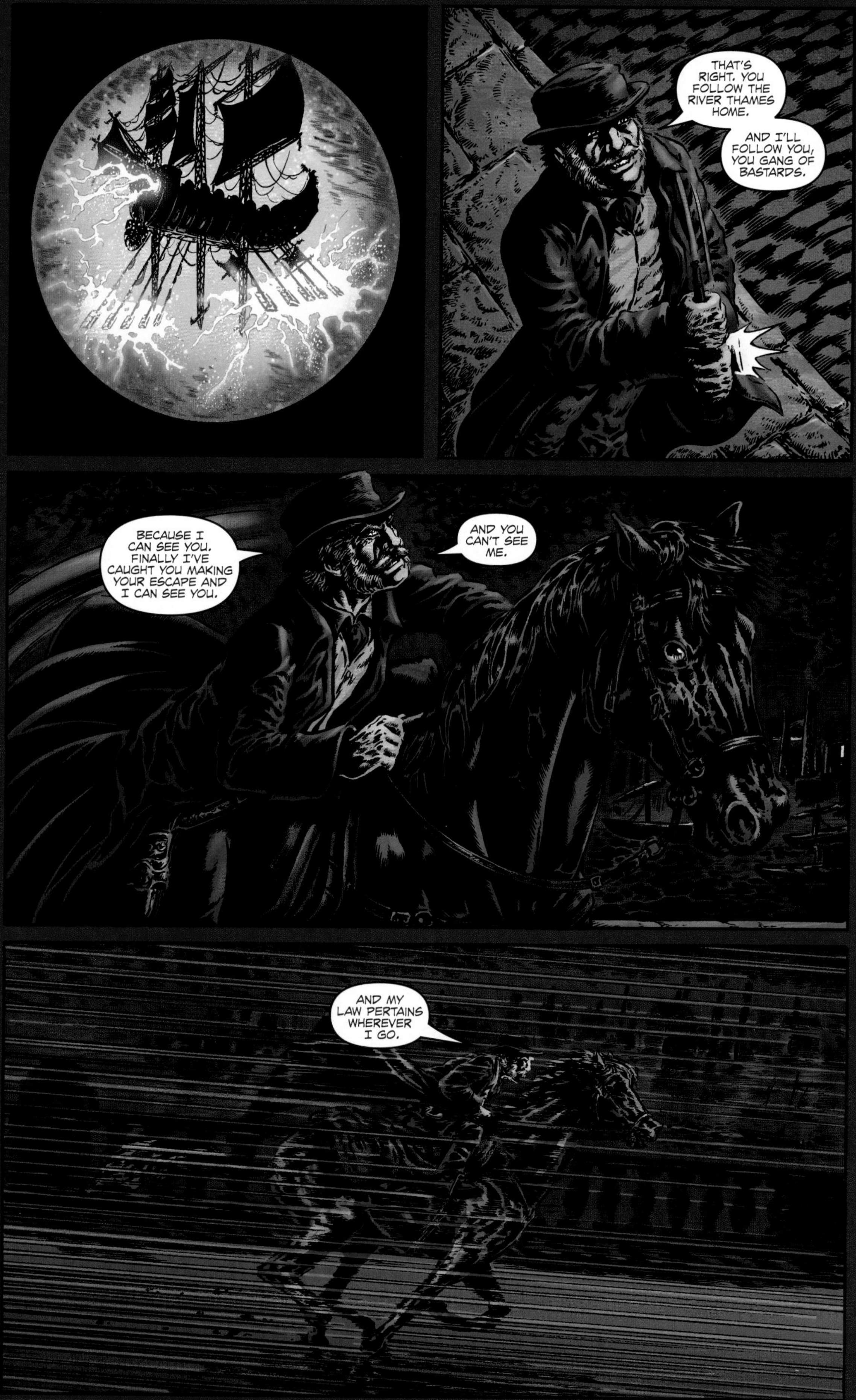
THAT'S RIGHT. YOU FOLLOW THE RIVER THAMES HOME.
AND I'LL FOLLOW YOU, YOU GANG OF BASTARDS.
BECAUSE I CAN SEE YOU. FINALLY I'VE CAUGHT YOU MAKING YOUR ESCAPE AND I CAN SEE YOU.
AND YOU CAN'T SEE ME.
AND MY LAW PERTAINS WHEREVER I GO.

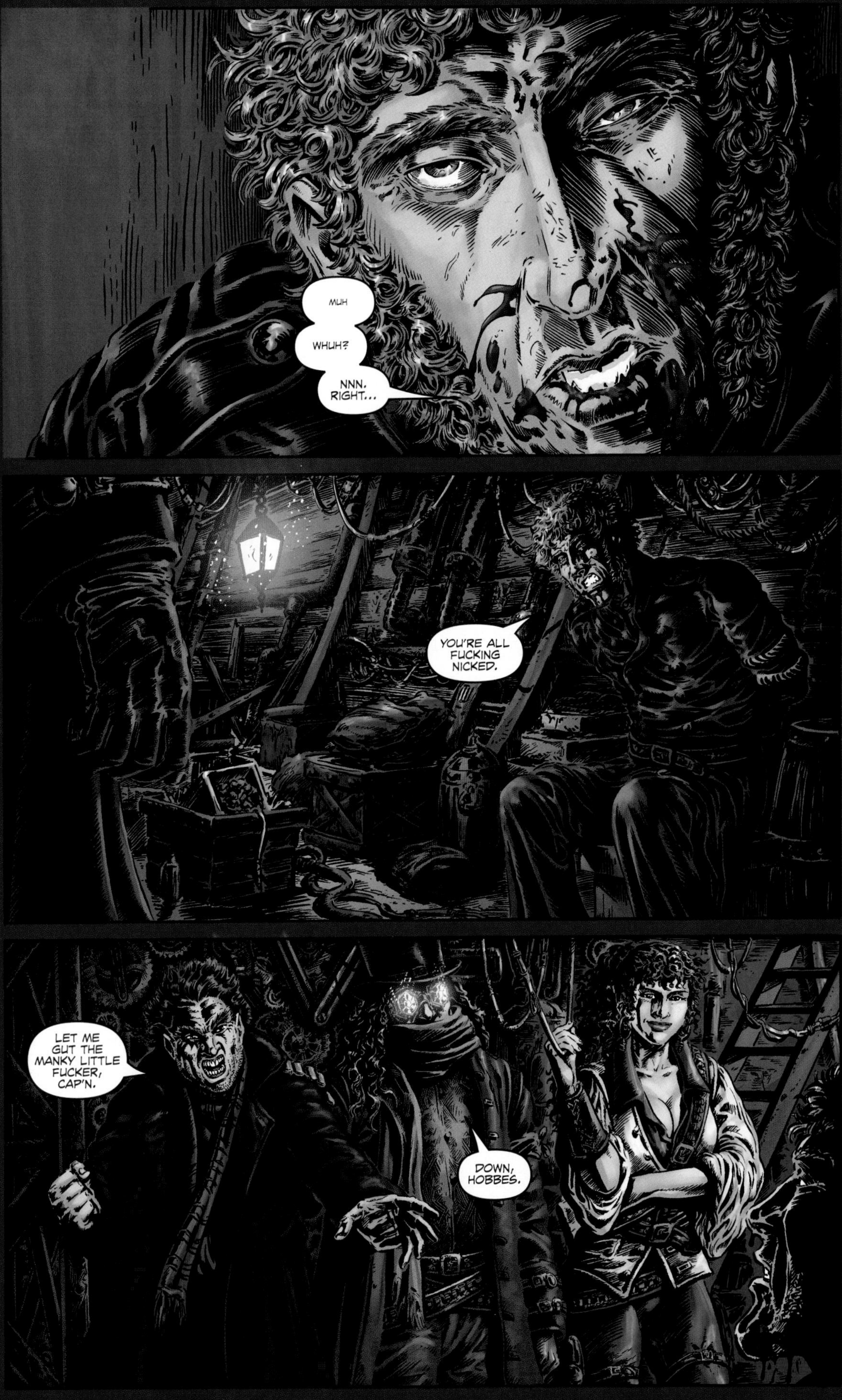
MUH
WHUH?
NNN. RIGHT...
YOU'RE ALL FUCKING NICKED.
LET ME GUT THE MANKY LITTLE FUCKER, CAP'N.
DOWN, HOBBES.

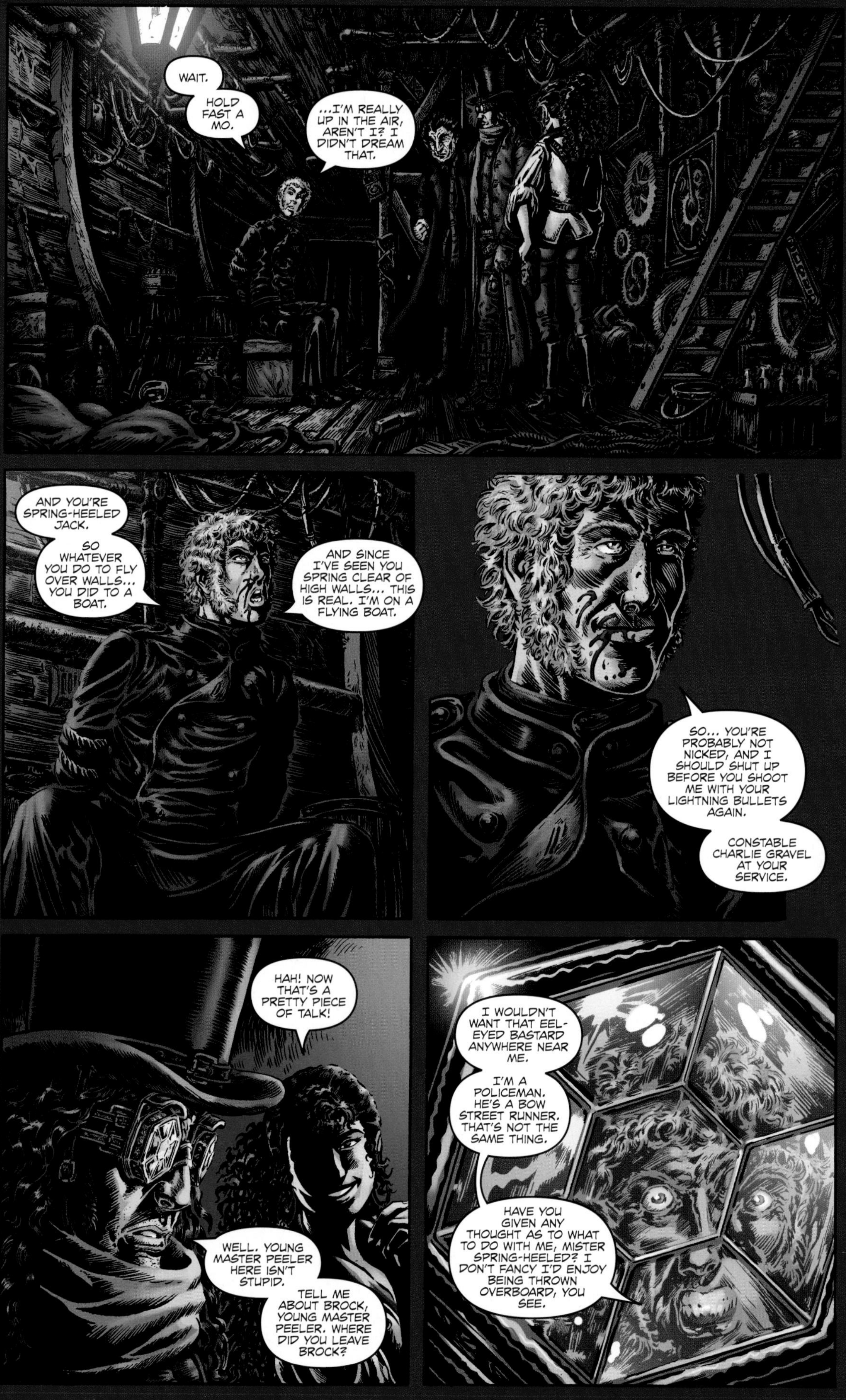
WAIT.
HOLD FAST A MO.
...I'M REALLY UP IN THE AIR, AREN'T I? I DIDN'T DREAM THAT.
AND YOU'RE SPRING-HEELED JACK.
SO WHATEVER YOU DO TO FLY OVER WALLS... YOU DID TO A BOAT.
AND SINCE I'VE SEEN YOU SPRING CLEAR OF HIGH WALLS... THIS IS REAL. I'M ON A FLYING BOAT.
SO... YOU'RE PROBABLY NOT NICKED, AND I SHOULD SHUT UP BEFORE YOU SHOOT ME WITH YOUR LIGHTNING BULLETS AGAIN.
CONSTABLE CHARLIE GRAVEL AT YOUR SERVICE.
HAH! NOW THAT'S A PRETTY PIECE OF TALK!
WELL. YOUNG MASTER PEELER HERE ISN'T STUPID.
TELL ME ABOUT BROCK, YOUNG MASTER PEELER. WHERE DID YOU LEAVE BROCK?
I WOULDN'T WANT THAT EEL-EYED BASTARD ANYWHERE NEAR ME.
I'M A POLICEMAN. HE'S A BOW STREET RUNNER. THAT'S NOT THE SAME THING.
HAVE YOU GIVEN ANY THOUGHT AS TO WHAT TO DO WITH ME, MISTER SPRING-HEELED? I DON'T FANCY I'D ENJOY BEING THROWN OVERBOARD, YOU SEE.

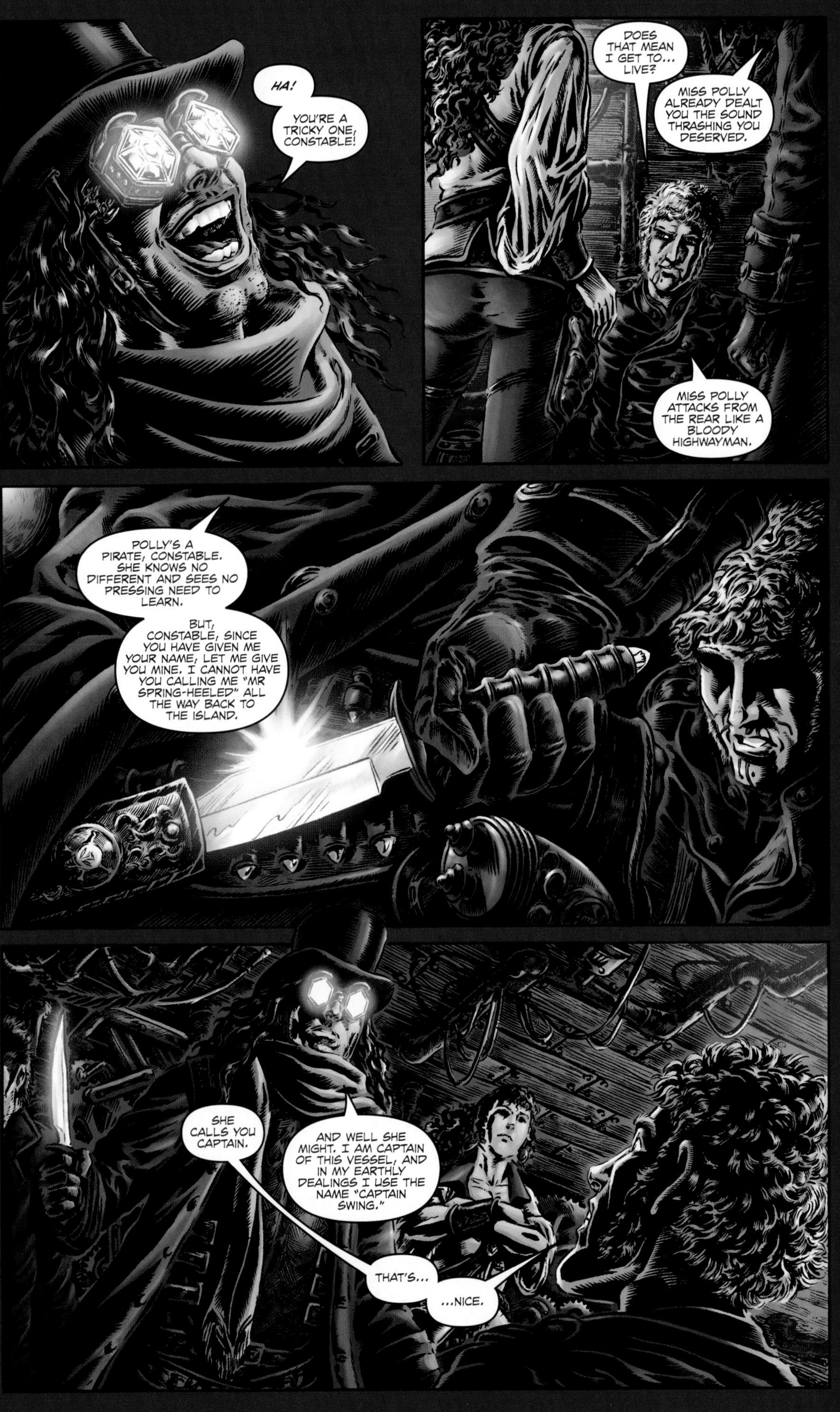

HA!
YOU'RE A TRICKY ONE, CONSTABLE!
DOES THAT MEAN I GET TO... LIVE?
MISS POLLY ALREADY DEALT YOU THE SOUND THRASHING YOU DESERVED.
MISS POLLY ATTACKS FROM THE REAR LIKE A BLOODY HIGHWAYMAN.
POLLY'S A PIRATE, CONSTABLE. SHE KNOWS NO DIFFERENT AND SEES NO PRESSING NEED TO LEARN.
BUT, CONSTABLE, SINCE YOU HAVE GIVEN ME YOUR NAME, LET ME GIVE YOU MINE. I CANNOT HAVE YOU CALLING ME "MR SPRING-HEELED" ALL THE WAY BACK TO THE ISLAND.
SHE CALLS YOU CAPTAIN.
AND WELL SHE MIGHT. I AM CAPTAIN OF THIS VESSEL, AND IN MY EARTHLY DEALINGS I USE THE NAME "CAPTAIN SWING."
THAT'S...
...NICE.

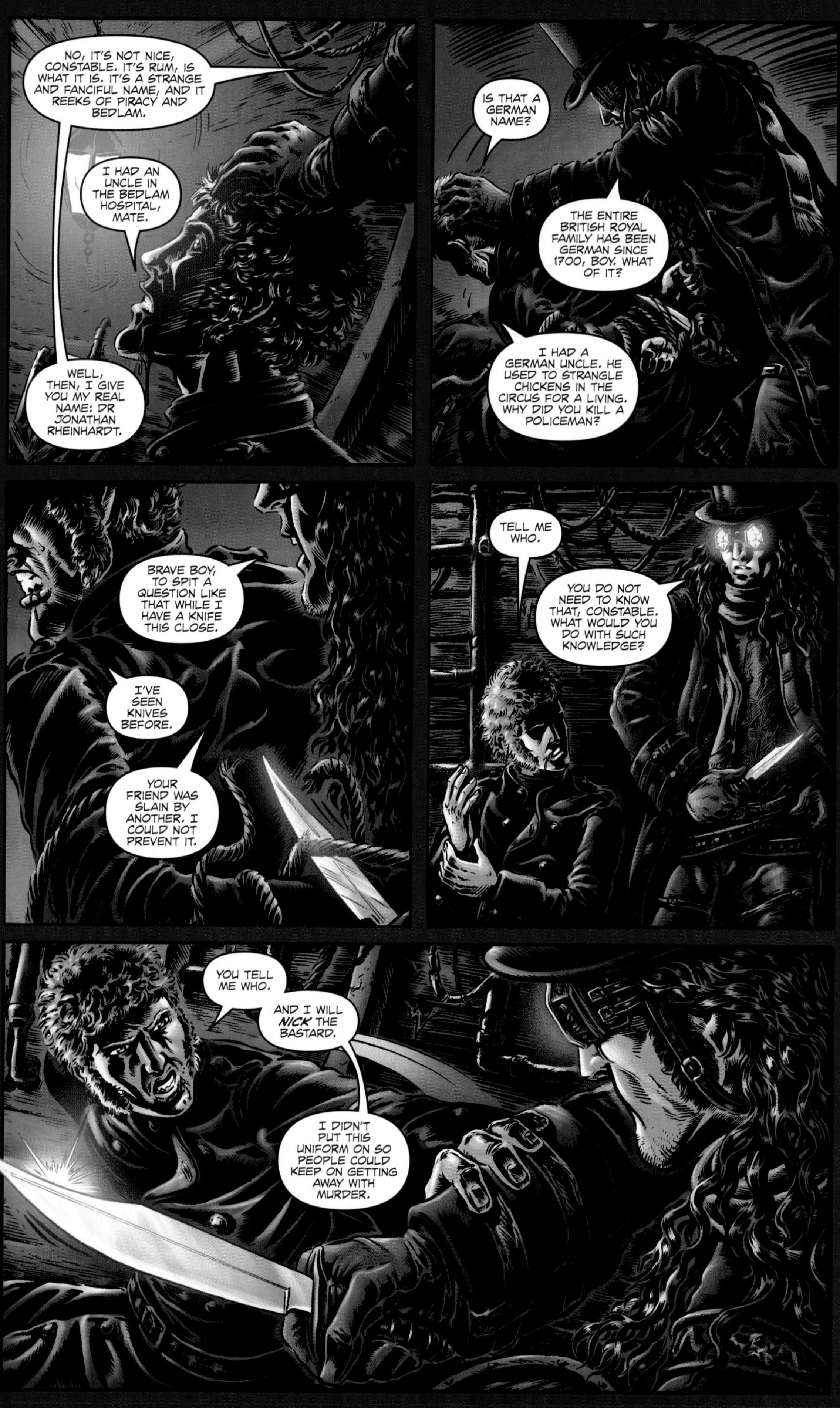
NO, IT'S NOT NICE, CONSTABLE. IT'S RUM, IS WHAT IT IS. IT'S A STRANGE AND FANCIFUL NAME, AND IT REEKS OF PIRACY AND BEDLAM.
I HAD AN UNCLE IN THE BEDLAM HOSPITAL, MATE.
WELL, THEN, I GIVE YOU MY REAL NAME: DR JONATHAN RHEINHARDT.
IS THAT A GERMAN NAME?
THE ENTIRE BRITISH ROYAL FAMILY HAS BEEN GERMAN SINCE 1700, BOY. WHAT OF IT?
I HAD A GERMAN UNCLE. HE USED TO STRANGLE CHICKENS IN THE CIRCUS FOR A LIVING. WHY DID YOU KILL A POLICEMAN?
BRAVE BOY, TO SPIT A QUESTION LIKE THAT WHILE I HAVE A KNIFE THIS CLOSE.
I'VE SEEN KNIVES BEFORE.
YOUR FRIEND WAS SLAIN BY ANOTHER. I COULD NOT PREVENT IT.
TELL ME WHO.
YOU DO NOT NEED TO KNOW THAT, CONSTABLE. WHAT WOULD YOU DO WITH SUCH KNOWLEDGE?
YOU TELL ME WHO.
AND I WILL *NICK* THE BASTARD.
I DIDN'T PUT THIS UNIFORM ON SO PEOPLE COULD KEEP ON GETTING AWAY WITH MURDER.

Doctor Jonathan Rheinhardt am I, oh yes. A name I barely dare to repeat to myself, studying my own face in the sooty and cracked little shaving mirror I take from my case at nights. A man of science, a Natural Philosopher. Easier, perhaps, to be Captain Swing, frightening agent of magic lights, than Jonathan Rheinhardt, a man cast out because he refused to turn the world over to magic. Some nights, being even the Spring-Heeled Jack of the Metropolitan Police's mythology would seem preferable to being a Natural Philosopher who has to leap around London dressed as a nightmare to try and put the world to rights.

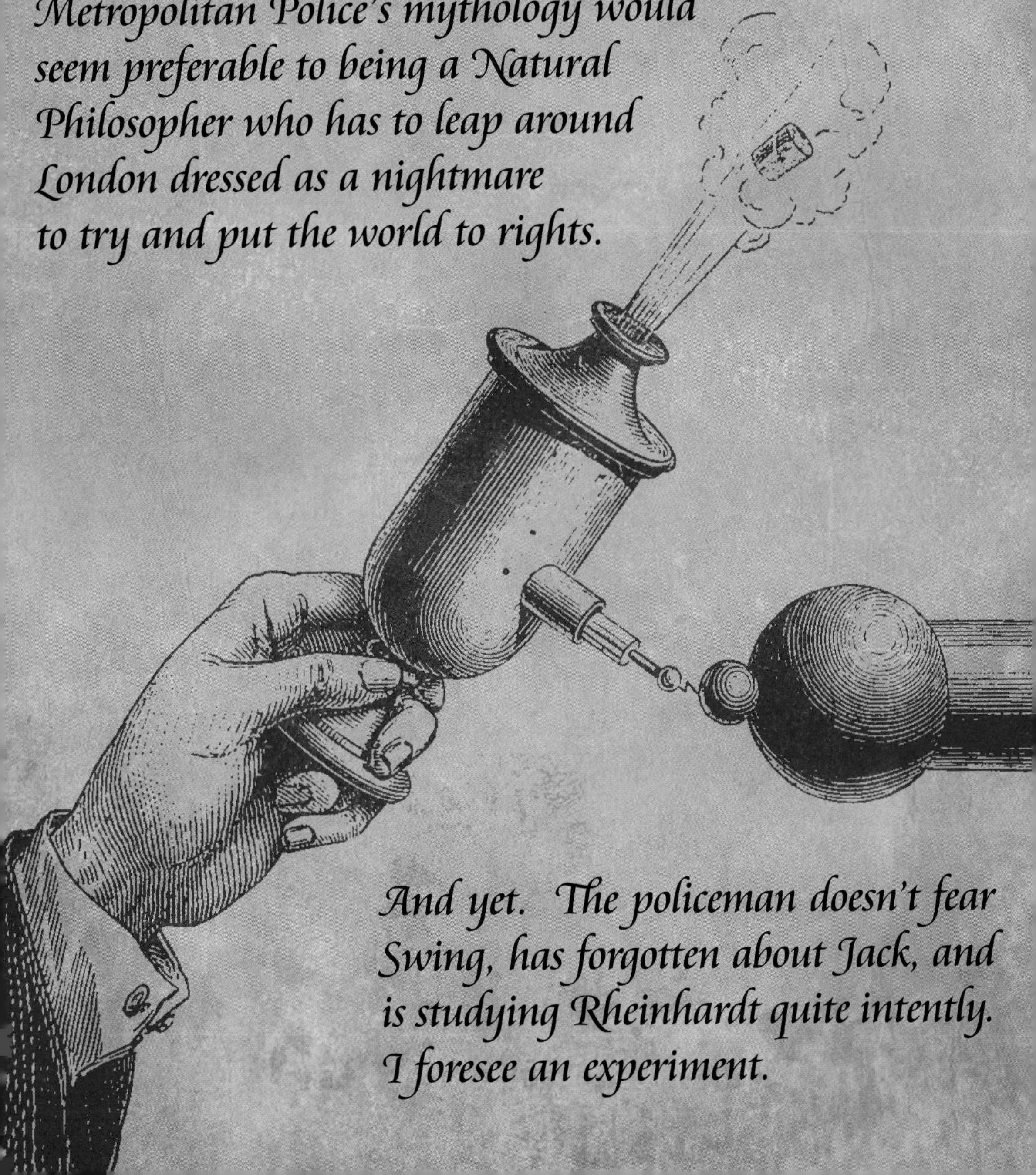

And yet. The policeman doesn't fear Swing, has forgotten about Jack, and is studying Rheinhardt quite intently. I foresee an experiment.

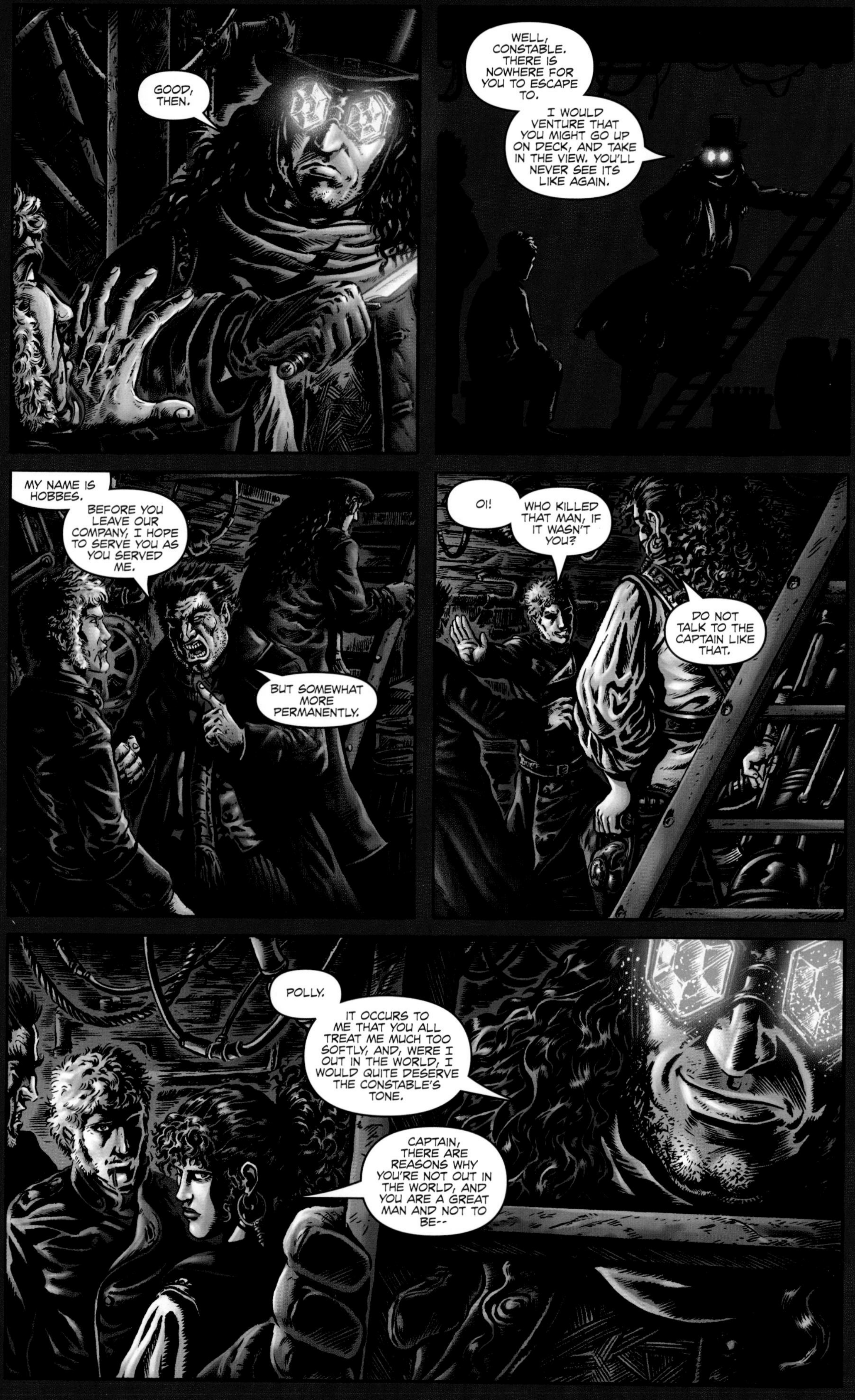
GOOD, THEN.
WELL, CONSTABLE. THERE IS NOWHERE FOR YOU TO ESCAPE TO.
I WOULD VENTURE THAT YOU MIGHT GO UP ON DECK, AND TAKE IN THE VIEW. YOU'LL NEVER SEE ITS LIKE AGAIN.
MY NAME IS HOBBES.
BEFORE YOU LEAVE OUR COMPANY, I HOPE TO SERVE YOU AS YOU SERVED ME.
BUT SOMEWHAT MORE PERMANENTLY.
OI!
WHO KILLED THAT MAN, IF IT WASN'T YOU?
DO NOT TALK TO THE CAPTAIN LIKE THAT.
POLLY.
IT OCCURS TO ME THAT YOU ALL TREAT ME MUCH TOO SOFTLY, AND, WERE I OUT IN THE WORLD, I WOULD QUITE DESERVE THE CONSTABLE'S TONE.
CAPTAIN, THERE ARE REASONS WHY YOU'RE NOT OUT IN THE WORLD, AND YOU ARE A GREAT MAN AND NOT TO BE--

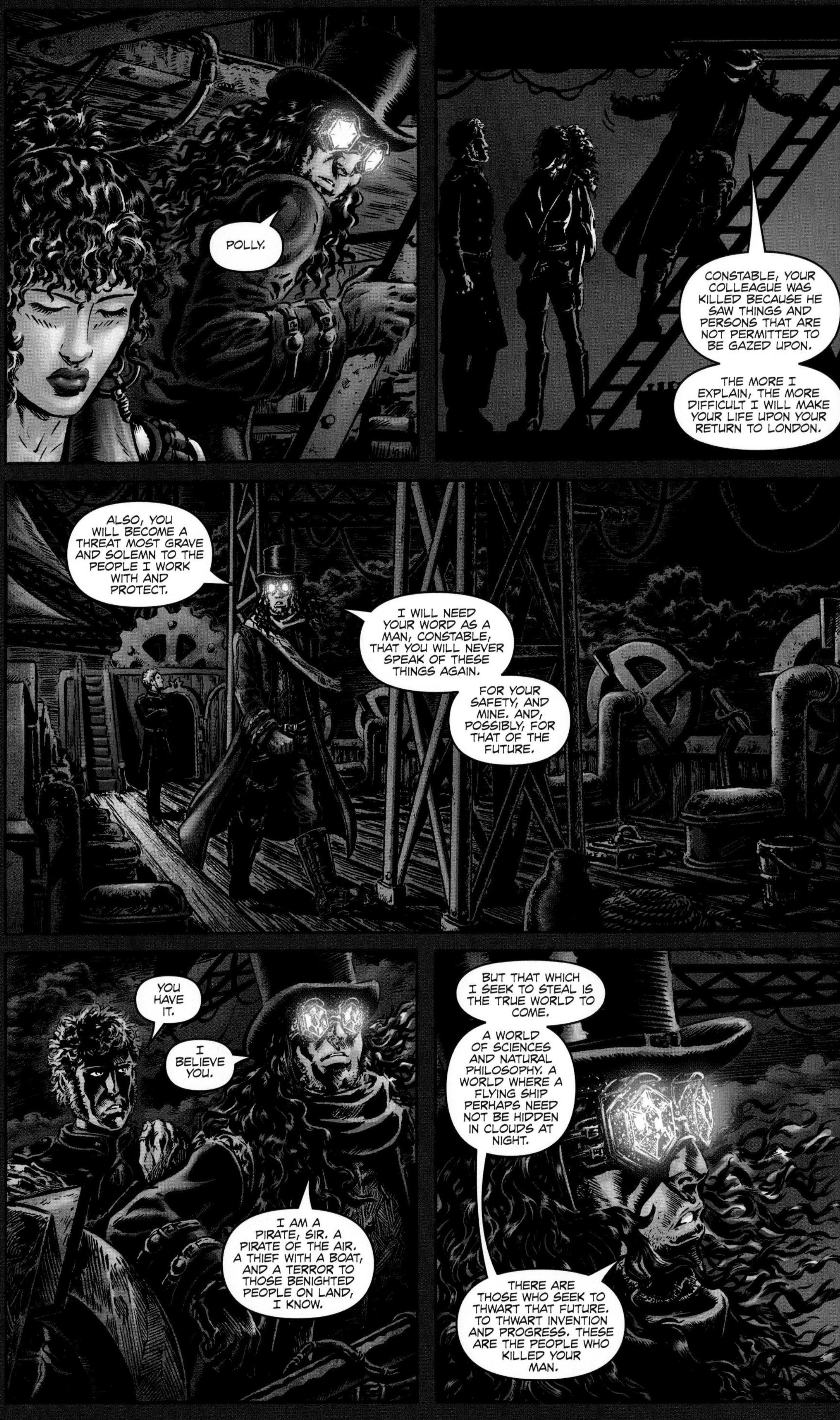
POLLY.
CONSTABLE, YOUR COLLEAGUE WAS KILLED BECAUSE HE SAW THINGS AND PERSONS THAT ARE NOT PERMITTED TO BE GAZED UPON.
THE MORE I EXPLAIN, THE MORE DIFFICULT I WILL MAKE YOUR LIFE UPON YOUR RETURN TO LONDON.
ALSO, YOU WILL BECOME A THREAT MOST GRAVE AND SOLEMN TO THE PEOPLE I WORK WITH AND PROTECT.
I WILL NEED YOUR WORD AS A MAN, CONSTABLE, THAT YOU WILL NEVER SPEAK OF THESE THINGS AGAIN.
FOR YOUR SAFETY, AND MINE. AND, POSSIBLY, FOR THAT OF THE FUTURE.
YOU HAVE IT.
I BELIEVE YOU.
I AM A PIRATE, SIR. A PIRATE OF THE AIR. A THIEF WITH A BOAT, AND A TERROR TO THOSE BENIGHTED PEOPLE ON LAND, I KNOW.
BUT THAT WHICH I SEEK TO STEAL IS THE TRUE WORLD TO COME.
A WORLD OF SCIENCES AND NATURAL PHILOSOPHY. A WORLD WHERE A FLYING SHIP PERHAPS NEED NOT BE HIDDEN IN CLOUDS AT NIGHT.
THERE ARE THOSE WHO SEEK TO THWART THAT FUTURE. TO THWART INVENTION AND PROGRESS. THESE ARE THE PEOPLE WHO KILLED YOUR MAN.

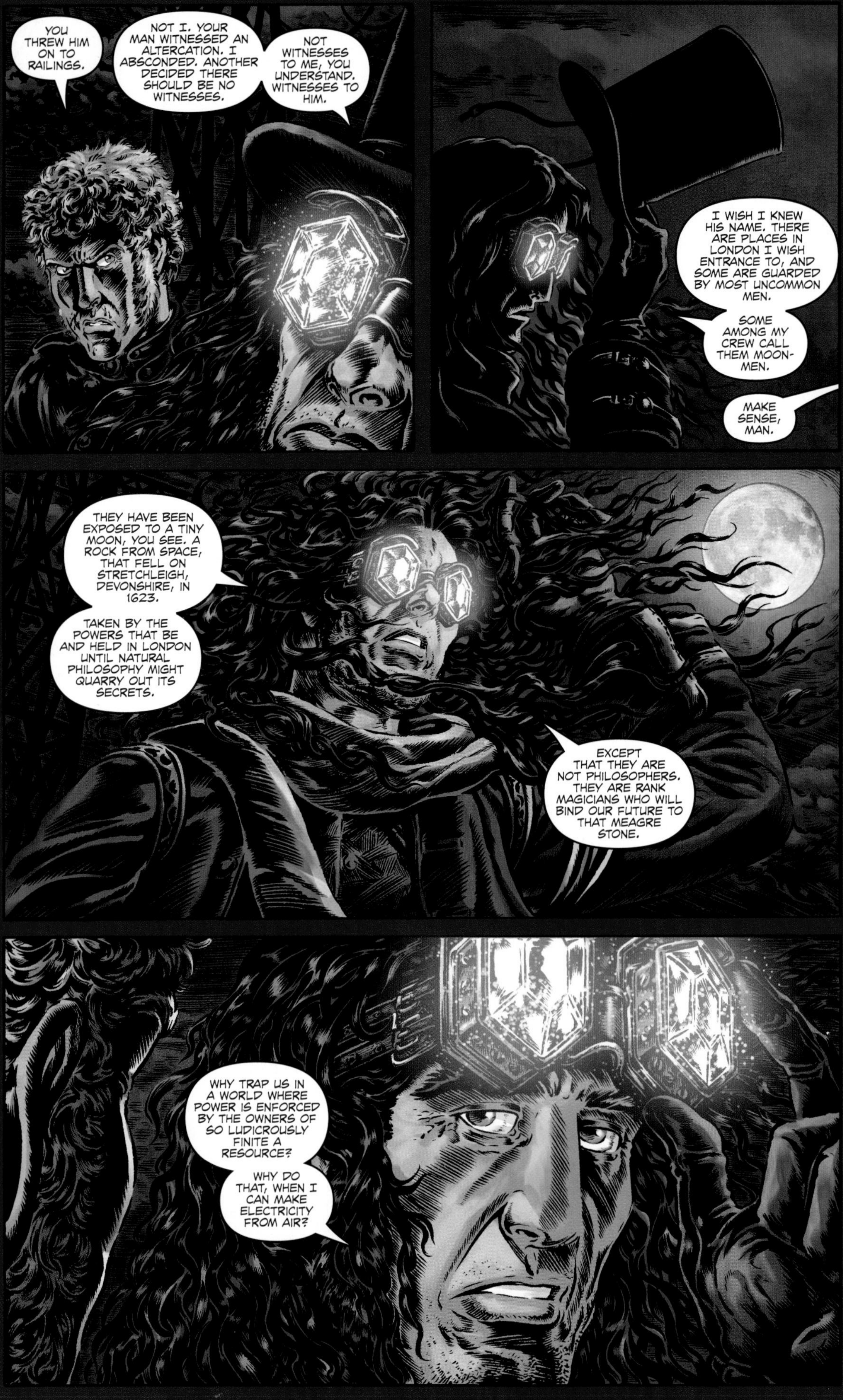
YOU THREW HIM ON TO RAILINGS.
NOT I. YOUR MAN WITNESSED AN ALTERCATION. I ABSCONDED. ANOTHER DECIDED THERE SHOULD BE NO WITNESSES.
NOT WITNESSES TO ME, YOU UNDERSTAND. WITNESSES TO HIM.
I WISH I KNEW HIS NAME. THERE ARE PLACES IN LONDON I WISH ENTRANCE TO, AND SOME ARE GUARDED BY MOST UNCOMMON MEN.
SOME AMONG MY CREW CALL THEM MOON-MEN.
MAKE SENSE, MAN.
THEY HAVE BEEN EXPOSED TO A TINY MOON, YOU SEE. A ROCK FROM SPACE, THAT FELL ON STRETCHLEIGH, DEVONSHIRE, IN 1623.
TAKEN BY THE POWERS THAT BE AND HELD IN LONDON UNTIL NATURAL PHILOSOPHY MIGHT QUARRY OUT ITS SECRETS.
EXCEPT THAT THEY ARE NOT PHILOSOPHERS. THEY ARE RANK MAGICIANS WHO WILL BIND OUR FUTURE TO THAT MEAGRE STONE.
WHY TRAP US IN A WORLD WHERE POWER IS ENFORCED BY THE OWNERS OF SO LUDICROUSLY FINITE A RESOURCE?
WHY DO THAT, WHEN I CAN MAKE ELECTRICITY FROM AIR?

It is so hard to make people understand, sometimes. With the pirates, I could frame my conceit in one way, and then turn it to show its golden hull, and they would see, instinctively. With Hobbes, who learned how to invent shipbuilding tricks and traps at his grandfather's knee (or, rather, his peg leg), it was the work of moments. Hobbes, shipwright to pirates, knew in his soul that the making of things could in so many ways be consonant with freedom from tyranny. Tyranny of all kinds. Poor Polly, born on a gaolhouse floor, had both rebellion and the need for freedom in her very blood.

But to convince a policeman, the very symbol of a country ever more watched by dry authority, the agent of the ever smaller enclosures we are required to live in...

I am all at sea.

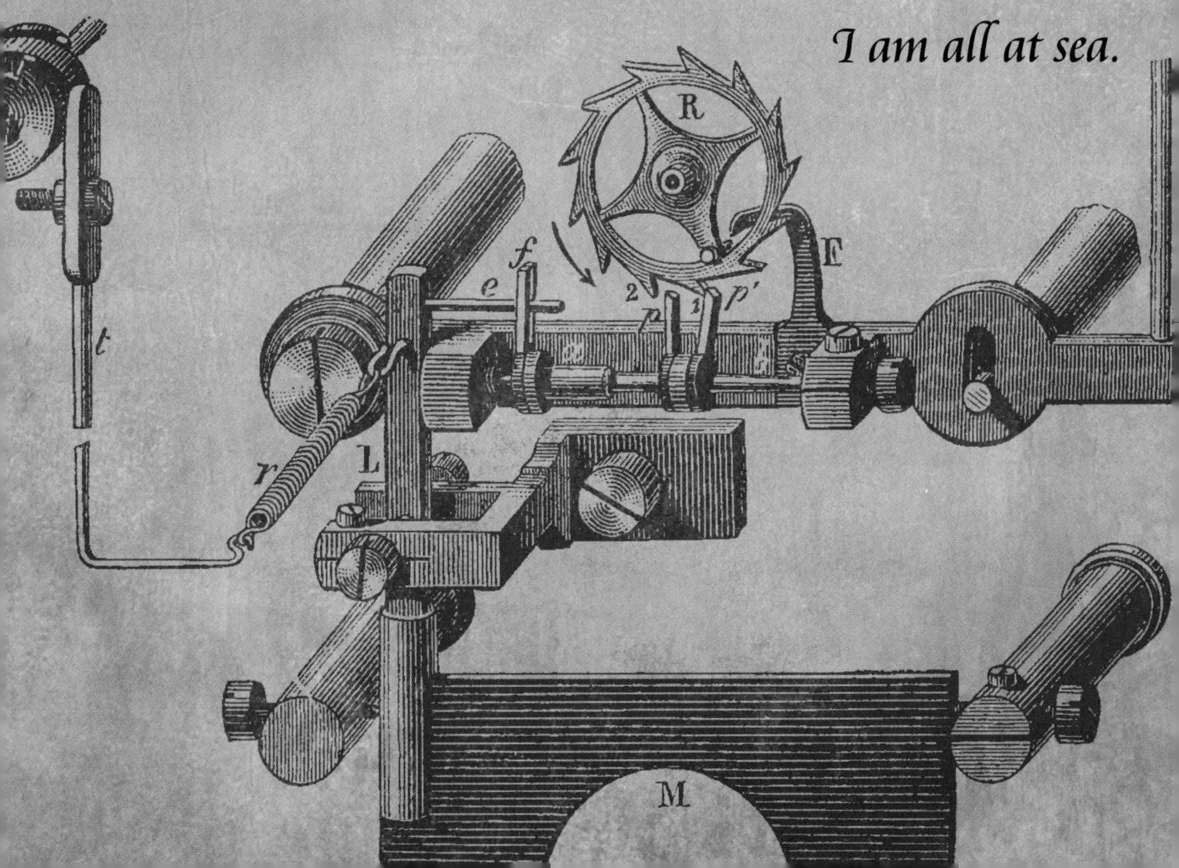
R
F
f
e
2
1
p
p'
t
r
L
M

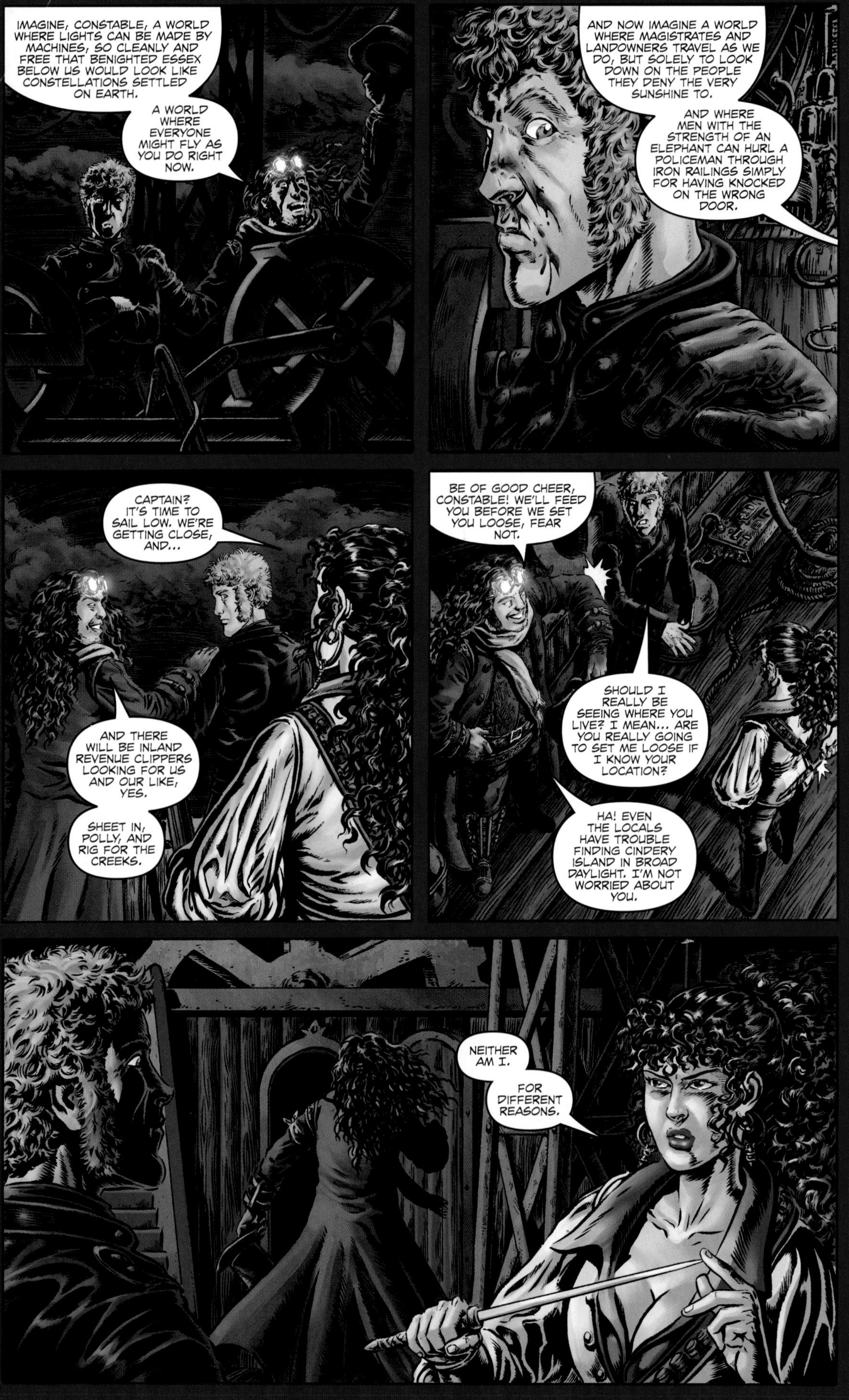
IMAGINE, CONSTABLE, A WORLD WHERE LIGHTS CAN BE MADE BY MACHINES, SO CLEANLY AND FREE THAT BENIGHTED ESSEX BELOW US WOULD LOOK LIKE CONSTELLATIONS SETTLED ON EARTH.
A WORLD WHERE EVERYONE MIGHT FLY AS YOU DO RIGHT NOW.
AND NOW IMAGINE A WORLD WHERE MAGISTRATES AND LANDOWNERS TRAVEL AS WE DO, BUT SOLELY TO LOOK DOWN ON THE PEOPLE THEY DENY THE VERY SUNSHINE TO.
AND WHERE MEN WITH THE STRENGTH OF AN ELEPHANT CAN HURL A POLICEMAN THROUGH IRON RAILINGS SIMPLY FOR HAVING KNOCKED ON THE WRONG DOOR.
CAPTAIN? IT'S TIME TO SAIL LOW. WE'RE GETTING CLOSE, AND...
AND THERE WILL BE INLAND REVENUE CLIPPERS LOOKING FOR US AND OUR LIKE, YES.
SHEET IN, POLLY, AND RIG FOR THE CREEKS.
BE OF GOOD CHEER, CONSTABLE! WE'LL FEED YOU BEFORE WE SET YOU LOOSE, FEAR NOT.
SHOULD I REALLY BE SEEING WHERE YOU LIVE? I MEAN... ARE YOU REALLY GOING TO SET ME LOOSE IF I KNOW YOUR LOCATION?
HA! EVEN THE LOCALS HAVE TROUBLE FINDING CINDERY ISLAND IN BROAD DAYLIGHT. I'M NOT WORRIED ABOUT YOU.
NEITHER AM I.
FOR DIFFERENT REASONS.

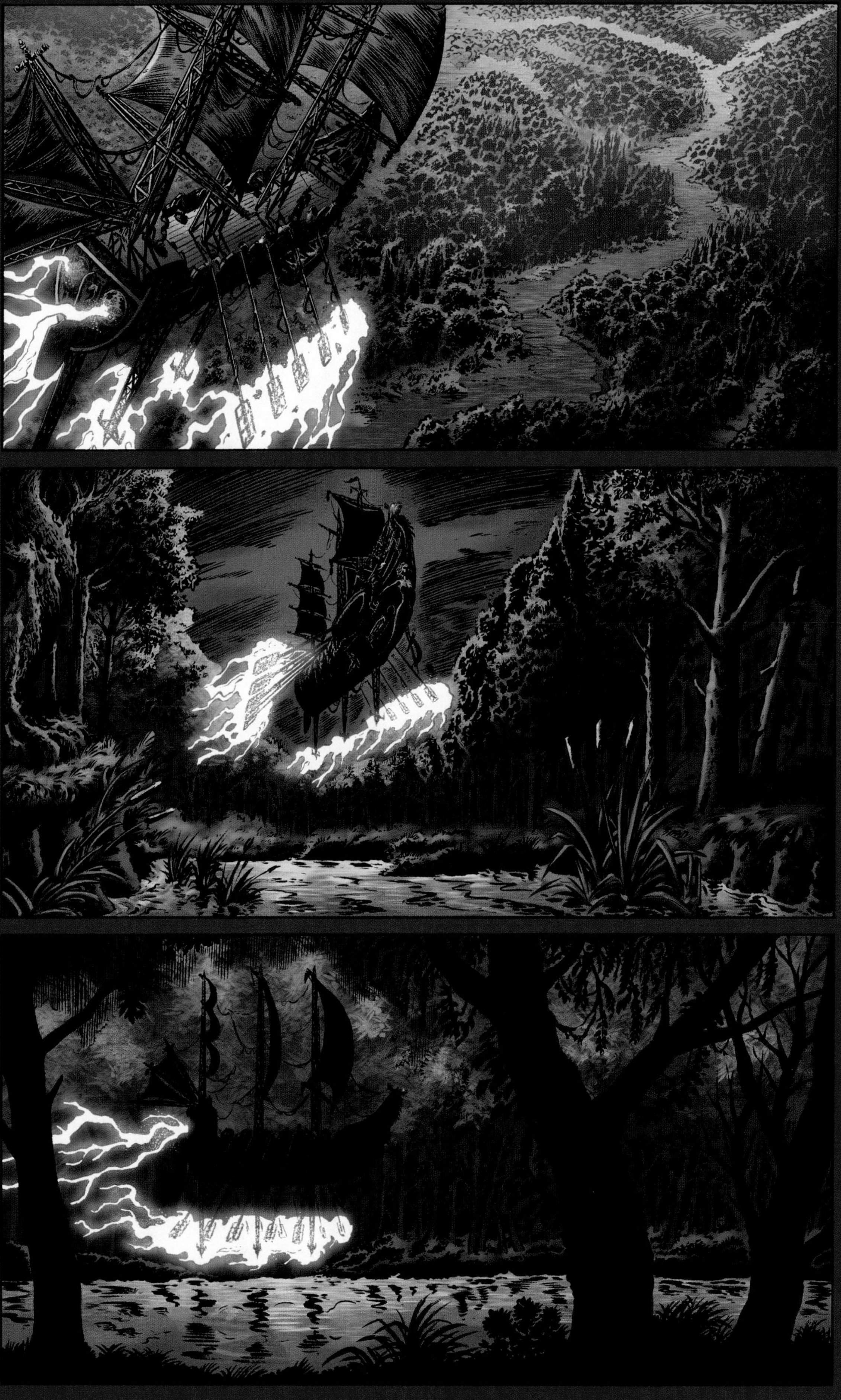

On into dark Essex we sailed. Past Mucking Marshes and on towards Foulness, then north past Paglesham towards Fingringhoe, through Little Ditch and the Thorn Fleet for the Brightlingsea Creek. The Strood Channel, the Besom Fleet and Point Clear Bay. Names to conjure with. The Blackwater. Northey Island, where Byrhtnoþ, Elderman of the Blackwater, stood off a horde of Norsemen i' viking: defeated only when he acceded to the Norse demands for a fair fight and allowed them on to the mainland. Sixty years old and more than six feet he stood, this man of too much heart, and it took three Norse at once to kill him.

Fairness is a quality I admire and seek to tend within myself. Whenever I sailed by Northey Island, I questioned it anew.

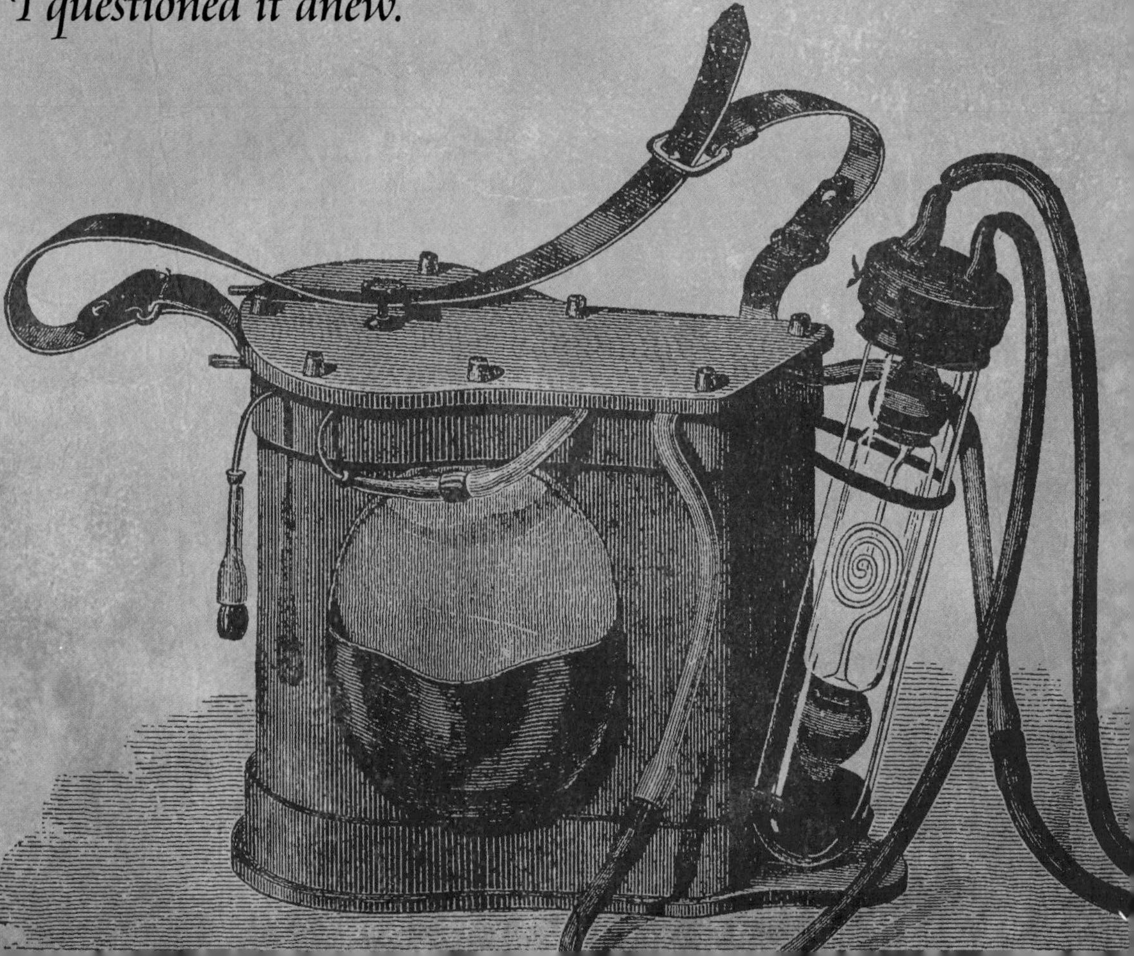

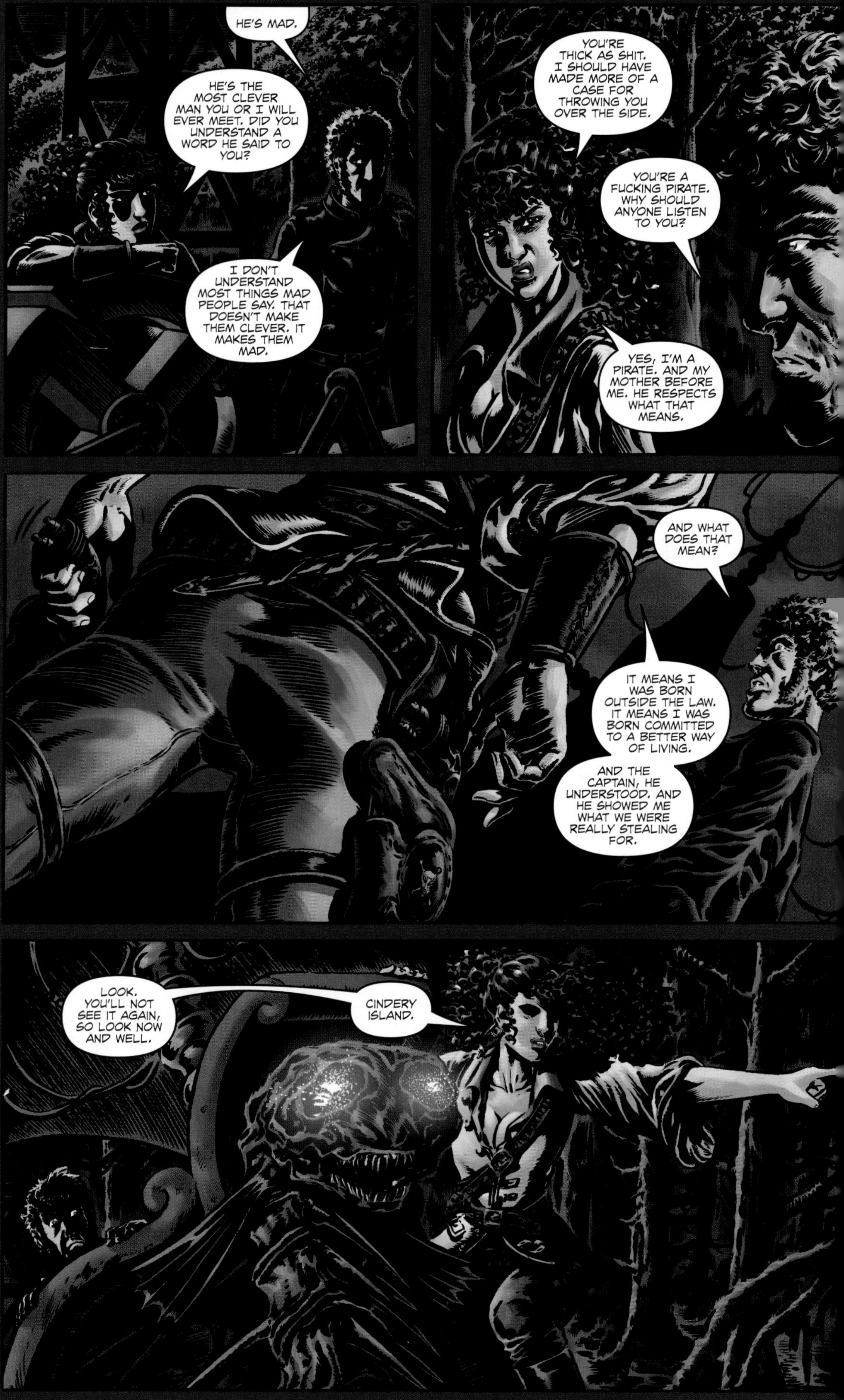
HE'S MAD.
HE'S THE MOST CLEVER MAN YOU OR I WILL EVER MEET. DID YOU UNDERSTAND A WORD HE SAID TO YOU?
I DON'T UNDERSTAND MOST THINGS MAD PEOPLE SAY. THAT DOESN'T MAKE THEM CLEVER. IT MAKES THEM MAD.
YOU'RE THICK AS SHIT. I SHOULD HAVE MADE MORE OF A CASE FOR THROWING YOU OVER THE SIDE.
YOU'RE A FUCKING PIRATE. WHY SHOULD ANYONE LISTEN TO YOU?
YES, I'M A PIRATE. AND MY MOTHER BEFORE ME. HE RESPECTS WHAT THAT MEANS.
AND WHAT DOES THAT MEAN?
IT MEANS I WAS BORN OUTSIDE THE LAW. IT MEANS I WAS BORN COMMITTED TO A BETTER WAY OF LIVING.
AND THE CAPTAIN, HE UNDERSTOOD. AND HE SHOWED ME WHAT WE WERE REALLY STEALING FOR.
LOOK. YOU'LL NOT SEE IT AGAIN, SO LOOK NOW AND WELL.
CINDERY ISLAND.

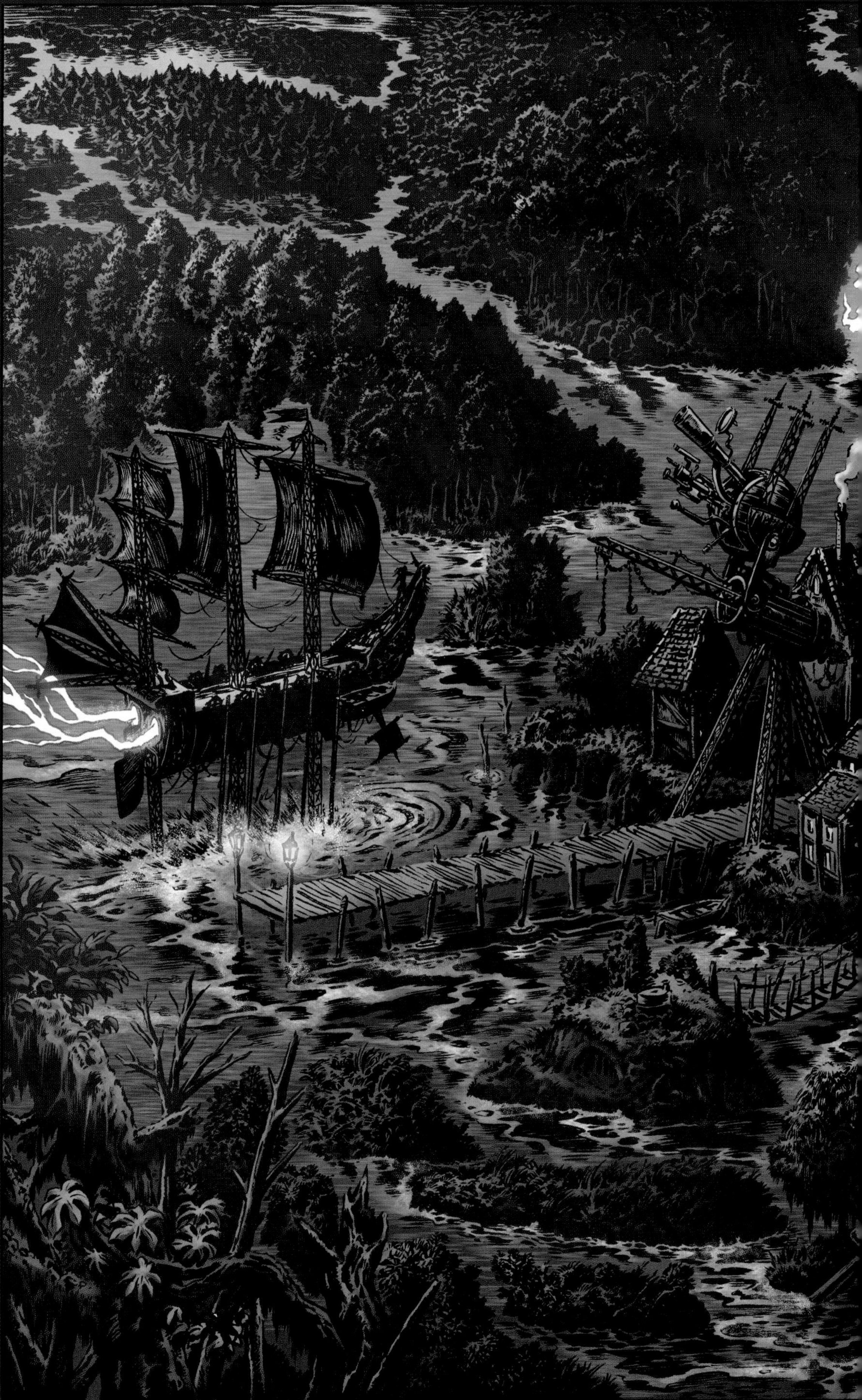

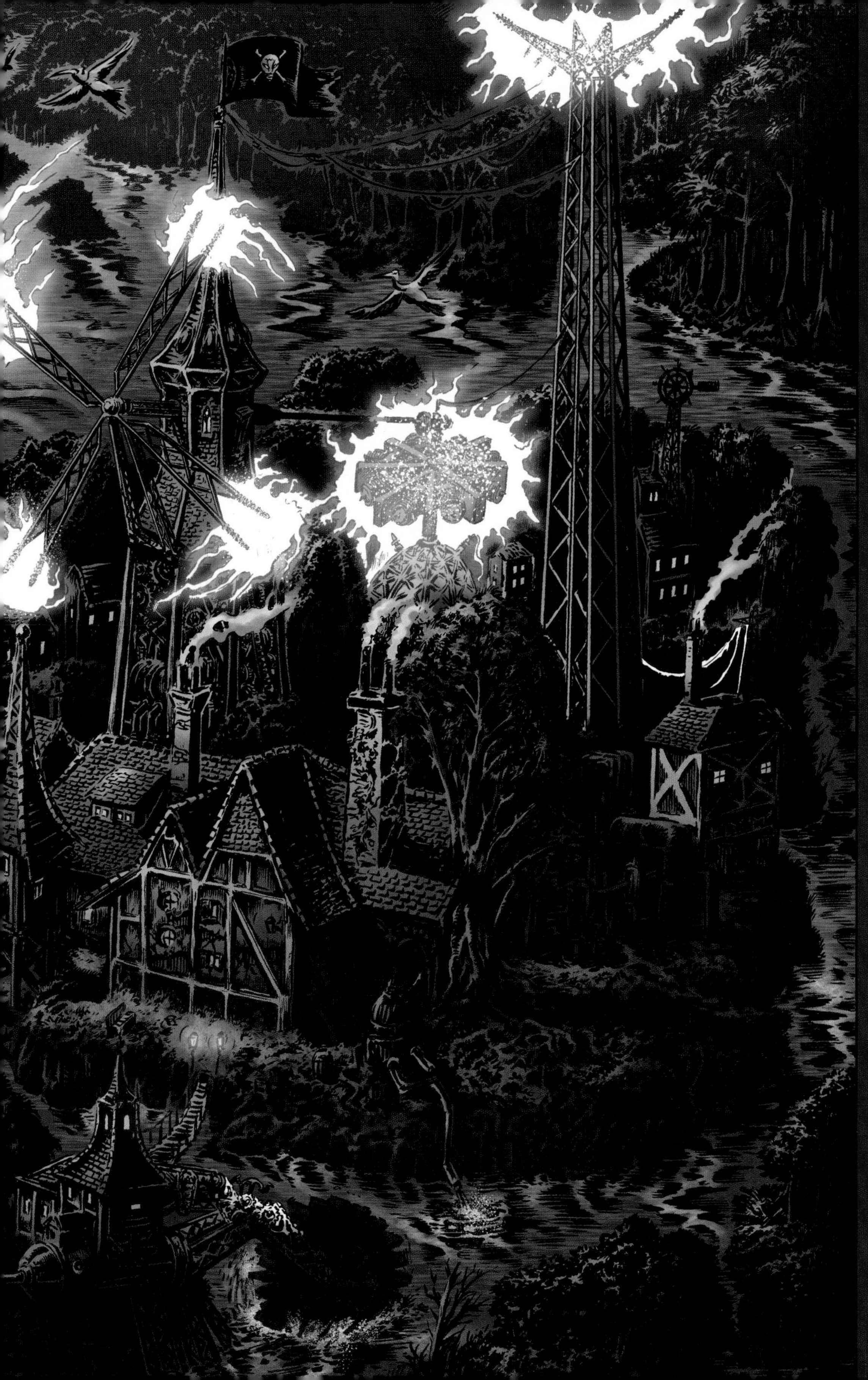

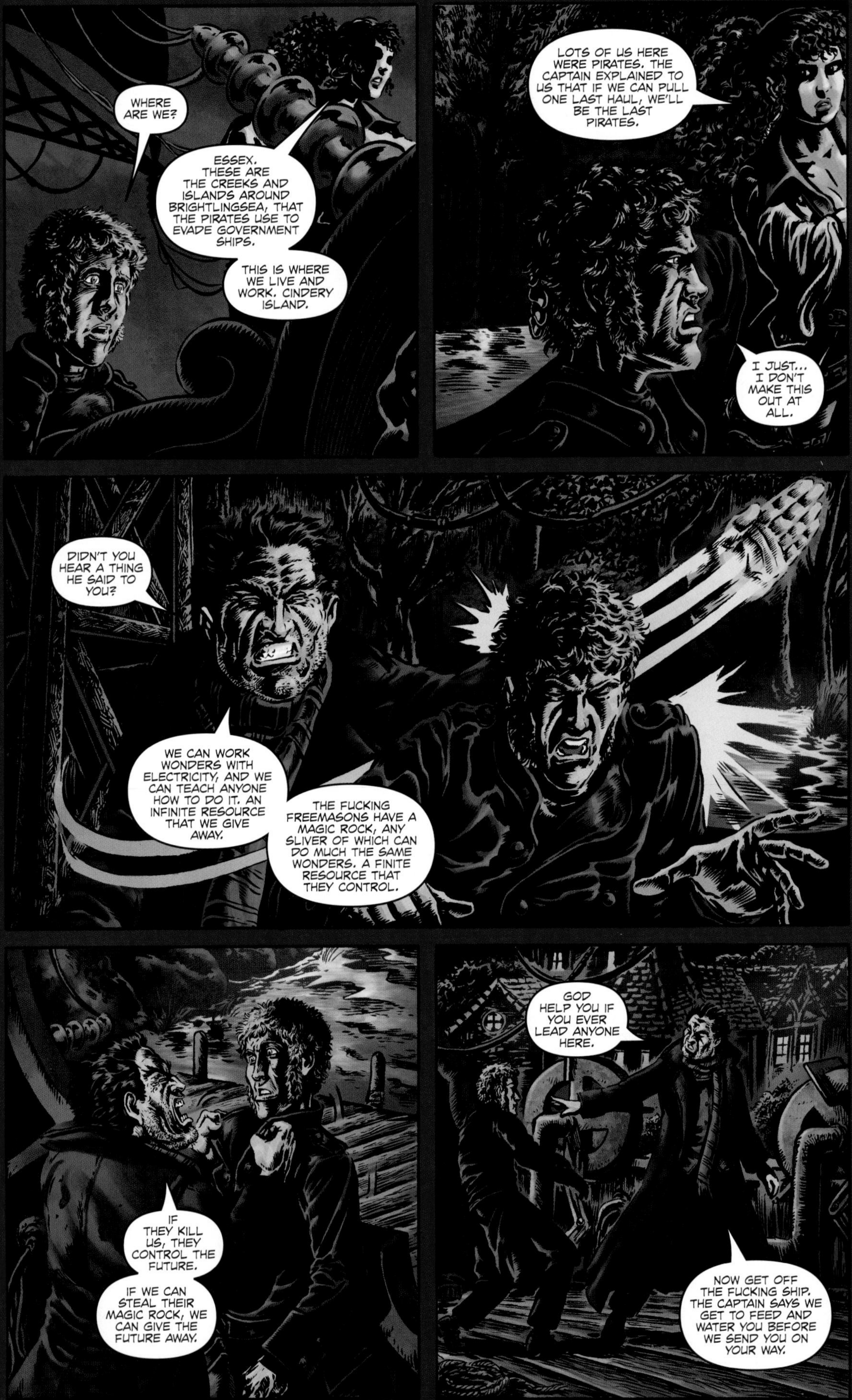
WHERE ARE WE?
ESSEX. THESE ARE THE CREEKS AND ISLANDS AROUND BRIGHTLINGSEA, THAT THE PIRATES USE TO EVADE GOVERNMENT SHIPS.
THIS IS WHERE WE LIVE AND WORK. CINDERY ISLAND.
LOTS OF US HERE WERE PIRATES. THE CAPTAIN EXPLAINED TO US THAT IF WE CAN PULL ONE LAST HAUL, WE'LL BE THE LAST PIRATES.
I JUST... I DON'T MAKE THIS OUT AT ALL.
DIDN'T YOU HEAR A THING HE SAID TO YOU?
WE CAN WORK WONDERS WITH ELECTRICITY, AND WE CAN TEACH ANYONE HOW TO DO IT. AN INFINITE RESOURCE THAT WE GIVE AWAY.
THE FUCKING FREEMASONS HAVE A MAGIC ROCK, ANY SLIVER OF WHICH CAN DO MUCH THE SAME WONDERS. A FINITE RESOURCE THAT THEY CONTROL.
IF THEY KILL US, THEY CONTROL THE FUTURE.
IF WE CAN STEAL THEIR MAGIC ROCK, WE CAN GIVE THE FUTURE AWAY.
GOD HELP YOU IF YOU EVER LEAD ANYONE HERE.
NOW GET OFF THE FUCKING SHIP. THE CAPTAIN SAYS WE GET TO FEED AND WATER YOU BEFORE WE SEND YOU ON YOUR WAY.

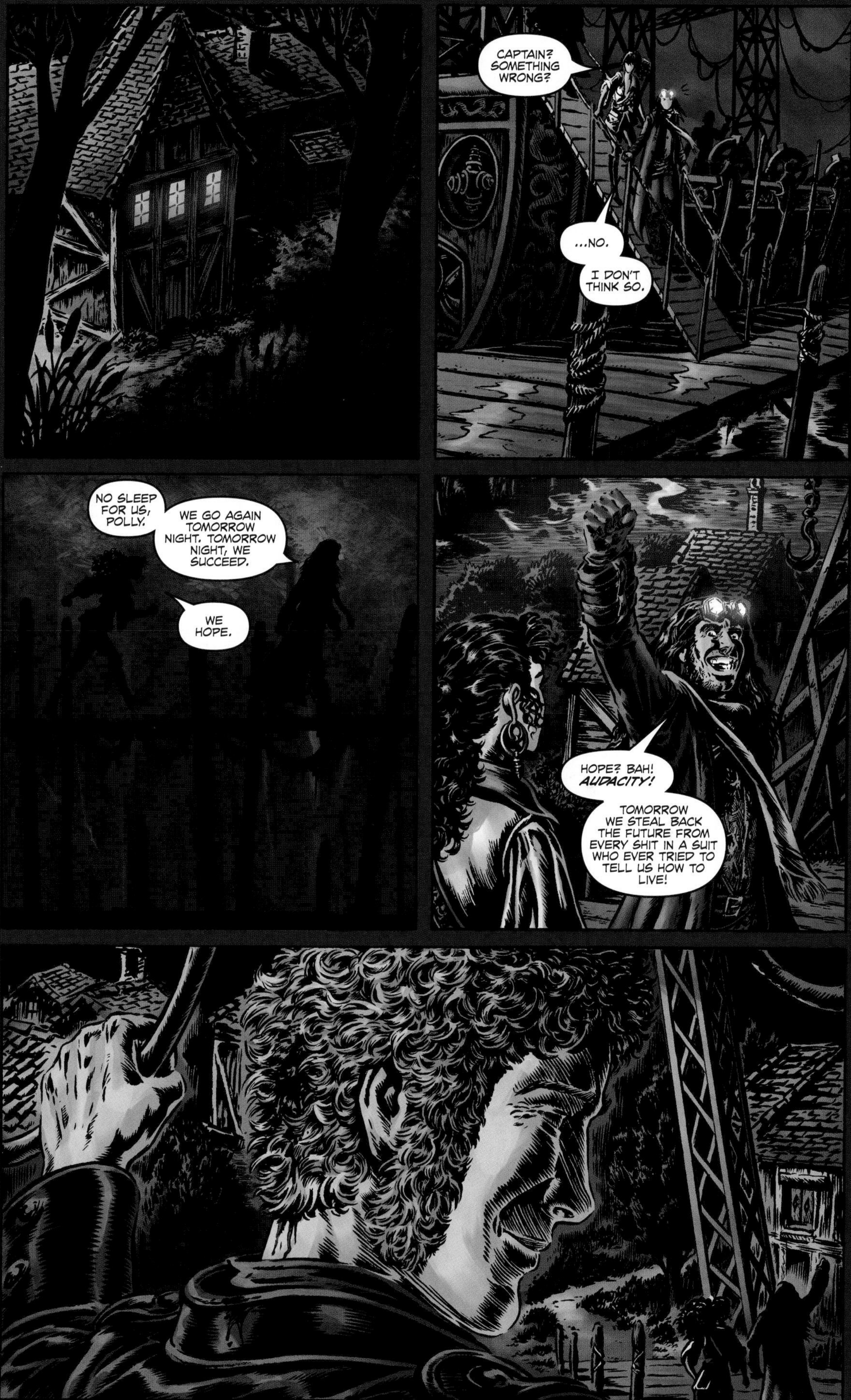
CAPTAIN? SOMETHING WRONG?
...NO.
I DON'T THINK SO.
NO SLEEP FOR US, POLLY.
WE GO AGAIN TOMORROW NIGHT. TOMORROW NIGHT, WE SUCCEED.
WE HOPE.
HOPE? BAH! AUDACITY!
TOMORROW WE STEAL BACK THE FUTURE FROM EVERY SHIT IN A SUIT WHO EVER TRIED TO TELL US HOW TO LIVE!

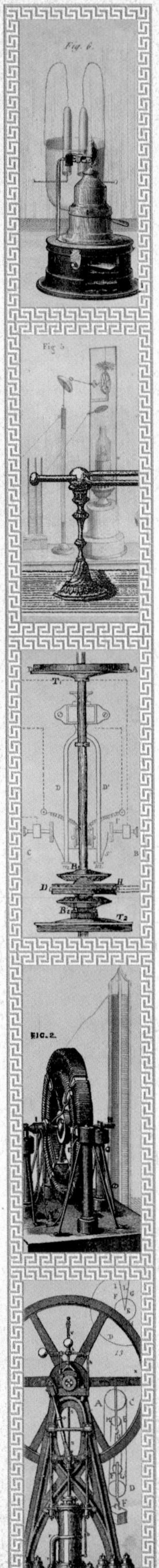

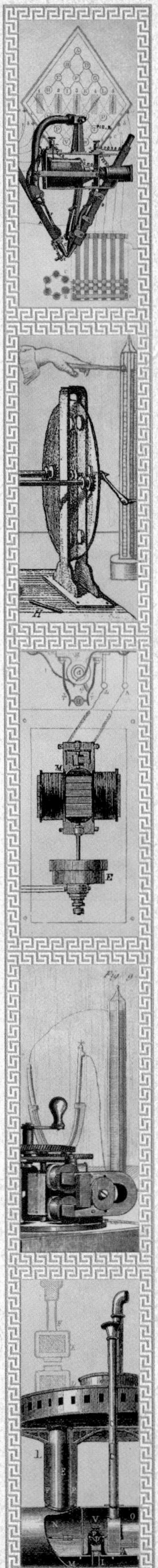

CAPTAIN SWING

and the ELECTRICAL PIRATES OF CINDERY ISLAND

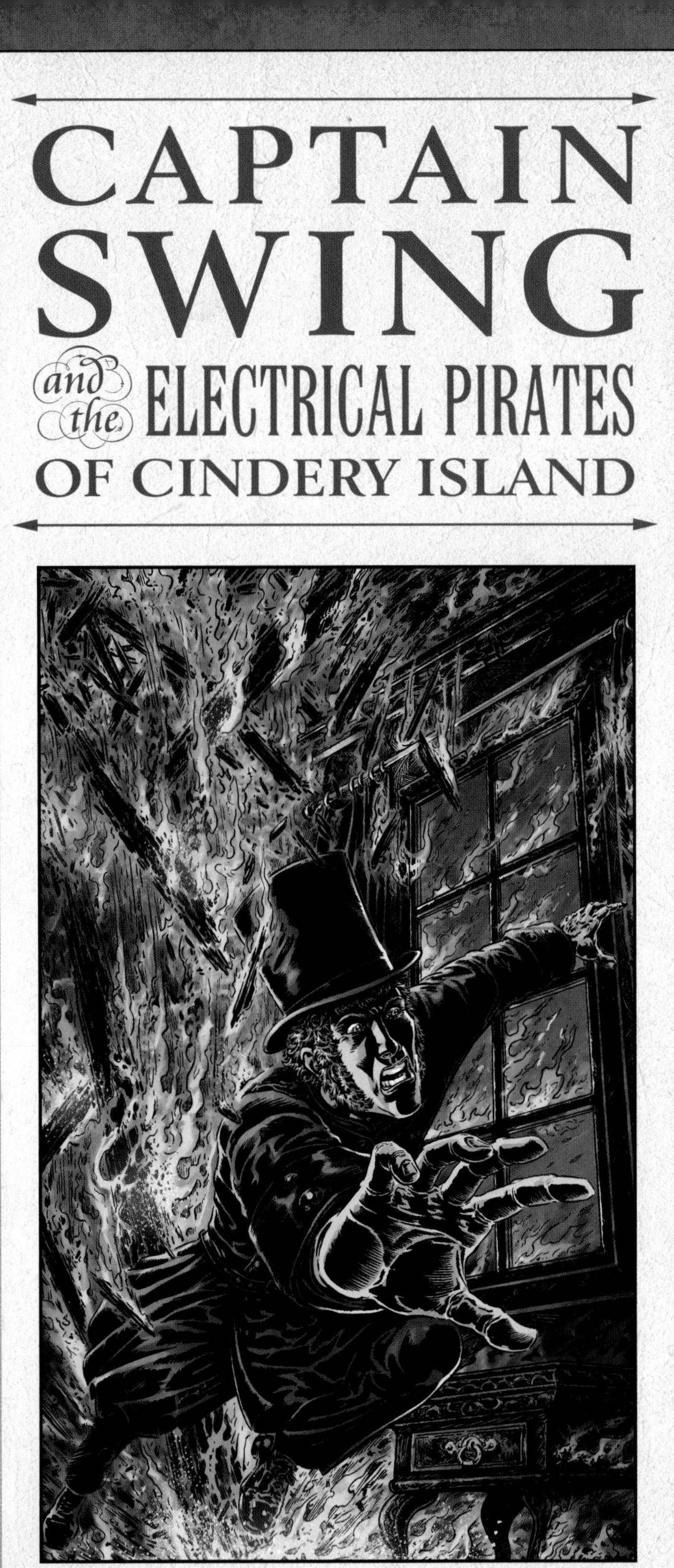

CHAPTER THREE

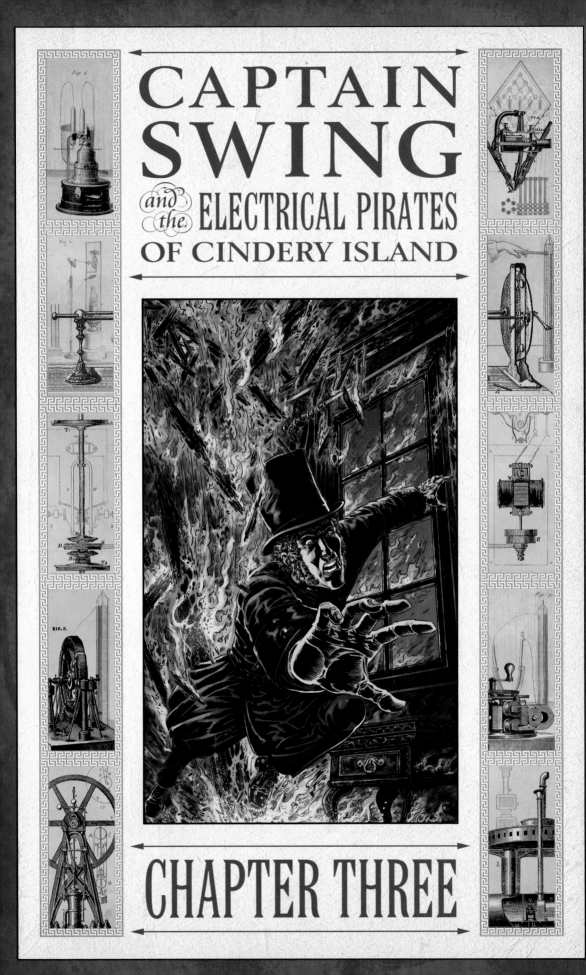

Cindery Island is two days' walk from London, give or take. A good horse, driven hard, can compress that into a matter of a few hours.

A horse in good health can reach thirty miles per hour with ease. Sustaining thirty miles an hour over two or three hours is another matter.

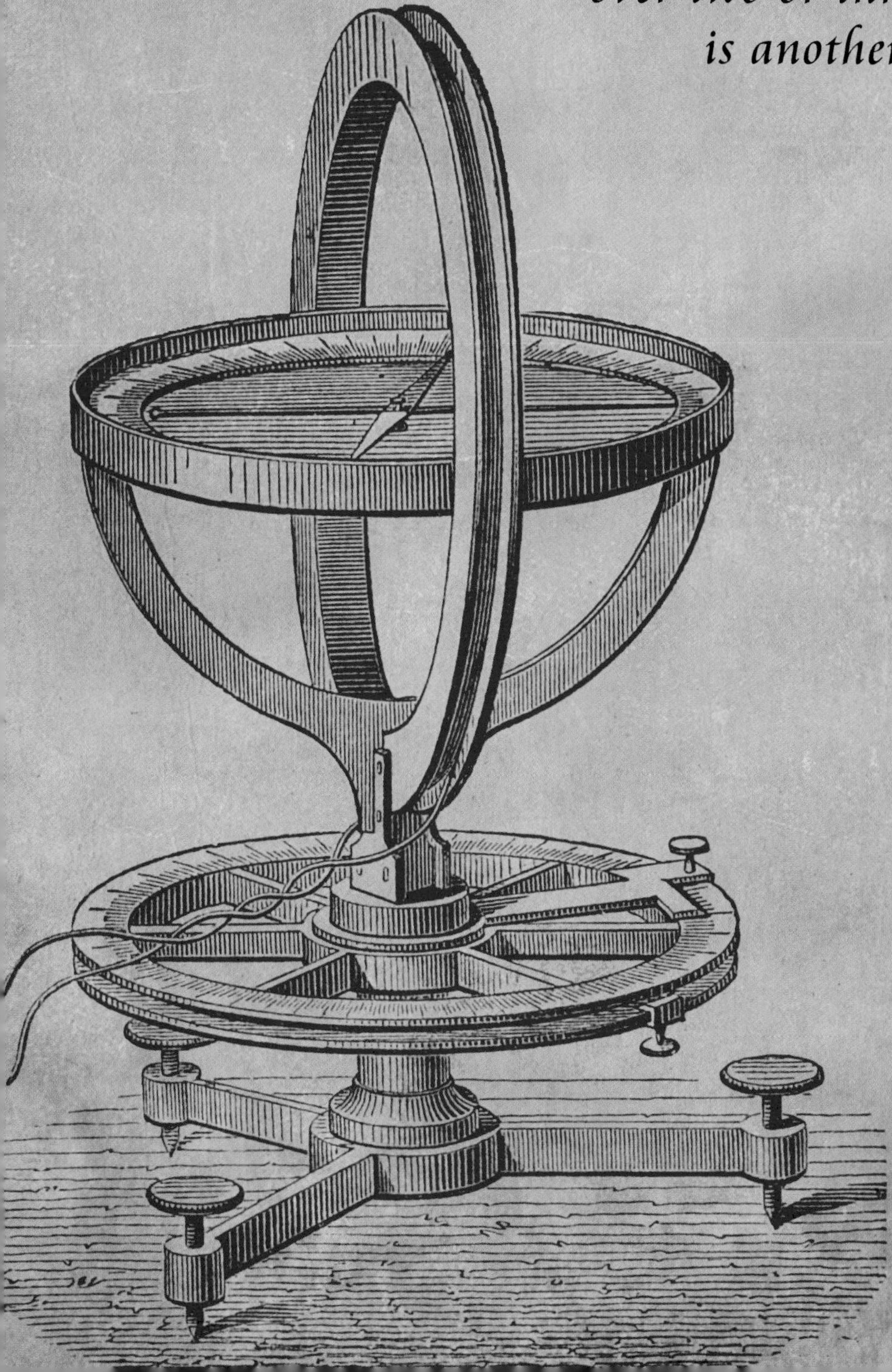

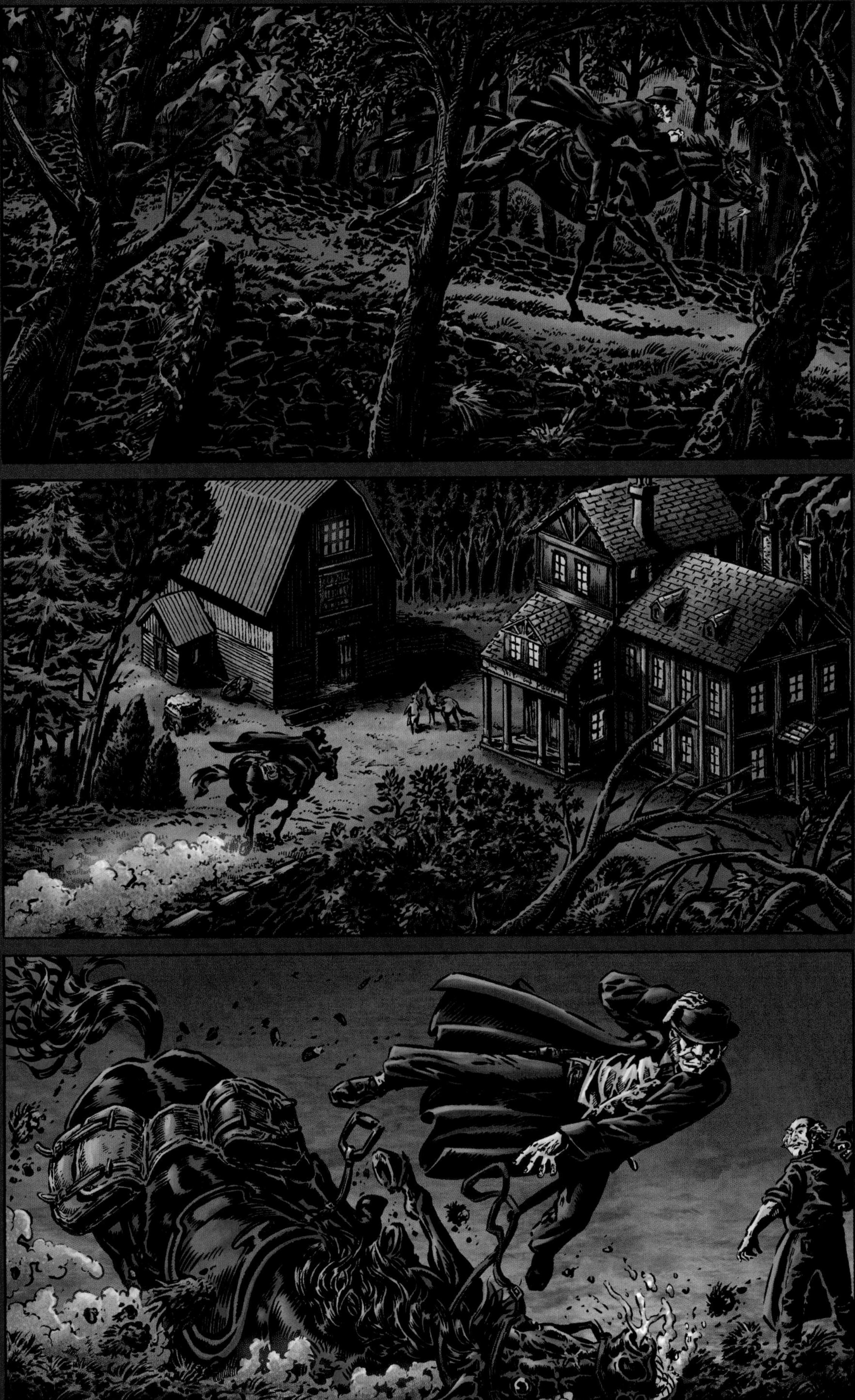

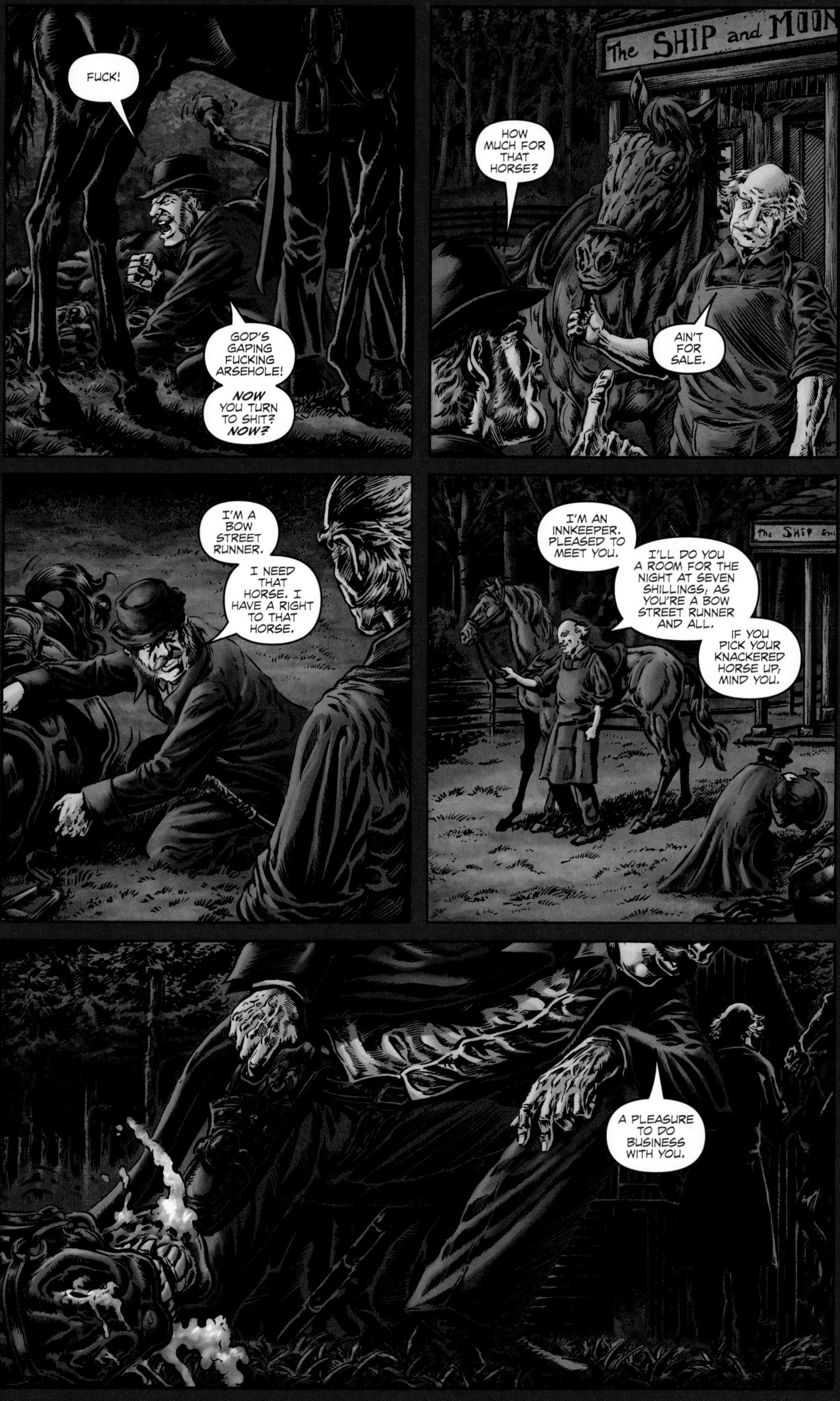
FUCK!
GOD'S GAPING FUCKING ARSEHOLE!
NOW YOU TURN TO SHIT? NOW?
The SHIP and MOON
HOW MUCH FOR THAT HORSE?
AIN'T FOR SALE.
I'M A BOW STREET RUNNER.
I NEED THAT HORSE. I HAVE A RIGHT TO THAT HORSE.
I'M AN INNKEEPER. PLEASED TO MEET YOU.
I'LL DO YOU A ROOM FOR THE NIGHT AT SEVEN SHILLINGS, AS YOU'RE A BOW STREET RUNNER AND ALL.
IF YOU PICK YOUR KNACKERED HORSE UP, MIND YOU.
A PLEASURE TO DO BUSINESS WITH YOU.

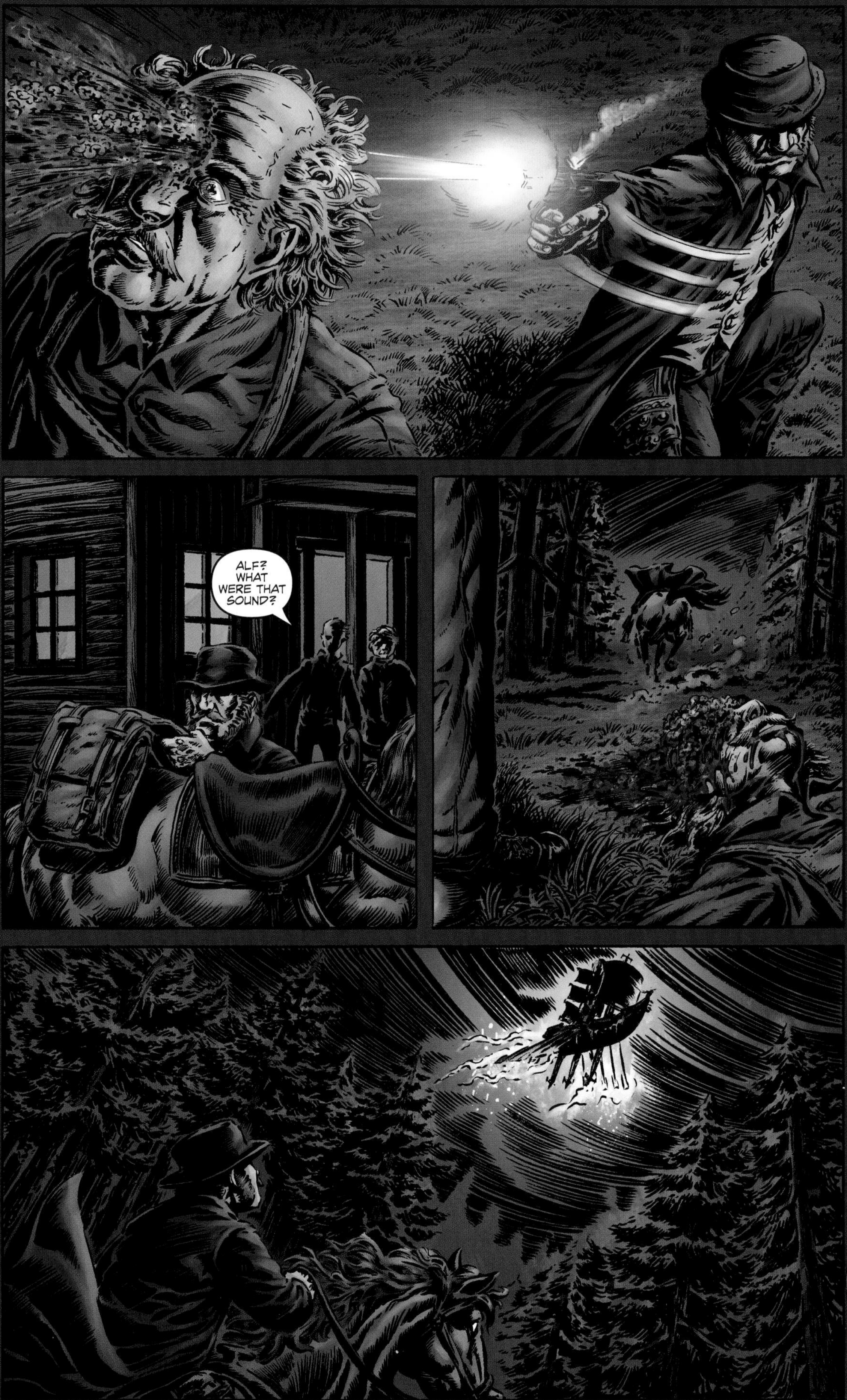
ALF? WHAT WERE THAT SOUND?

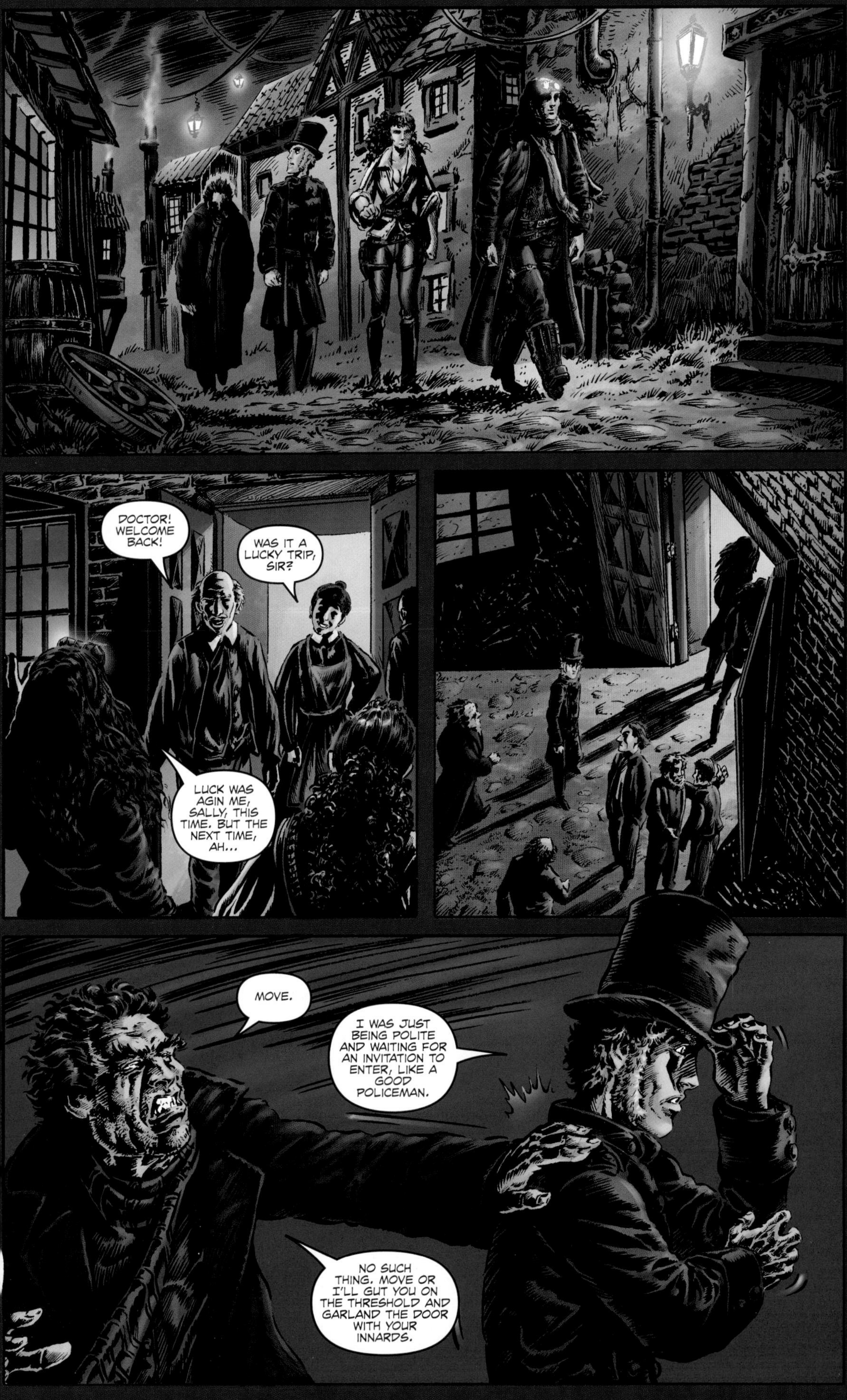
DOCTOR! WELCOME BACK!
WAS IT A LUCKY TRIP, SIR?
LUCK WAS AGIN ME, SALLY, THIS TIME. BUT THE NEXT TIME, AH...
MOVE.
I WAS JUST BEING POLITE AND WAITING FOR AN INVITATION TO ENTER, LIKE A GOOD POLICEMAN.
NO SUCH THING. MOVE OR I'LL GUT YOU ON THE THRESHOLD AND GARLAND THE DOOR WITH YOUR INNARDS.

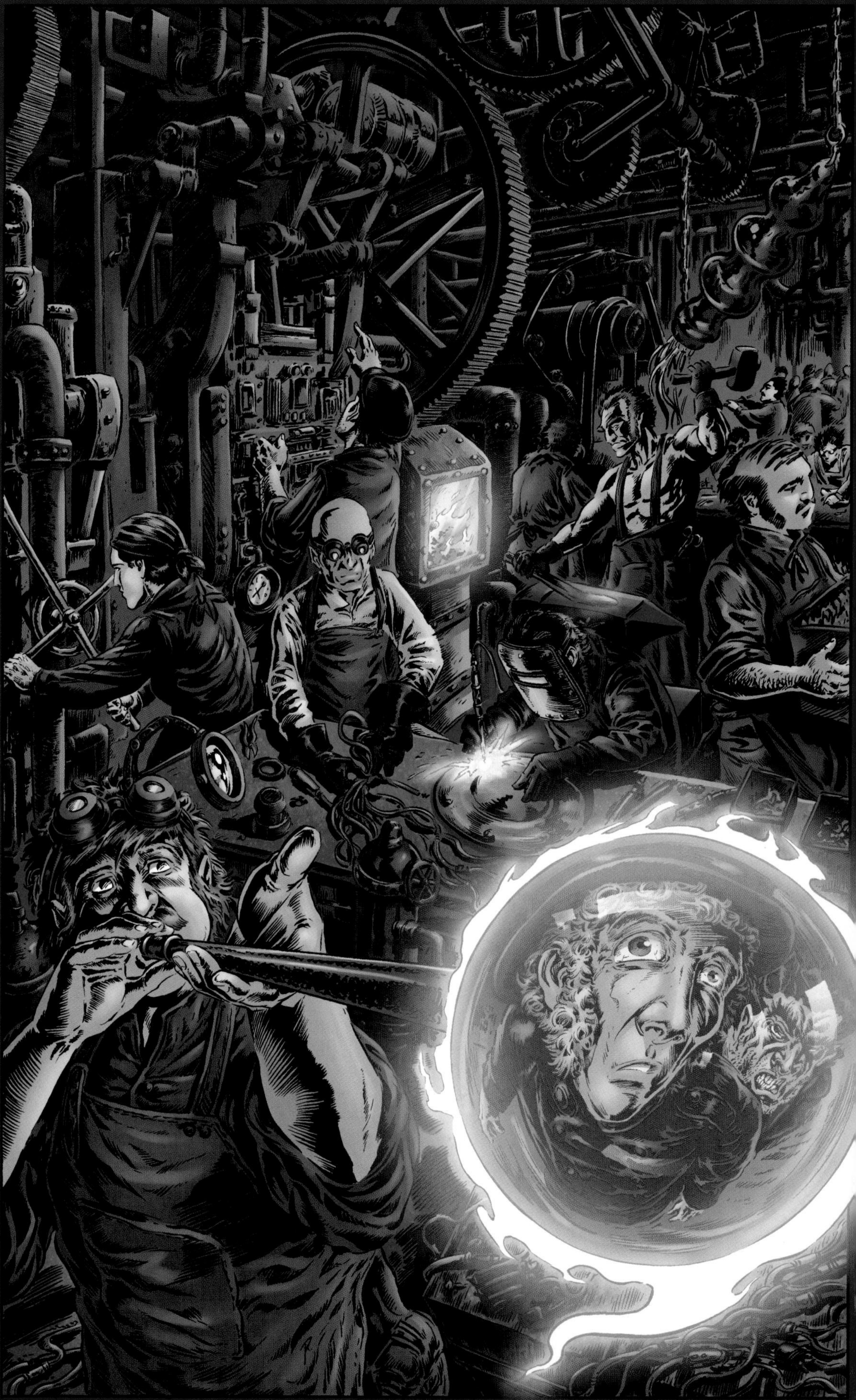

Where other people see wonder, or perhaps foolishness, I see only spilled blood and the work of years. It took so much from so many to build this place, and to this day I think only I understood the totality of what was crafted and forged there.

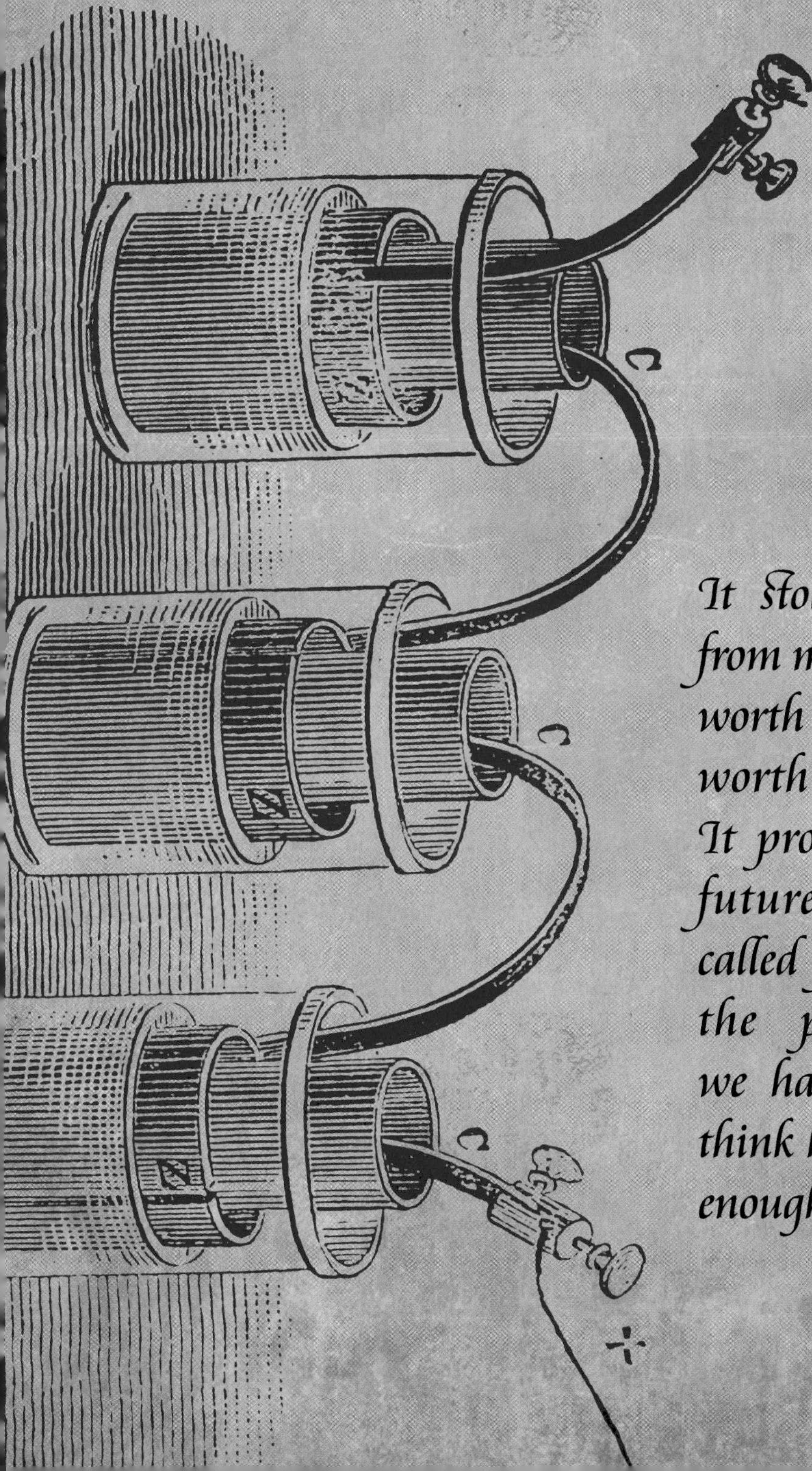

It stole everything from me. But it was worth it. It was worth everything. It proved that the future could be called forward into the present. All we had to do was think hard and care enough.

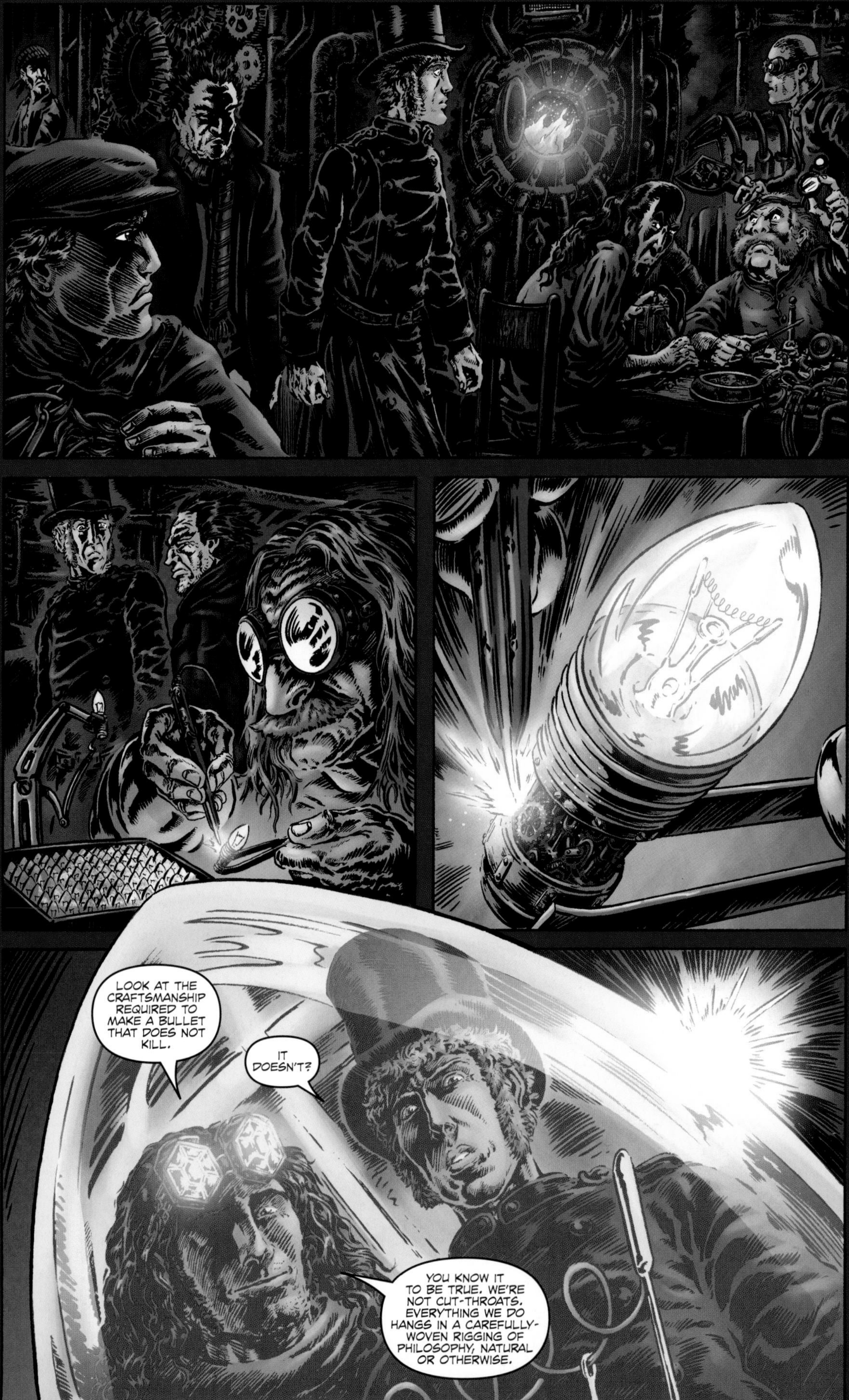
LOOK AT THE CRAFTSMANSHIP REQUIRED TO MAKE A BULLET THAT DOES NOT KILL.
IT DOESN'T?
YOU KNOW IT TO BE TRUE. WE'RE NOT CUT-THROATS. EVERYTHING WE DO HANGS IN A CAREFULLY-WOVEN RIGGING OF PHILOSOPHY, NATURAL OR OTHERWISE.

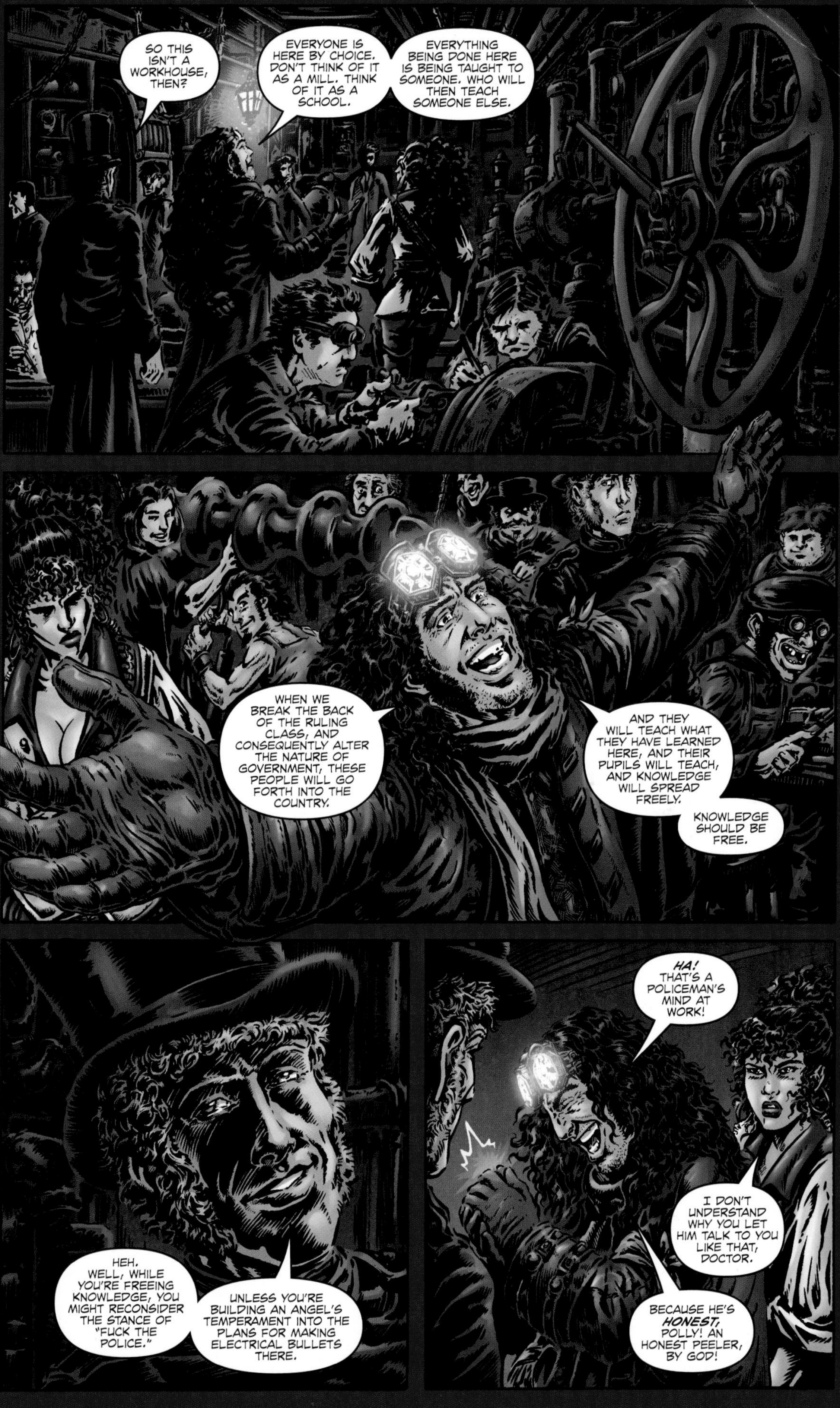

SO THIS ISN'T A WORKHOUSE, THEN?
EVERYONE IS HERE BY CHOICE. DON'T THINK OF IT AS A MILL. THINK OF IT AS A SCHOOL.
EVERYTHING BEING DONE HERE IS BEING TAUGHT TO SOMEONE. WHO WILL THEN TEACH SOMEONE ELSE.
WHEN WE BREAK THE BACK OF THE RULING CLASS, AND CONSEQUENTLY ALTER THE NATURE OF GOVERNMENT, THESE PEOPLE WILL GO FORTH INTO THE COUNTRY.
AND THEY WILL TEACH WHAT THEY HAVE LEARNED HERE, AND THEIR PUPILS WILL TEACH, AND KNOWLEDGE WILL SPREAD FREELY.
KNOWLEDGE SHOULD BE FREE.
HEH. WELL, WHILE YOU'RE FREEING KNOWLEDGE, YOU MIGHT RECONSIDER THE STANCE OF "FUCK THE POLICE."
UNLESS YOU'RE BUILDING AN ANGEL'S TEMPERAMENT INTO THE PLANS FOR MAKING ELECTRICAL BULLETS THERE.
HA! THAT'S A POLICEMAN'S MIND AT WORK!
I DON'T UNDERSTAND WHY YOU LET HIM TALK TO YOU LIKE THAT, DOCTOR.
BECAUSE HE'S *HONEST,* POLLY! AN HONEST PEELER, BY GOD!

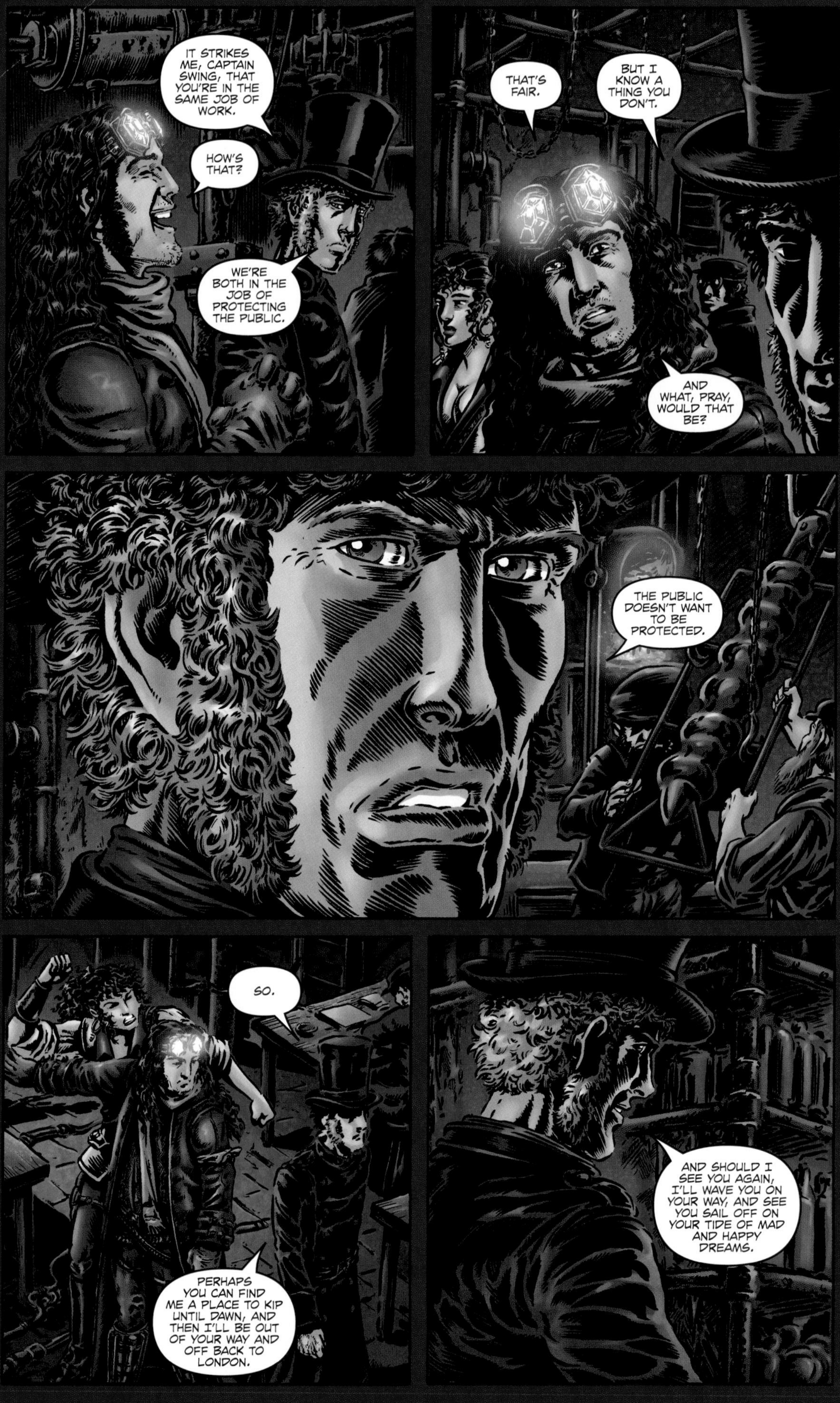
IT STRIKES ME, CAPTAIN SWING, THAT YOU'RE IN THE SAME JOB OF WORK.
HOW'S THAT?
WE'RE BOTH IN THE JOB OF PROTECTING THE PUBLIC.
THAT'S FAIR.
BUT I KNOW A THING YOU DON'T.
AND WHAT, PRAY, WOULD THAT BE?
THE PUBLIC DOESN'T WANT TO BE PROTECTED.
SO.
PERHAPS YOU CAN FIND ME A PLACE TO KIP UNTIL DAWN, AND THEN I'LL BE OUT OF YOUR WAY AND OFF BACK TO LONDON.
AND SHOULD I SEE YOU AGAIN, I'LL WAVE YOU ON YOUR WAY, AND SEE YOU SAIL OFF ON YOUR TIDE OF MAD AND HAPPY DREAMS.

I believe that perhaps we invented a new kind of man, when we (They) designated some of us as Police. They chose men to have the veils of society, big and small, torn from their eyes. Some men, it will drive mad. Some men, it will turn into brutal and unquestioning functionaries of a callous State. And some men... this man, I think... some men will be unable to see the world as anything but an ugly, unfair, unsaveable zoo filled with animals who would savage them at the first available opportunity just for being zookeepers. Just for keeping them alive and safe.

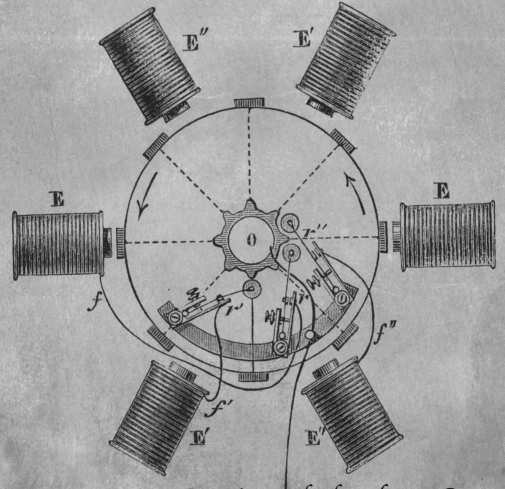

Utopian fool that I am, I feel that to be the cruelest thing of all.

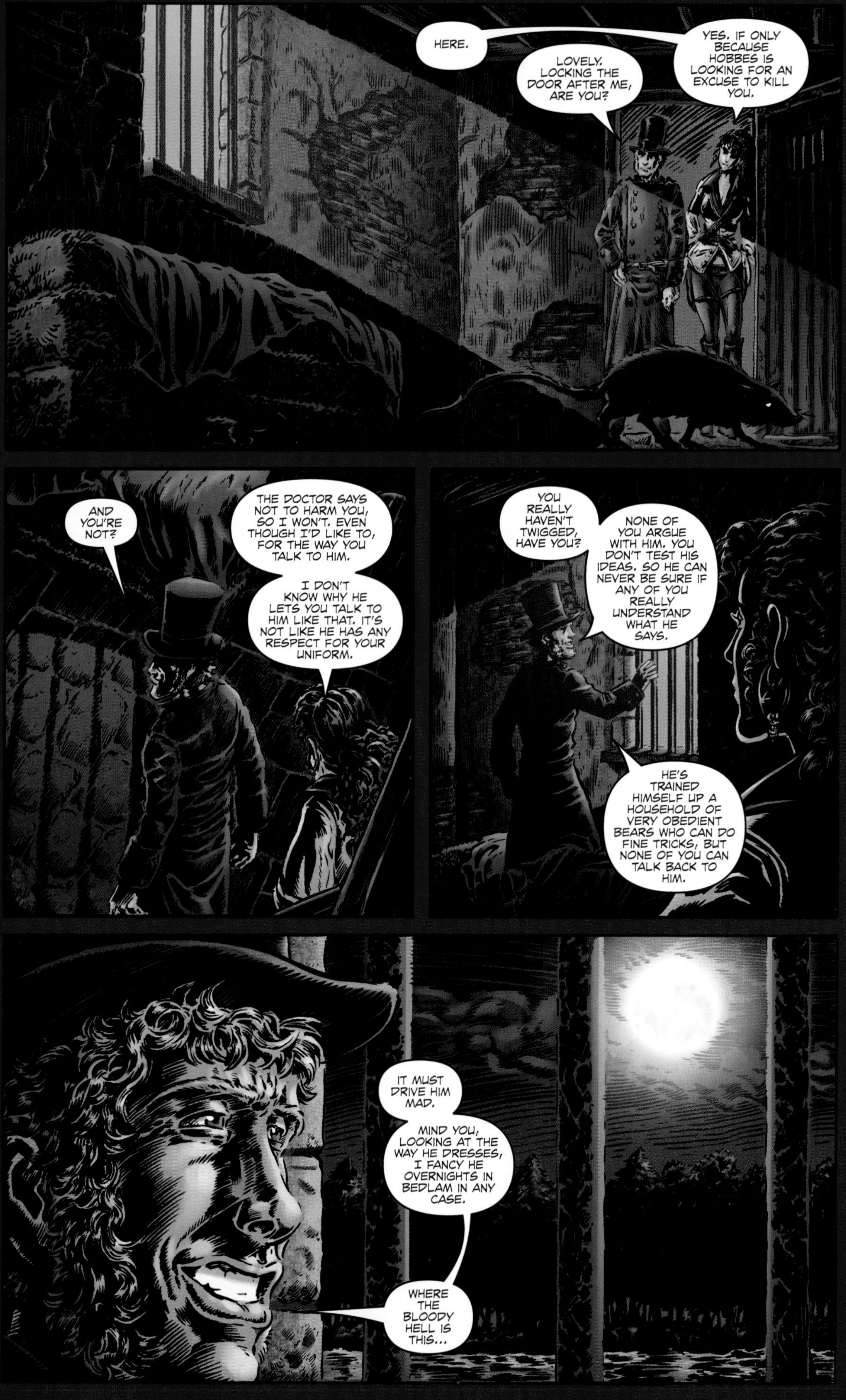
HERE.
LOVELY. LOCKING THE DOOR AFTER ME, ARE YOU?
YES. IF ONLY BECAUSE HOBBES IS LOOKING FOR AN EXCUSE TO KILL YOU.
THE DOCTOR SAYS NOT TO HARM YOU, SO I WON'T. EVEN THOUGH I'D LIKE TO, FOR THE WAY YOU TALK TO HIM.
I DON'T KNOW WHY HE LETS YOU TALK TO HIM LIKE THAT. IT'S NOT LIKE HE HAS ANY RESPECT FOR YOUR UNIFORM.
AND YOU'RE NOT?
YOU REALLY HAVEN'T TWIGGED, HAVE YOU?
NONE OF YOU ARGUE WITH HIM. YOU DON'T TEST HIS IDEAS. SO HE CAN NEVER BE SURE IF ANY OF YOU REALLY UNDERSTAND WHAT HE SAYS.
HE'S TRAINED HIMSELF UP A HOUSEHOLD OF VERY OBEDIENT BEARS WHO CAN DO FINE TRICKS, BUT NONE OF YOU CAN TALK BACK TO HIM.
IT MUST DRIVE HIM MAD.
MIND YOU, LOOKING AT THE WAY HE DRESSES, I FANCY HE OVERNIGHTS IN BEDLAM IN ANY CASE.
WHERE THE BLOODY HELL IS THIS...

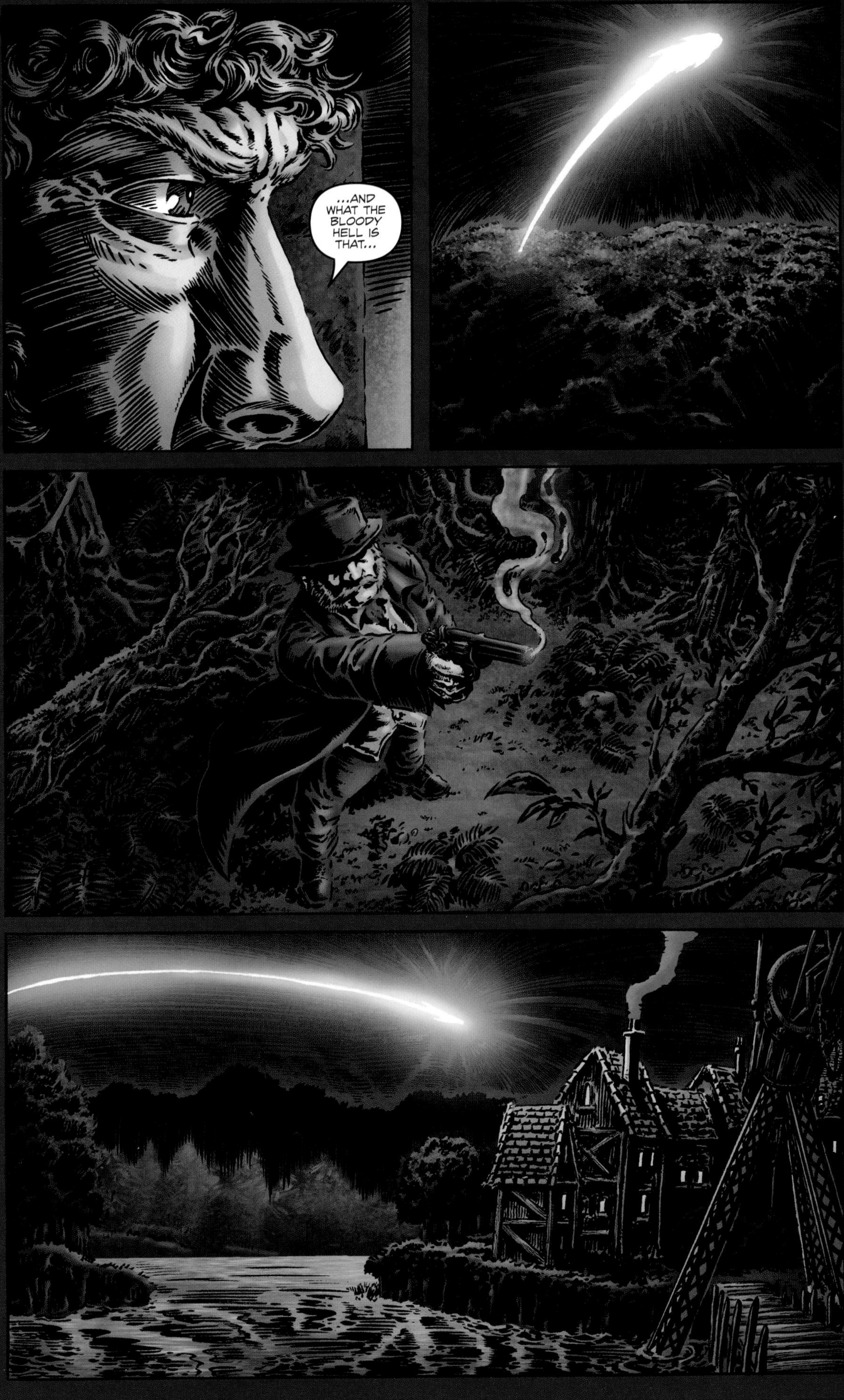
...AND WHAT THE BLOODY HELL IS THAT...

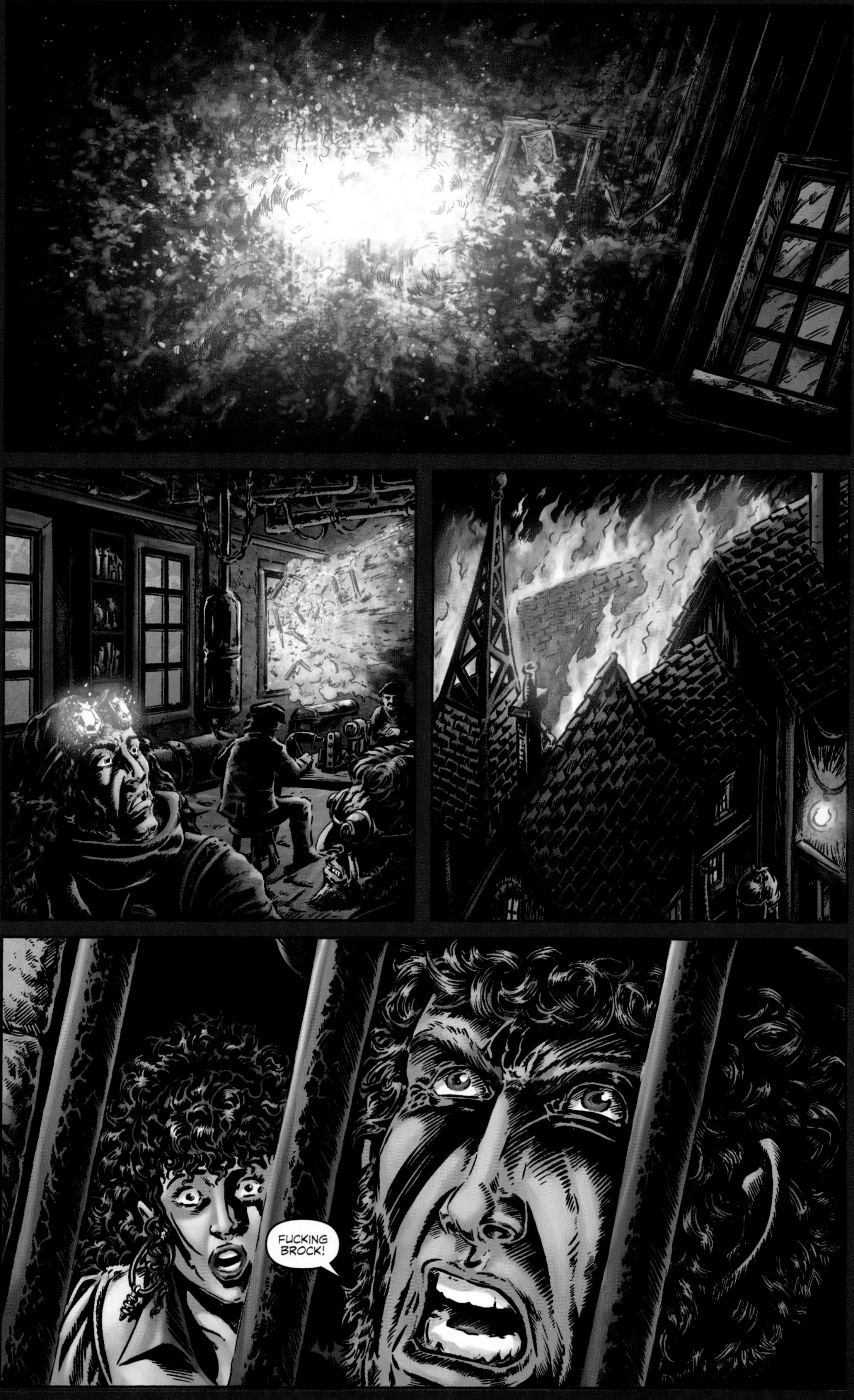
FUCKING BROCK!

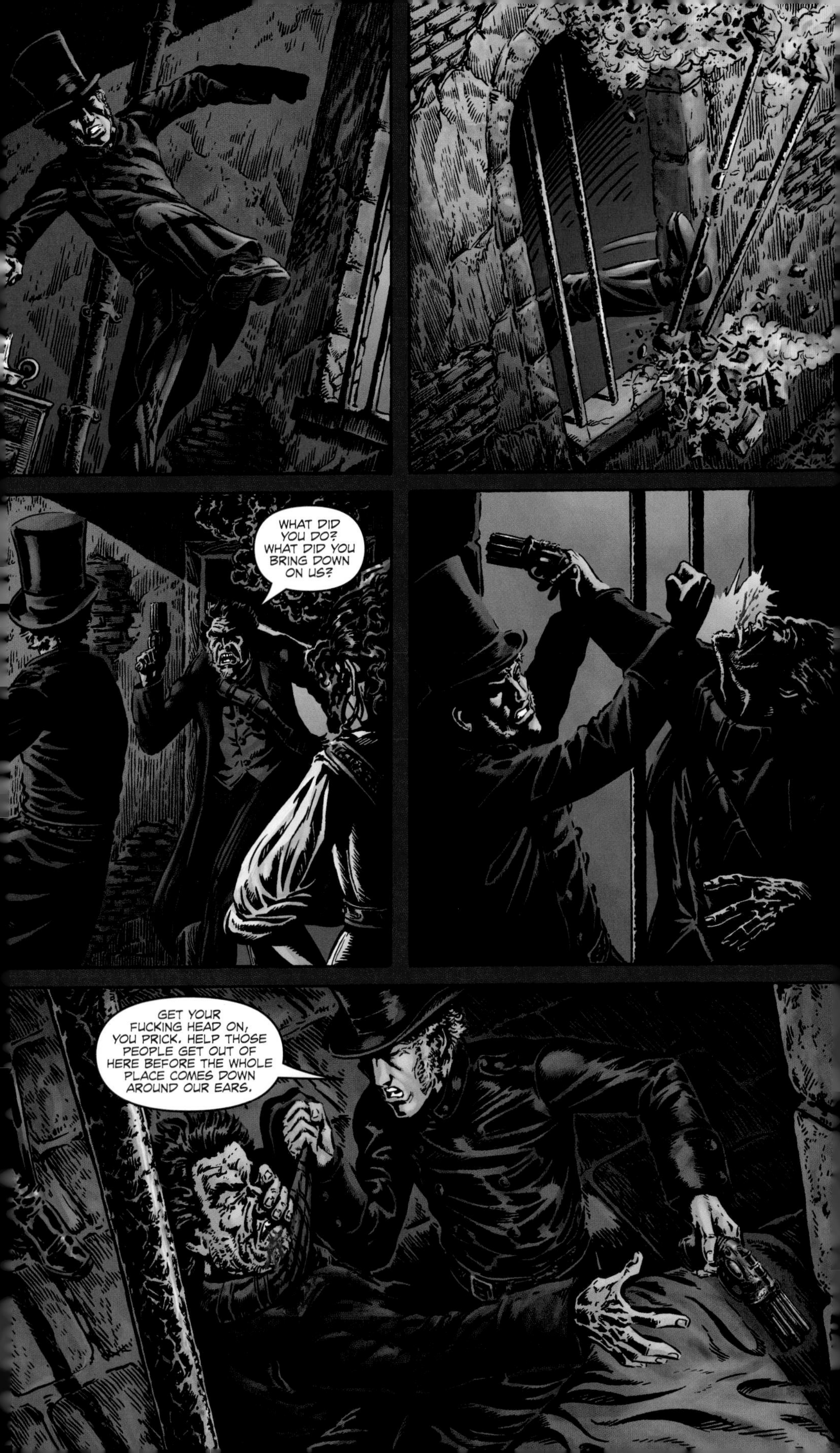
WHAT DID YOU DO? WHAT DID YOU BRING DOWN ON US?
GET YOUR FUCKING HEAD ON, YOU PRICK. HELP THOSE PEOPLE GET OUT OF HERE BEFORE THE WHOLE PLACE COMES DOWN AROUND OUR EARS.

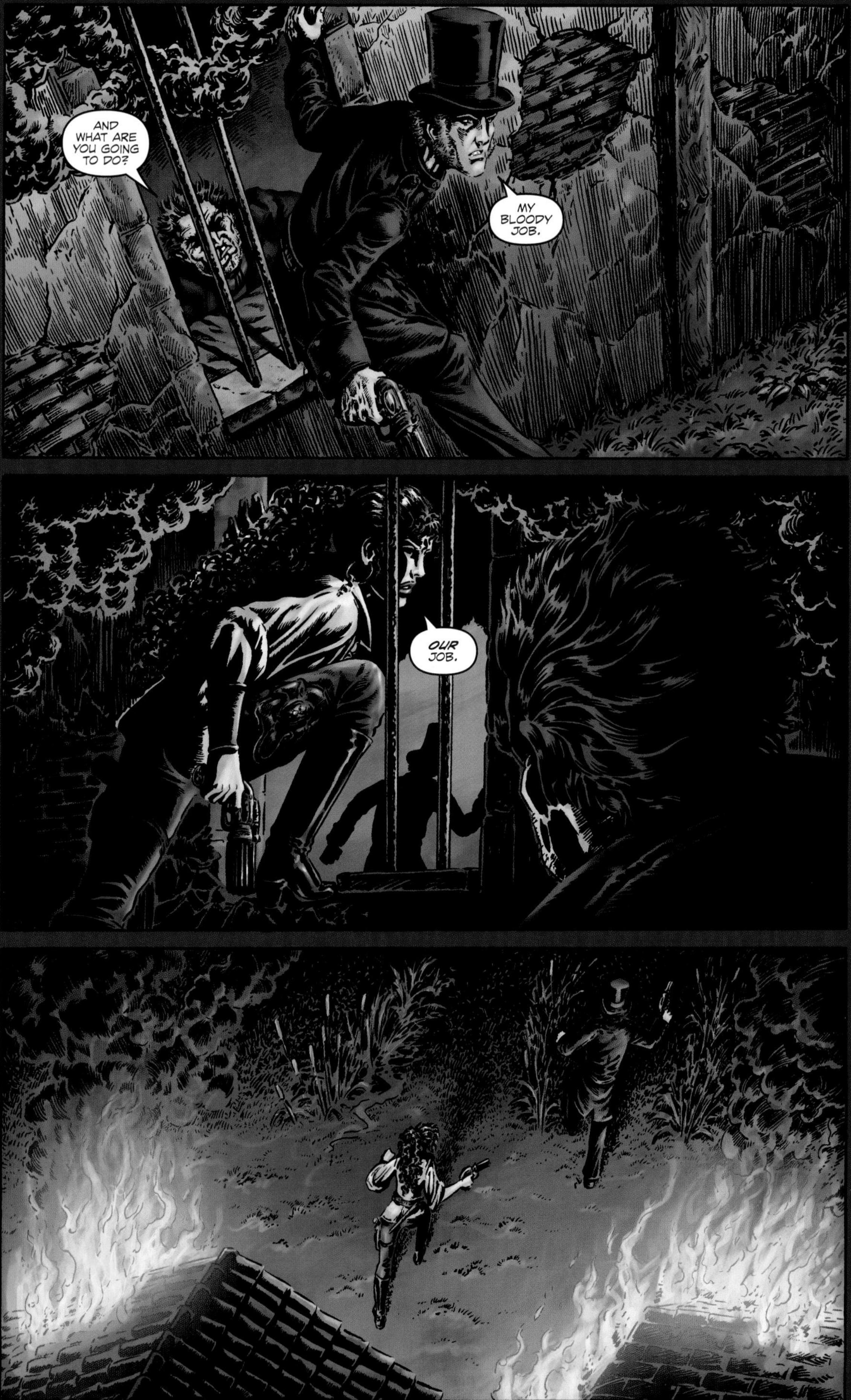
AND WHAT ARE YOU GOING TO DO?
MY BLOODY JOB.
OUR JOB.

In some ways, this was the proudest moment of my life. A London peeler and a pirate by blood, running together against an agent of the Courts.

I glimpsed them through a window as I was pushing my friends through the doors, and only for a moment. But that image remained burned on my eyes for the rest of my life.

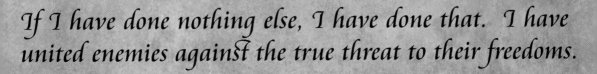

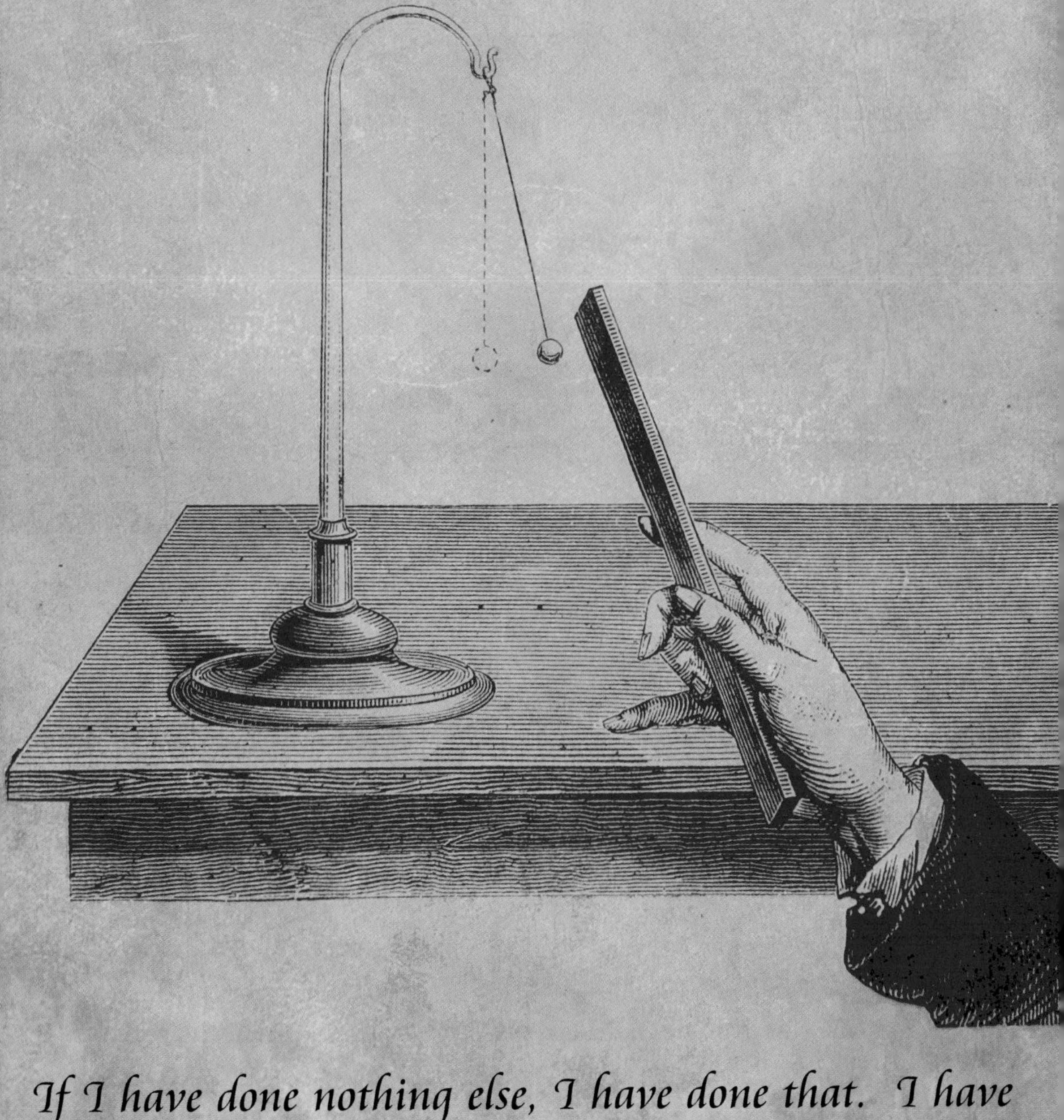

If I have done nothing else, I have done that. I have united enemies against the true threat to their freedoms.

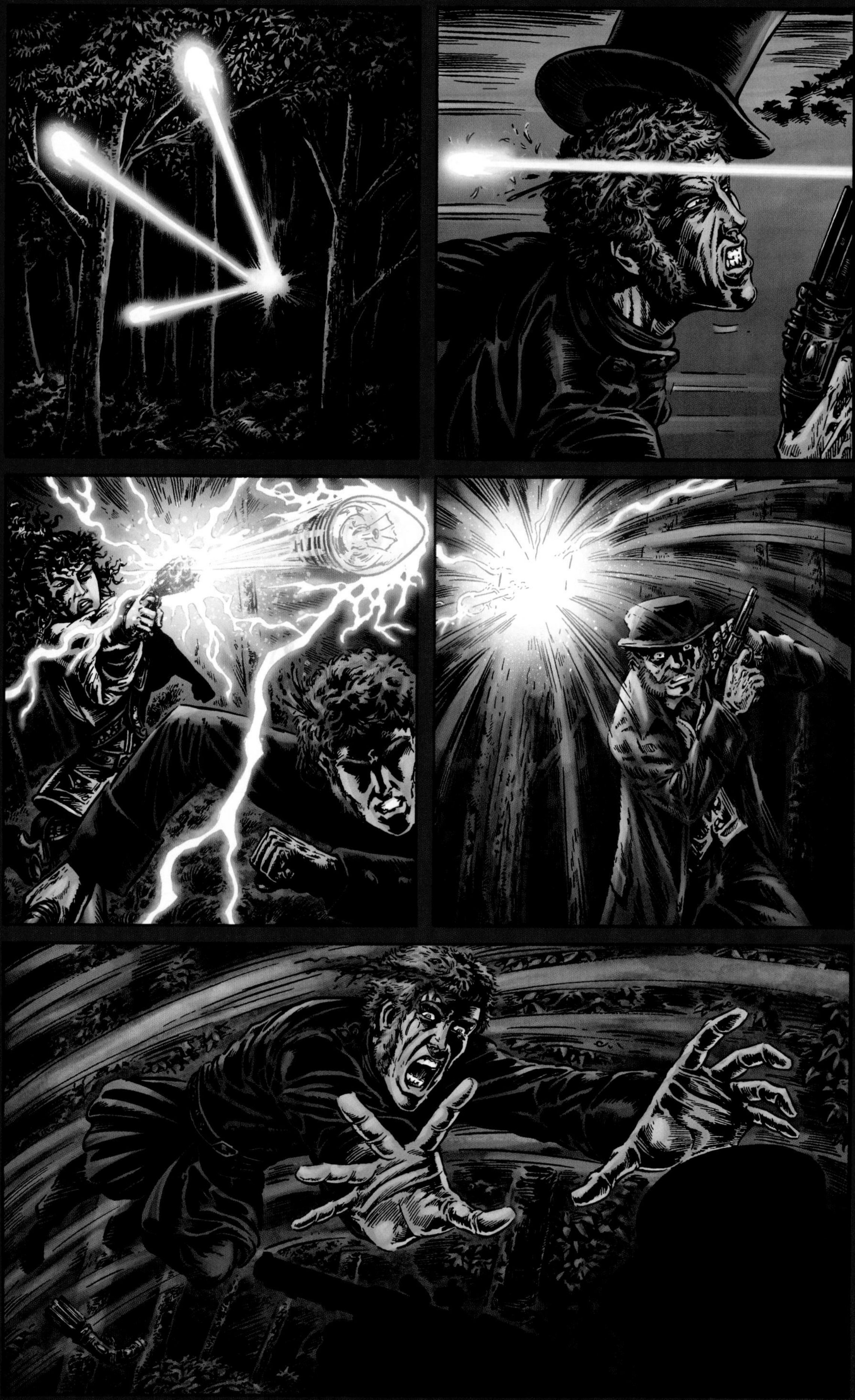

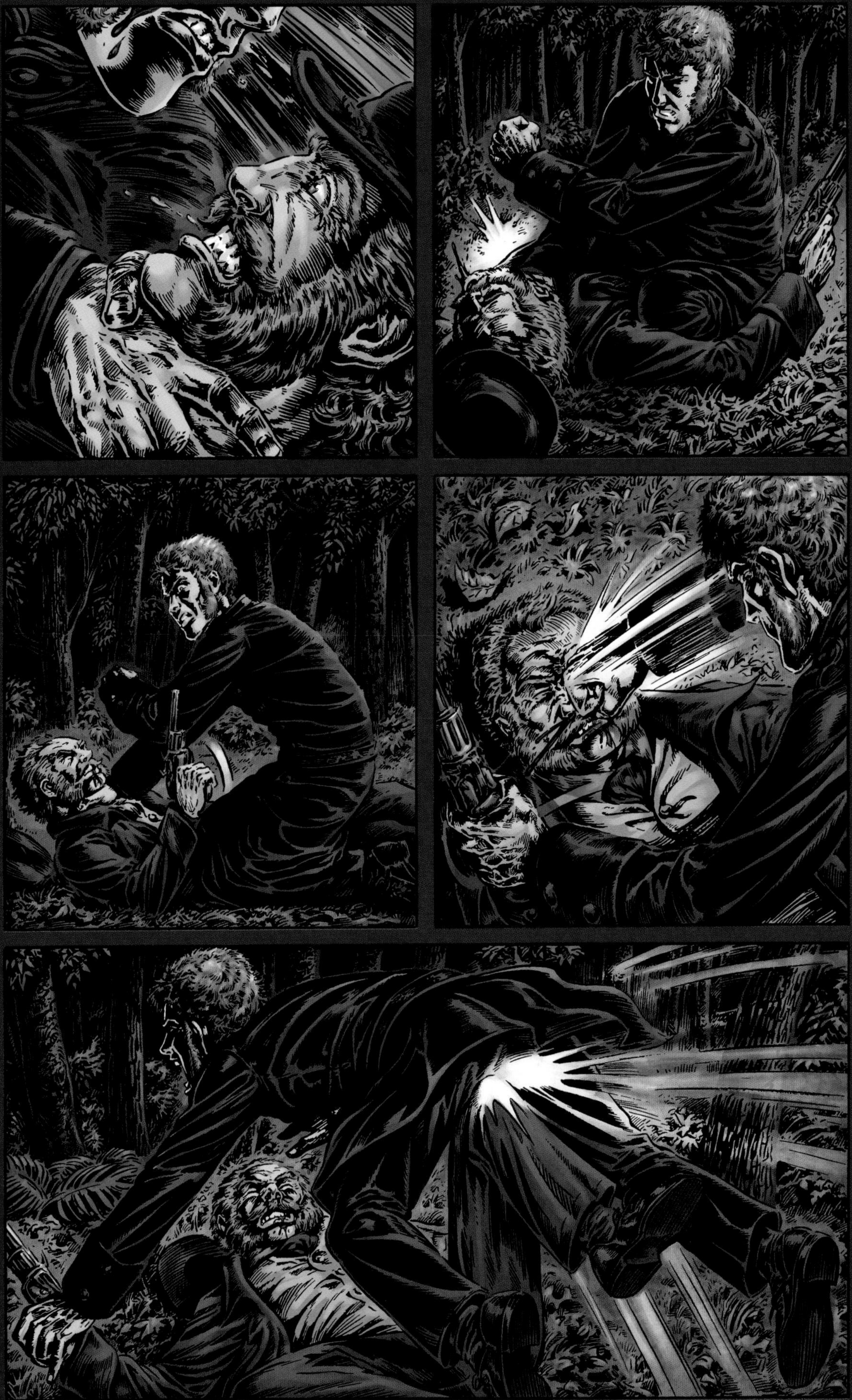

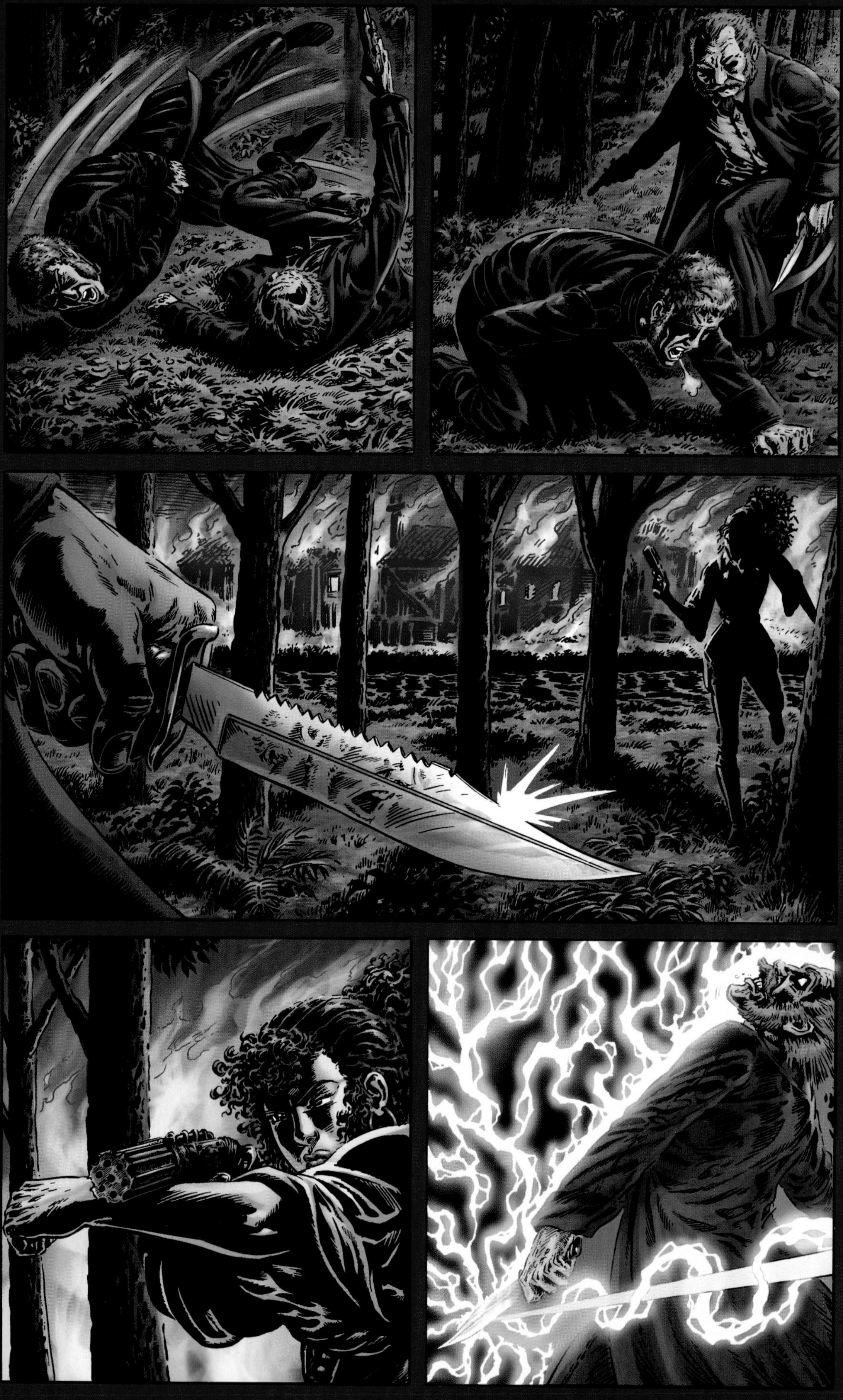

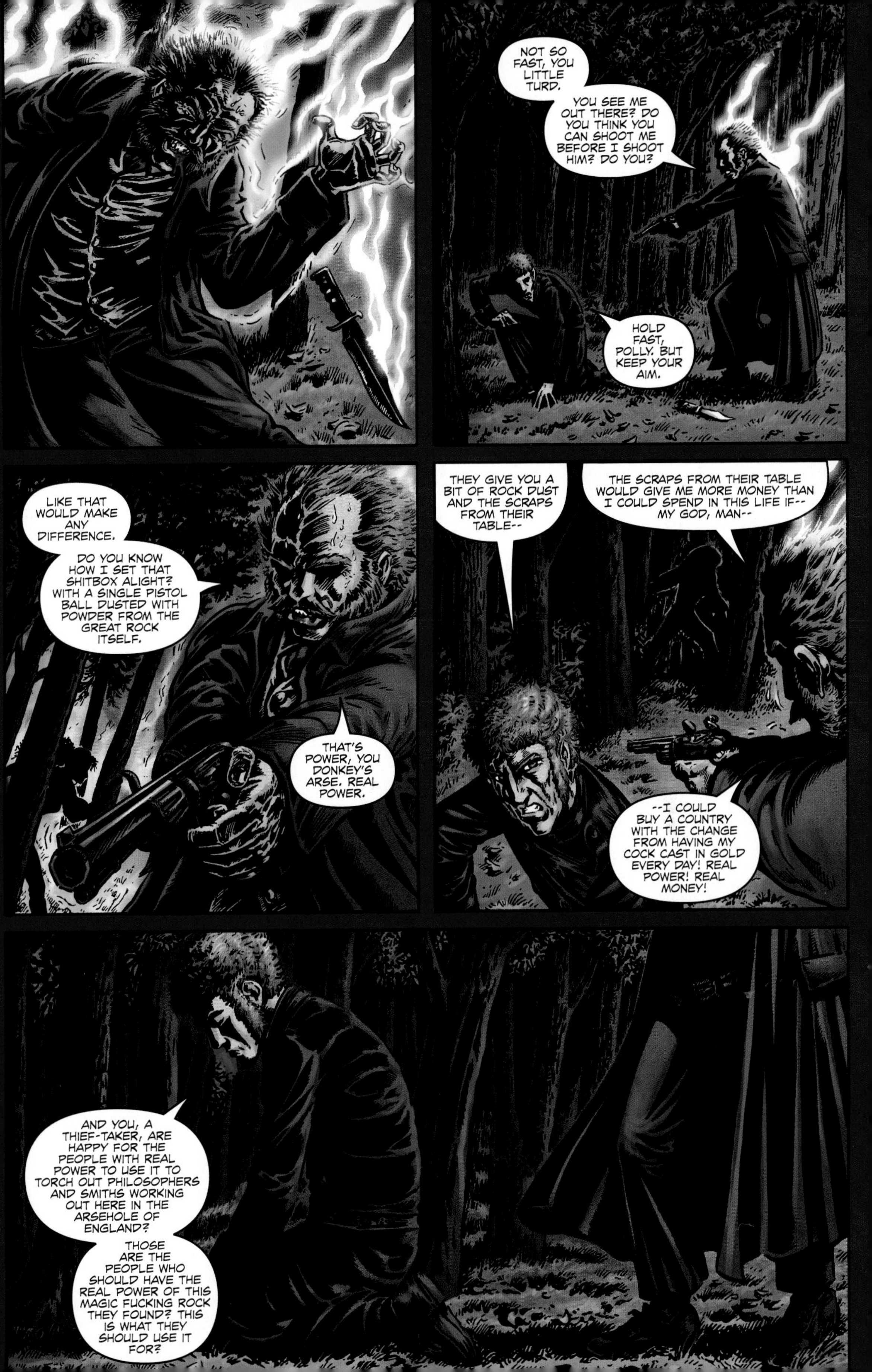
NOT SO FAST, YOU LITTLE TURD.
YOU SEE ME OUT THERE? DO YOU THINK YOU CAN SHOOT ME BEFORE I SHOOT HIM? DO YOU?
HOLD FAST, POLLY. BUT KEEP YOUR AIM.
LIKE THAT WOULD MAKE ANY DIFFERENCE.
DO YOU KNOW HOW I SET THAT SHITBOX ALIGHT? WITH A SINGLE PISTOL BALL DUSTED WITH POWDER FROM THE GREAT ROCK ITSELF.
THAT'S POWER, YOU DONKEY'S ARSE. REAL POWER.
THEY GIVE YOU A BIT OF ROCK DUST AND THE SCRAPS FROM THEIR TABLE--
THE SCRAPS FROM THEIR TABLE WOULD GIVE ME MORE MONEY THAN I COULD SPEND IN THIS LIFE IF-- MY GOD, MAN--
--I COULD BUY A COUNTRY WITH THE CHANGE FROM HAVING MY COCK CAST IN GOLD EVERY DAY! REAL POWER! REAL MONEY!
AND YOU, A THIEF-TAKER, ARE HAPPY FOR THE PEOPLE WITH REAL POWER TO USE IT TO TORCH OUT PHILOSOPHERS AND SMITHS WORKING OUT HERE IN THE ARSEHOLE OF ENGLAND?
THOSE ARE THE PEOPLE WHO SHOULD HAVE THE REAL POWER OF THIS MAGIC FUCKING ROCK THEY FOUND? THIS IS WHAT THEY SHOULD USE IT FOR?

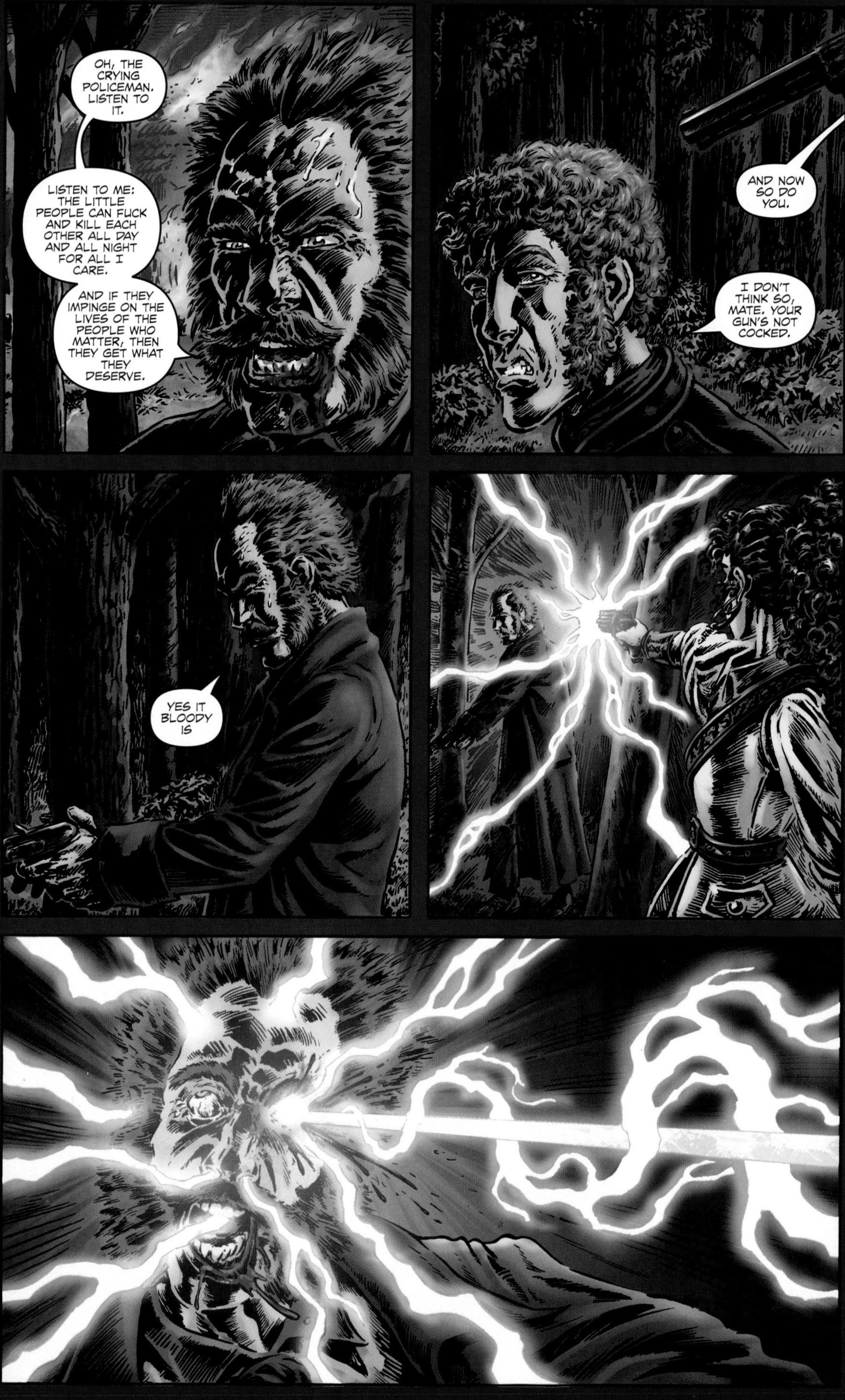
OH, THE CRYING POLICEMAN. LISTEN TO IT.
LISTEN TO ME: THE LITTLE PEOPLE CAN FUCK AND KILL EACH OTHER ALL DAY AND ALL NIGHT FOR ALL I CARE.
AND IF THEY IMPINGE ON THE LIVES OF THE PEOPLE WHO MATTER, THEN THEY GET WHAT THEY DESERVE.
AND NOW SO DO YOU.
I DON'T THINK SO, MATE. YOUR GUN'S NOT COCKED.
YES IT BLOODY IS

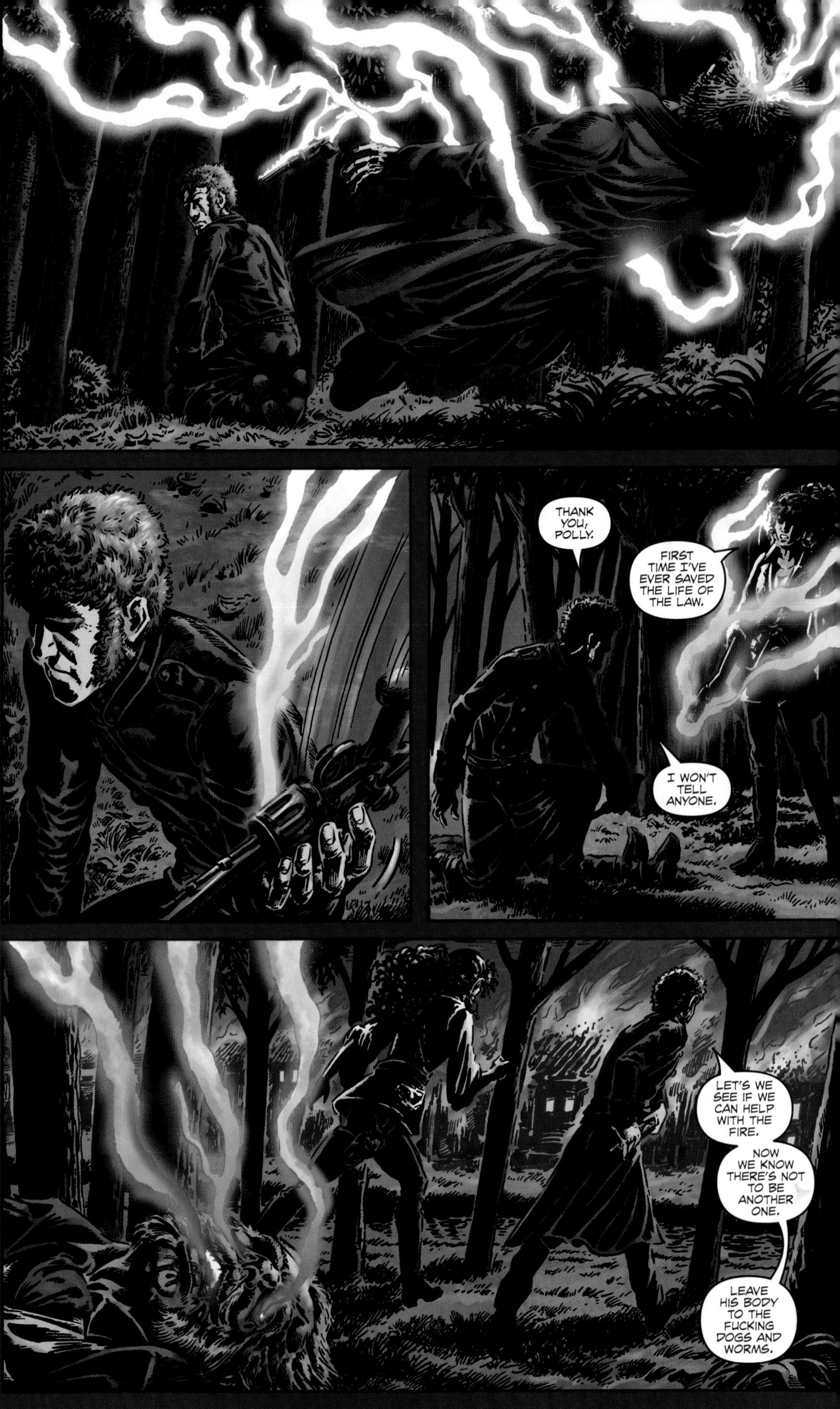
THANK YOU, POLLY.
FIRST TIME I'VE EVER SAVED THE LIFE OF THE LAW.
I WON'T TELL ANYONE.
LET'S WE SEE IF WE CAN HELP WITH THE FIRE.
NOW WE KNOW THERE'S NOT TO BE ANOTHER ONE.
LEAVE HIS BODY TO THE FUCKING DOGS AND WORMS.

I do not believe in heaven, or indeed a god. Even the blind or mad deities of the Gnostic schools. Nothing seems so elegant or philosophically correct to me as the notion that we emanate from the strict physical laws of the Universe.

But humans are electrical beings, and I like to dream that our electrical fields persist after death, perhaps drifting through the atmosphere. I have in this connection requested that I not be conventionally buried when I pass, for fear that my electricity be grounded in the earth. A sky burial, in the manner of the American Indian, would suit me well enough.

I have lived as an Electrical Pirate, and
I would wish to die the same way...

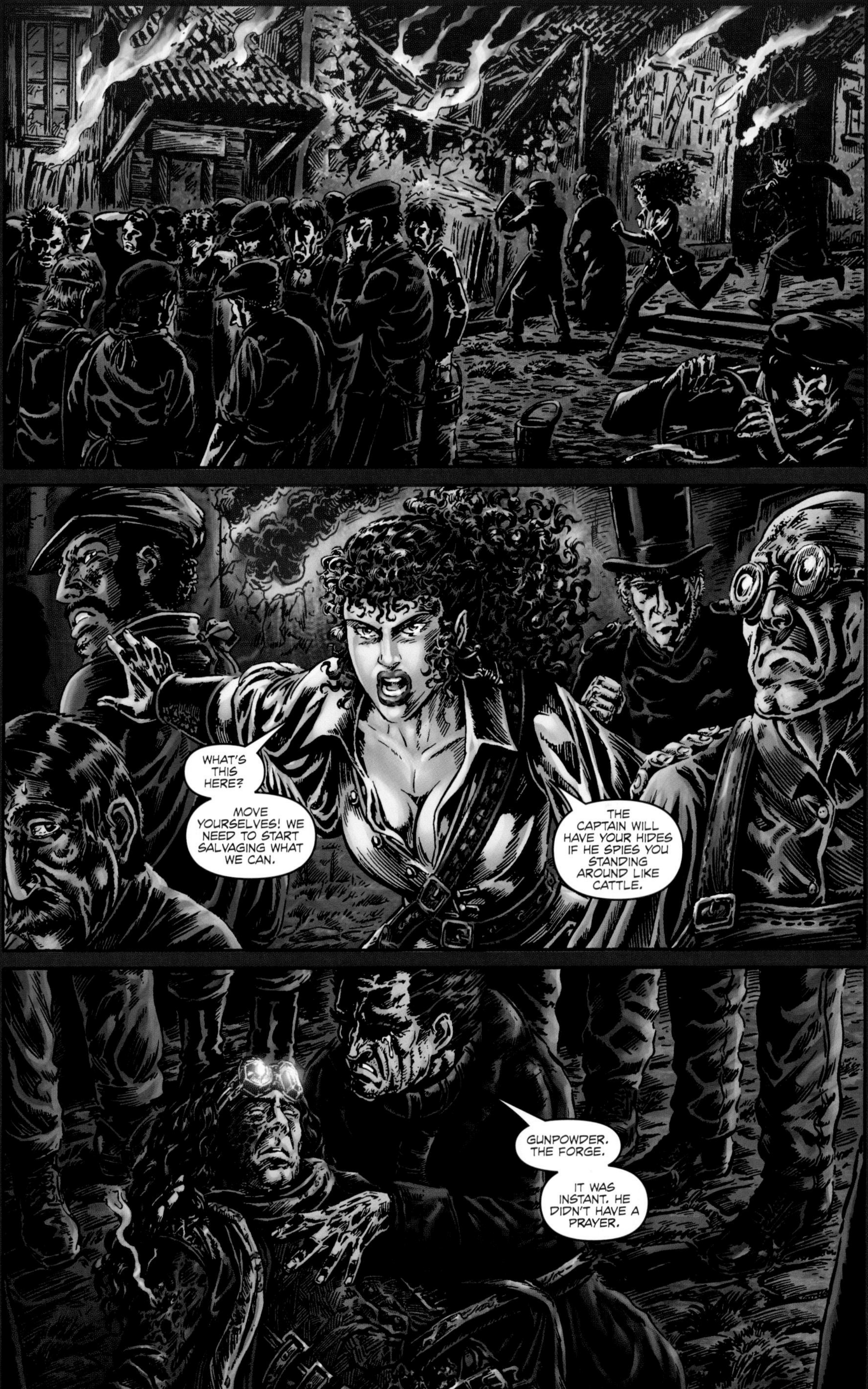

WHAT'S THIS HERE?
MOVE YOURSELVES! WE NEED TO START SALVAGING WHAT WE CAN.
THE CAPTAIN WILL HAVE YOUR HIDES IF HE SPIES YOU STANDING AROUND LIKE CATTLE.
GUNPOWDER. THE FORGE.
IT WAS INSTANT. HE DIDN'T HAVE A PRAYER.

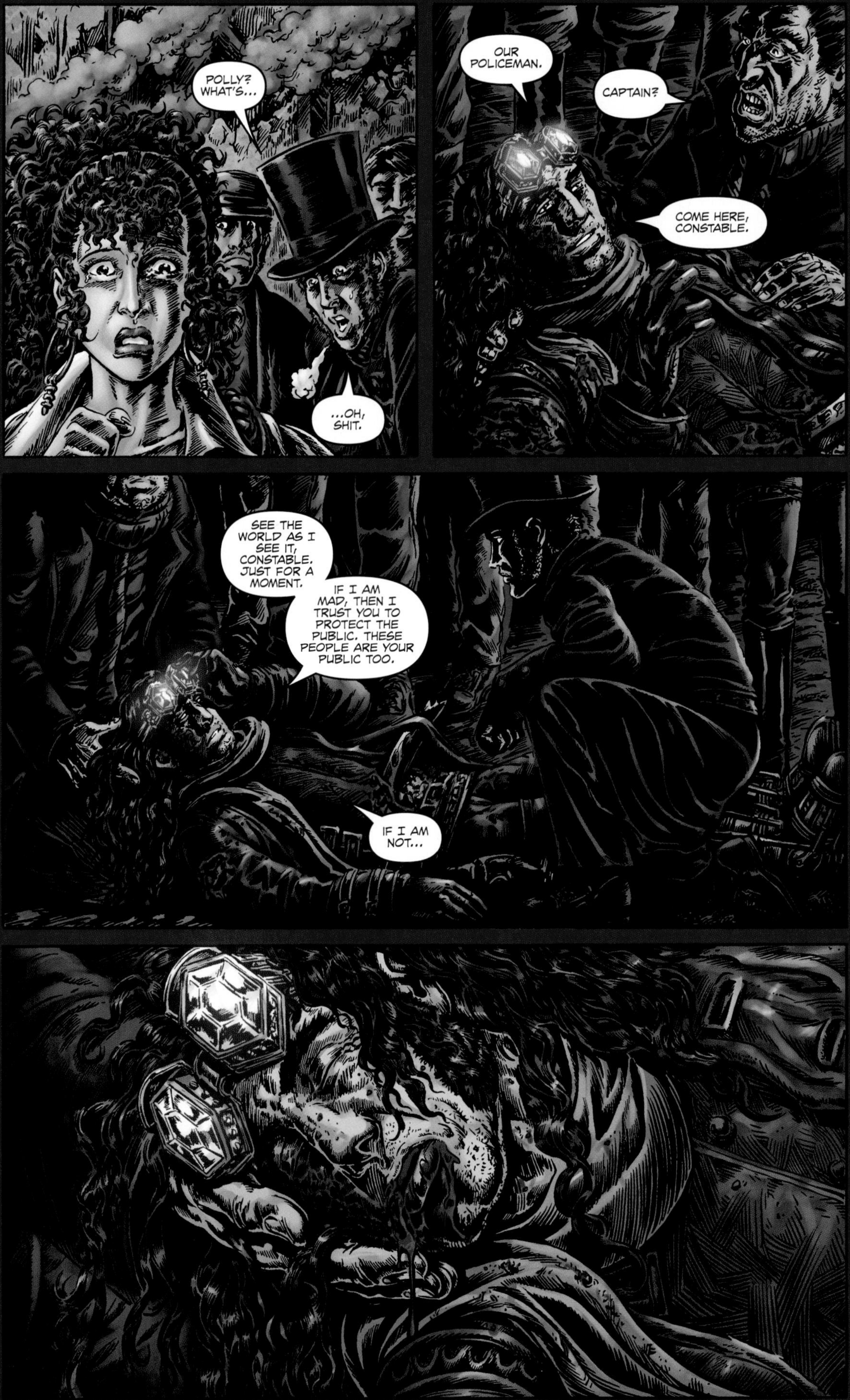
POLLY? WHAT'S...
...OH, SHIT.
OUR POLICEMAN.
CAPTAIN?
COME HERE, CONSTABLE.
SEE THE WORLD AS I SEE IT, CONSTABLE. JUST FOR A MOMENT.
IF I AM MAD, THEN I TRUST YOU TO PROTECT THE PUBLIC. THESE PEOPLE ARE YOUR PUBLIC TOO.
IF I AM NOT...

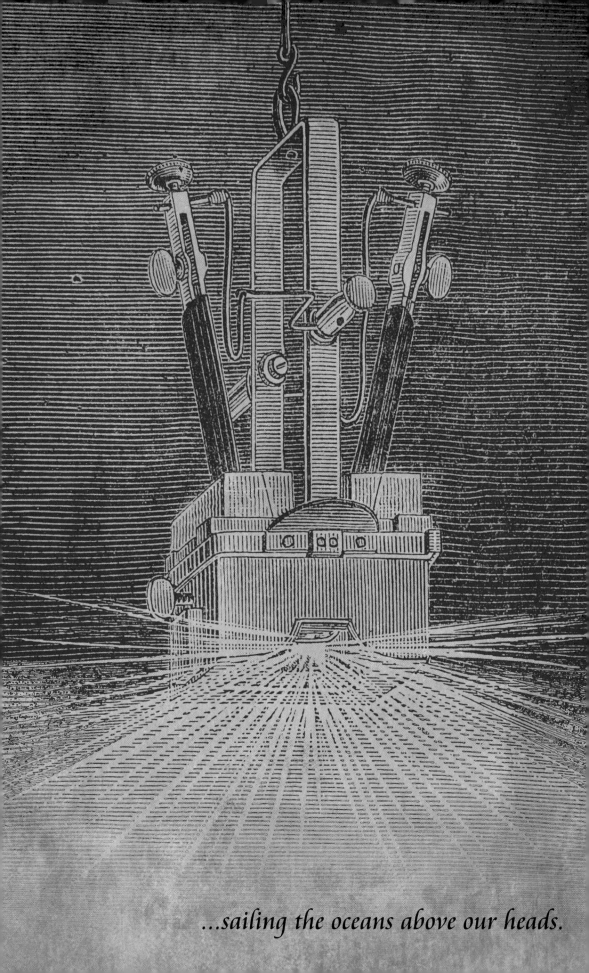

...*sailing the oceans above our heads.*

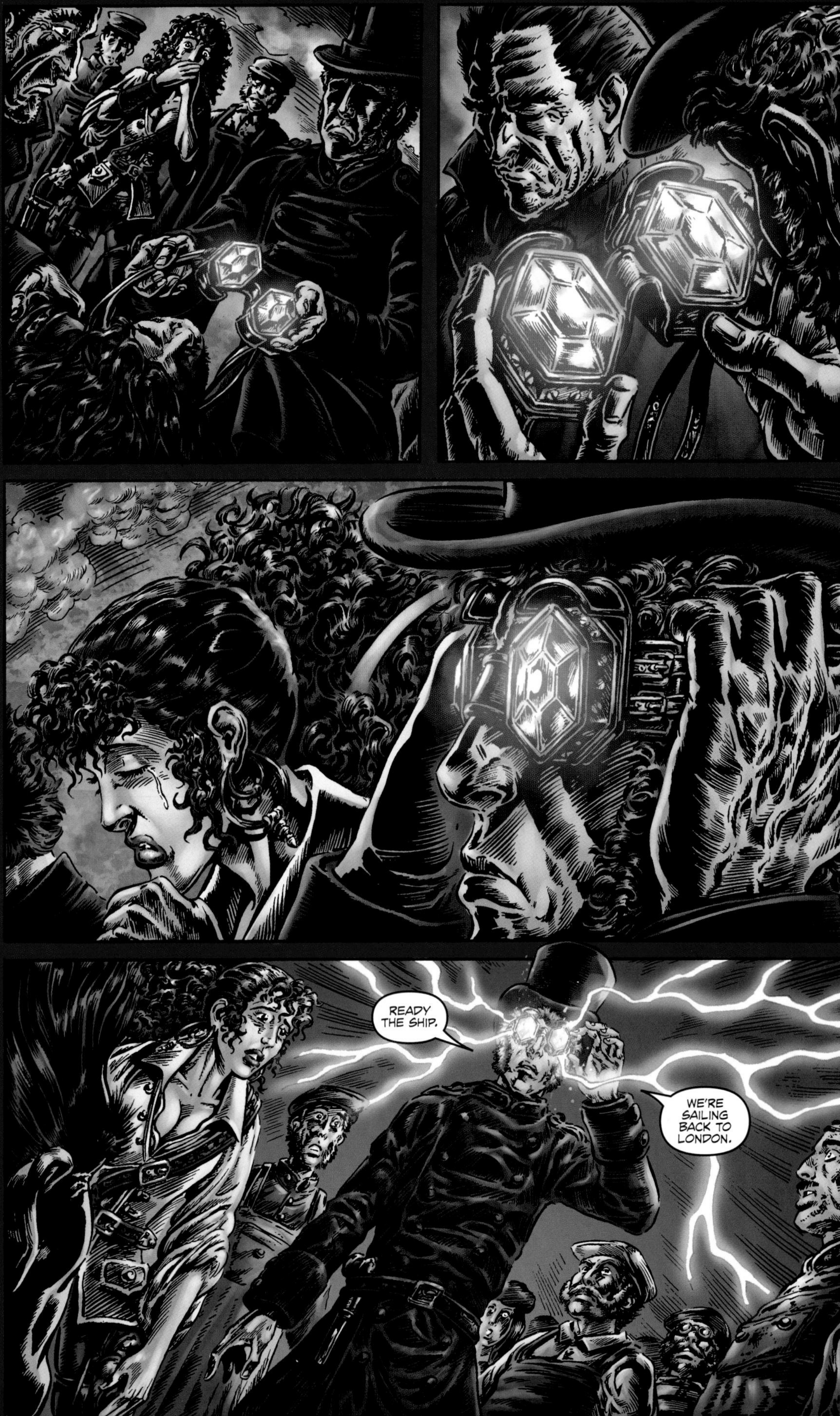
READY THE SHIP.
WE'RE SAILING BACK TO LONDON.

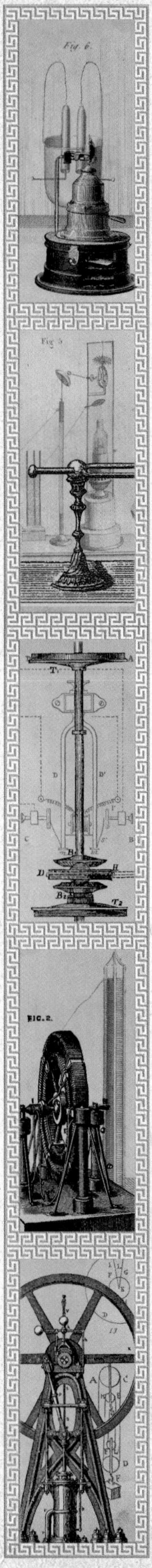

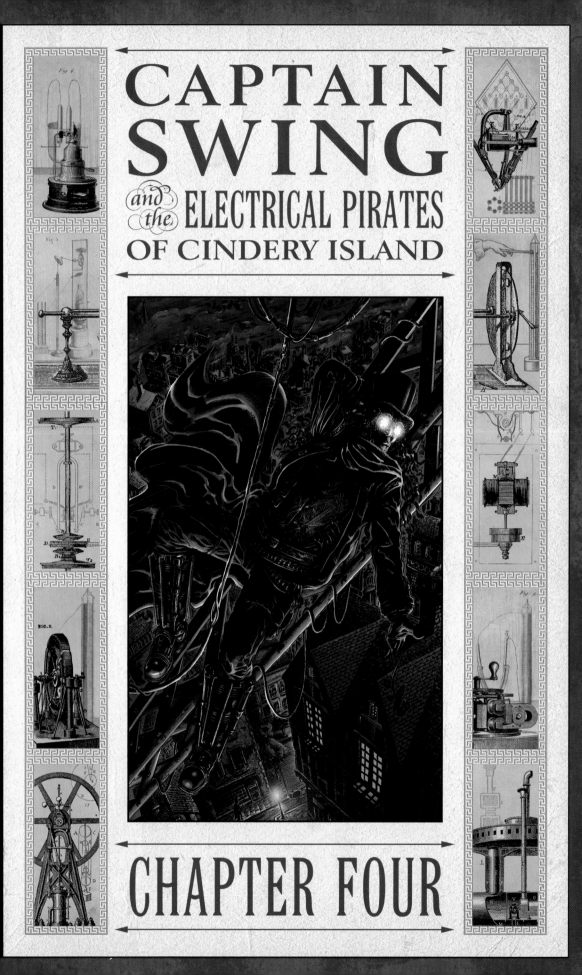

CAPTAIN SWING

and the ELECTRICAL PIRATES OF CINDERY ISLAND

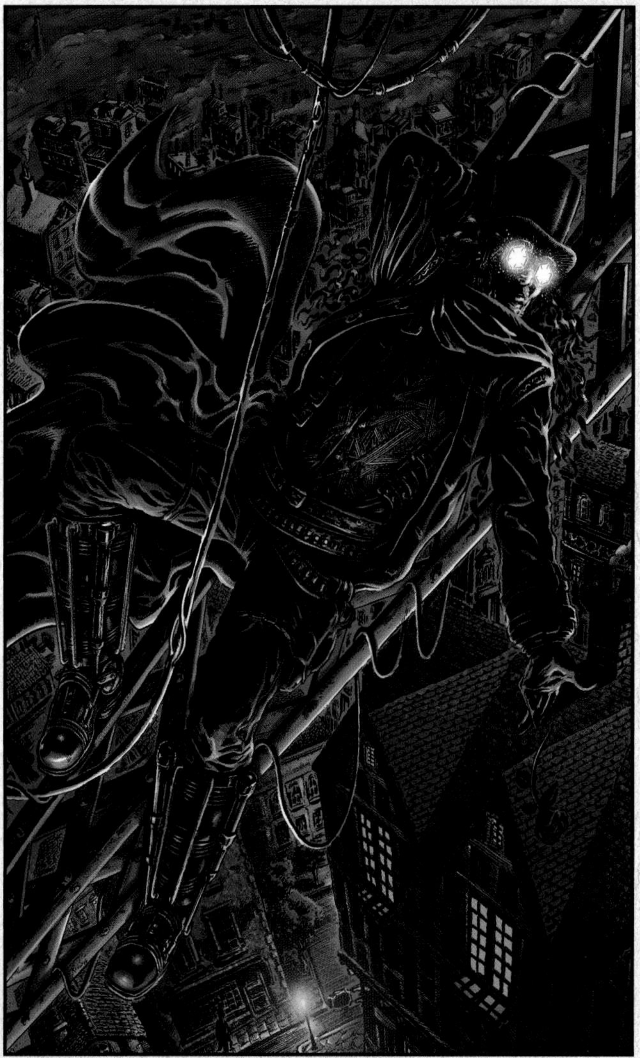

CHAPTER FOUR

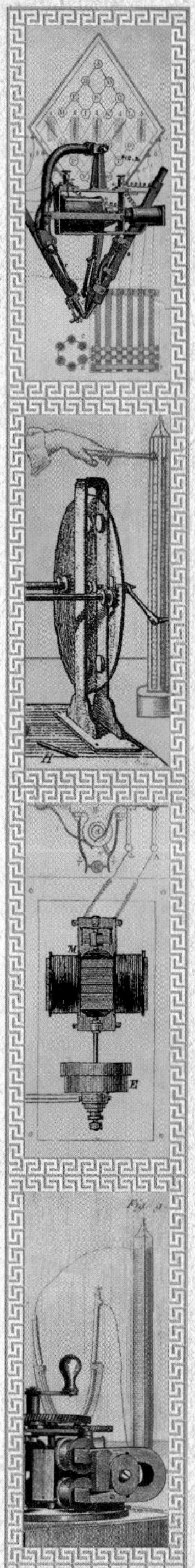

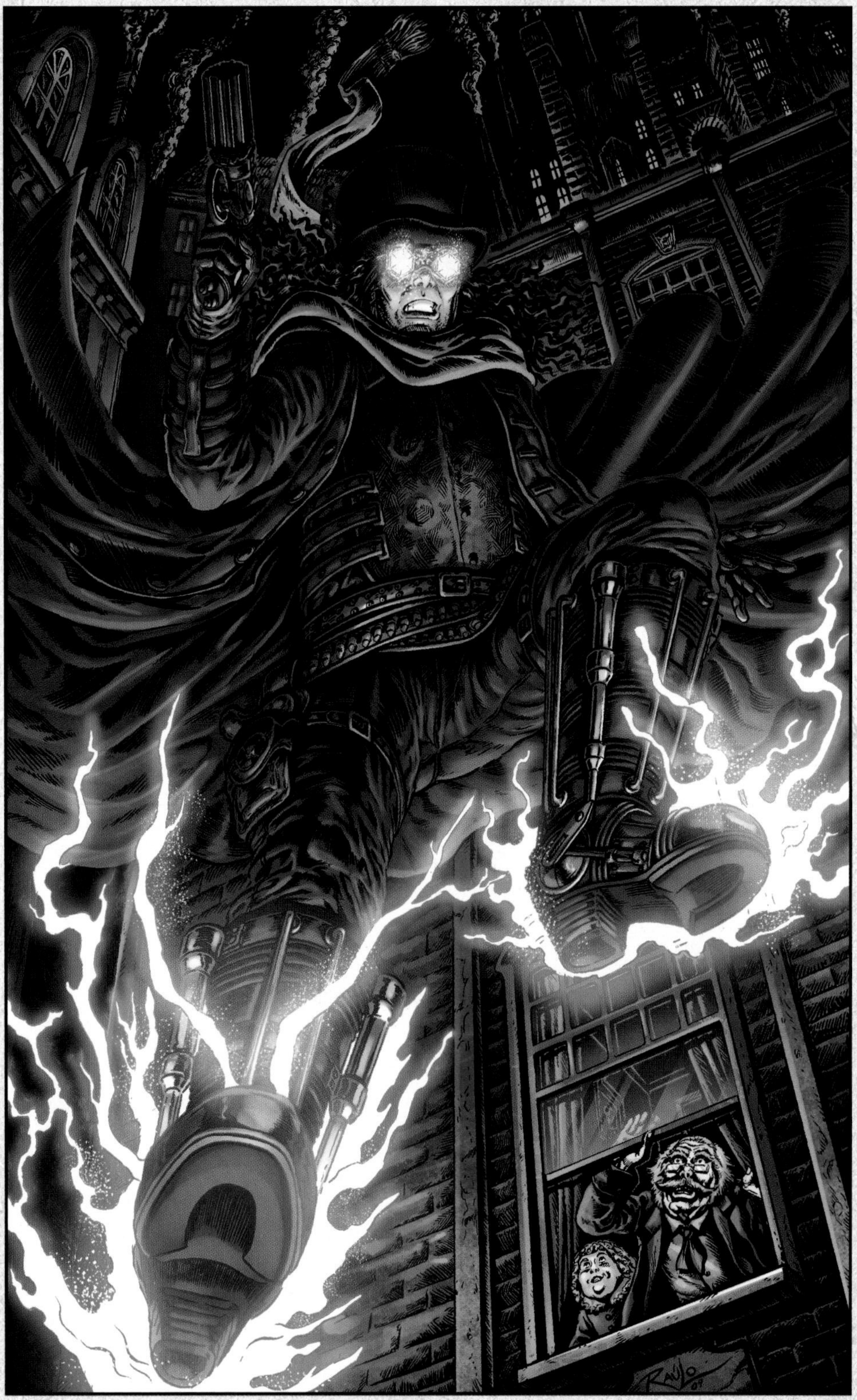

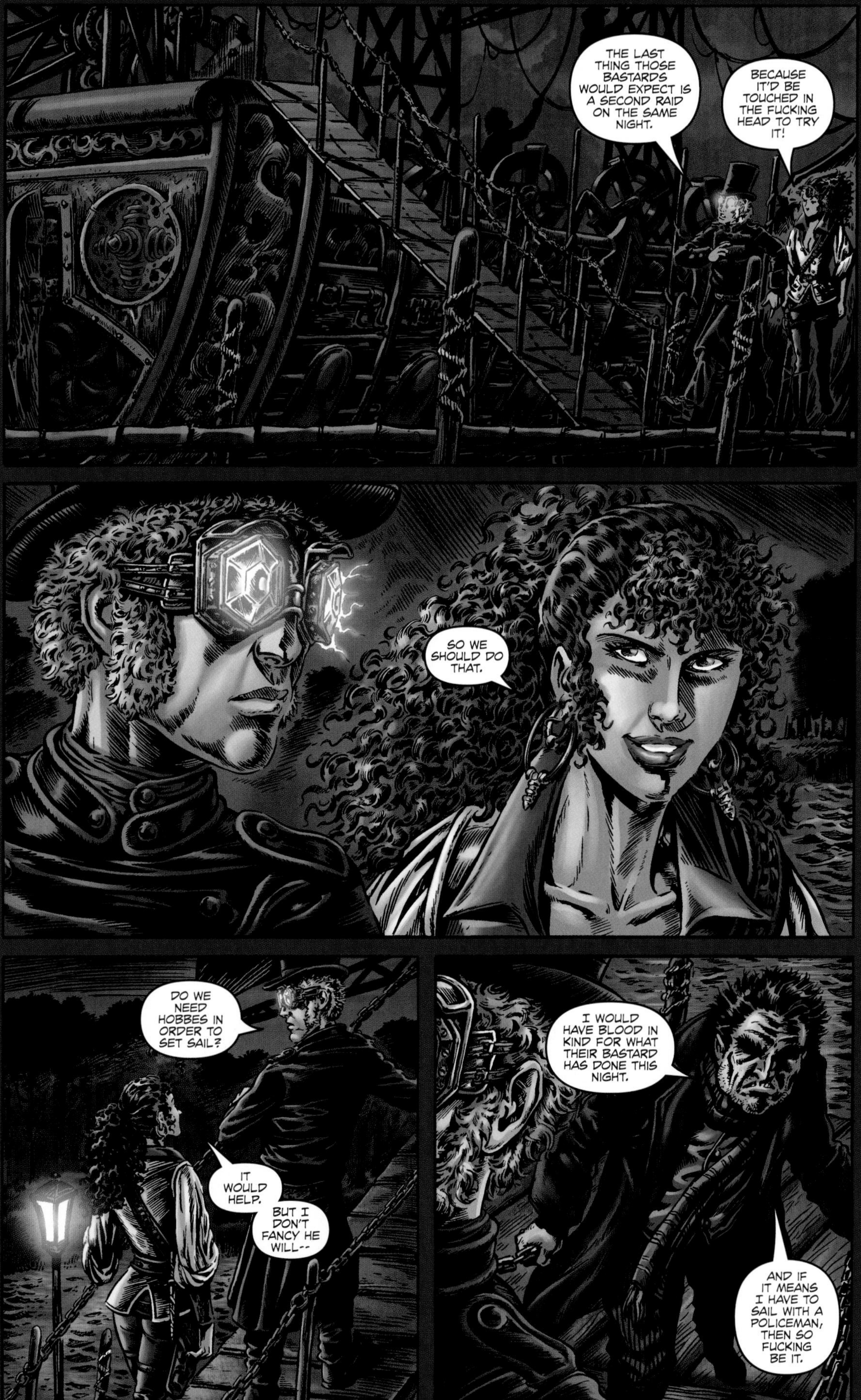
THE LAST THING THOSE BASTARDS WOULD EXPECT IS A SECOND RAID ON THE SAME NIGHT.
BECAUSE IT'D BE TOUCHED IN THE FUCKING HEAD TO TRY IT!
SO WE SHOULD DO THAT.
DO WE NEED HOBBES IN ORDER TO SET SAIL?
IT WOULD HELP.
BUT I DON'T FANCY HE WILL--
I WOULD HAVE BLOOD IN KIND FOR WHAT THEIR BASTARD HAS DONE THIS NIGHT.
AND IF IT MEANS I HAVE TO SAIL WITH A POLICEMAN, THEN SO FUCKING BE IT.

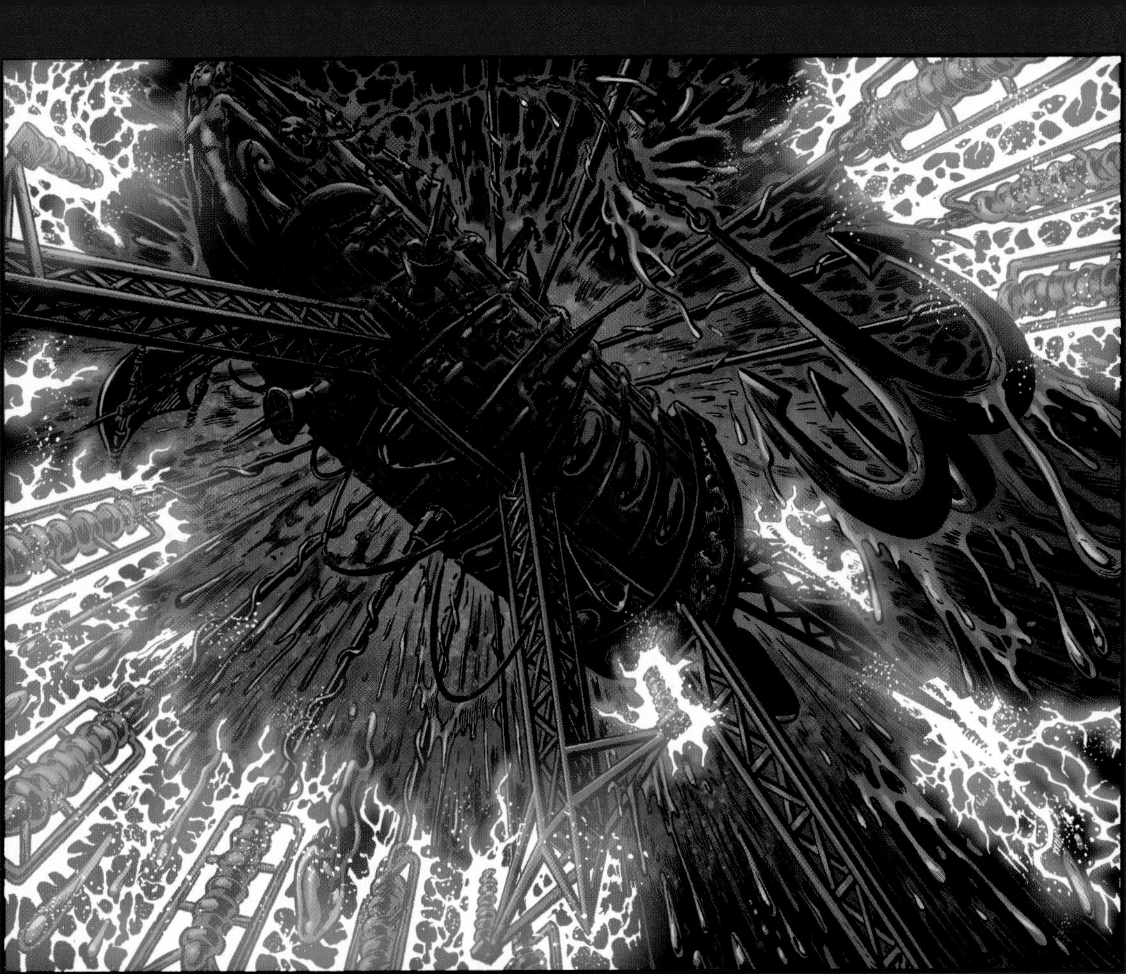

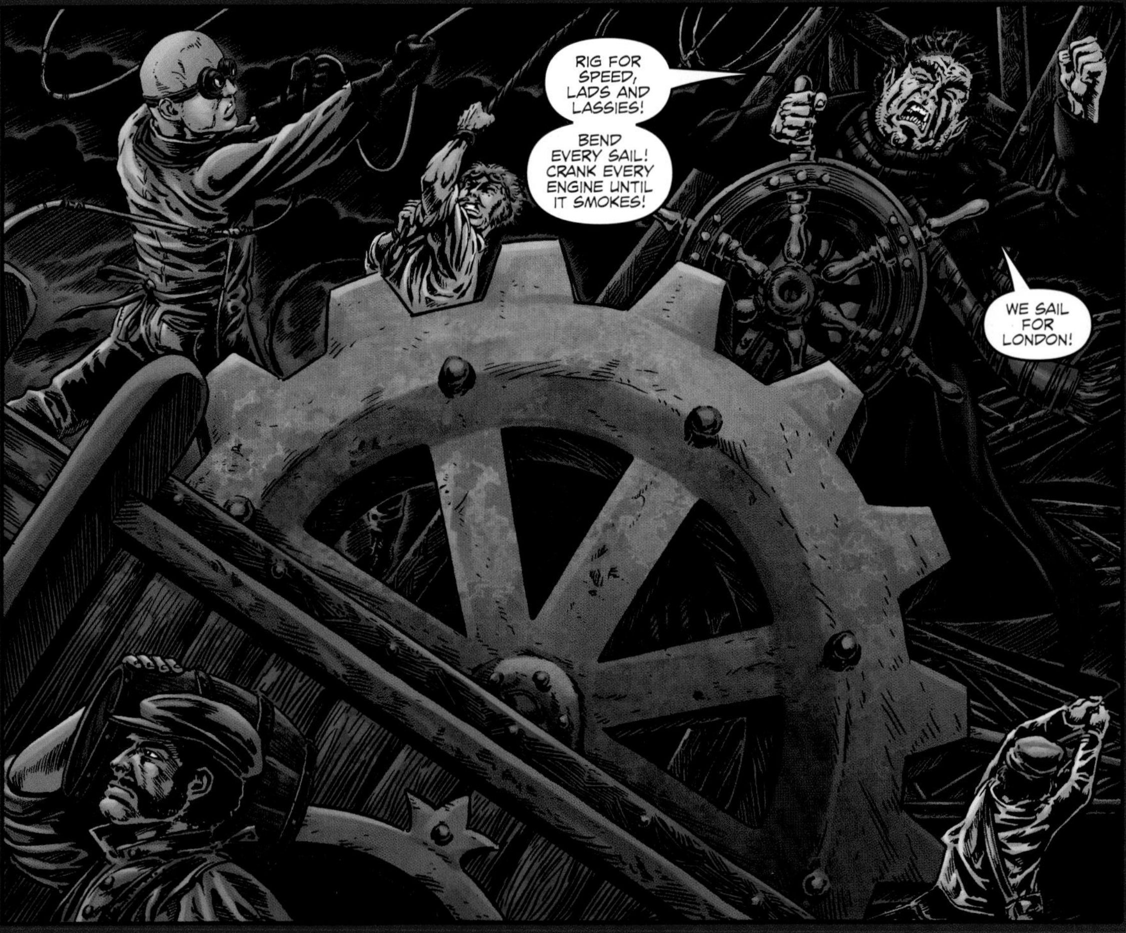
RIG FOR SPEED, LADS AND LASSIES!
BEND EVERY SAIL! CRANK EVERY ENGINE UNTIL IT SMOKES!
WE SAIL FOR LONDON!

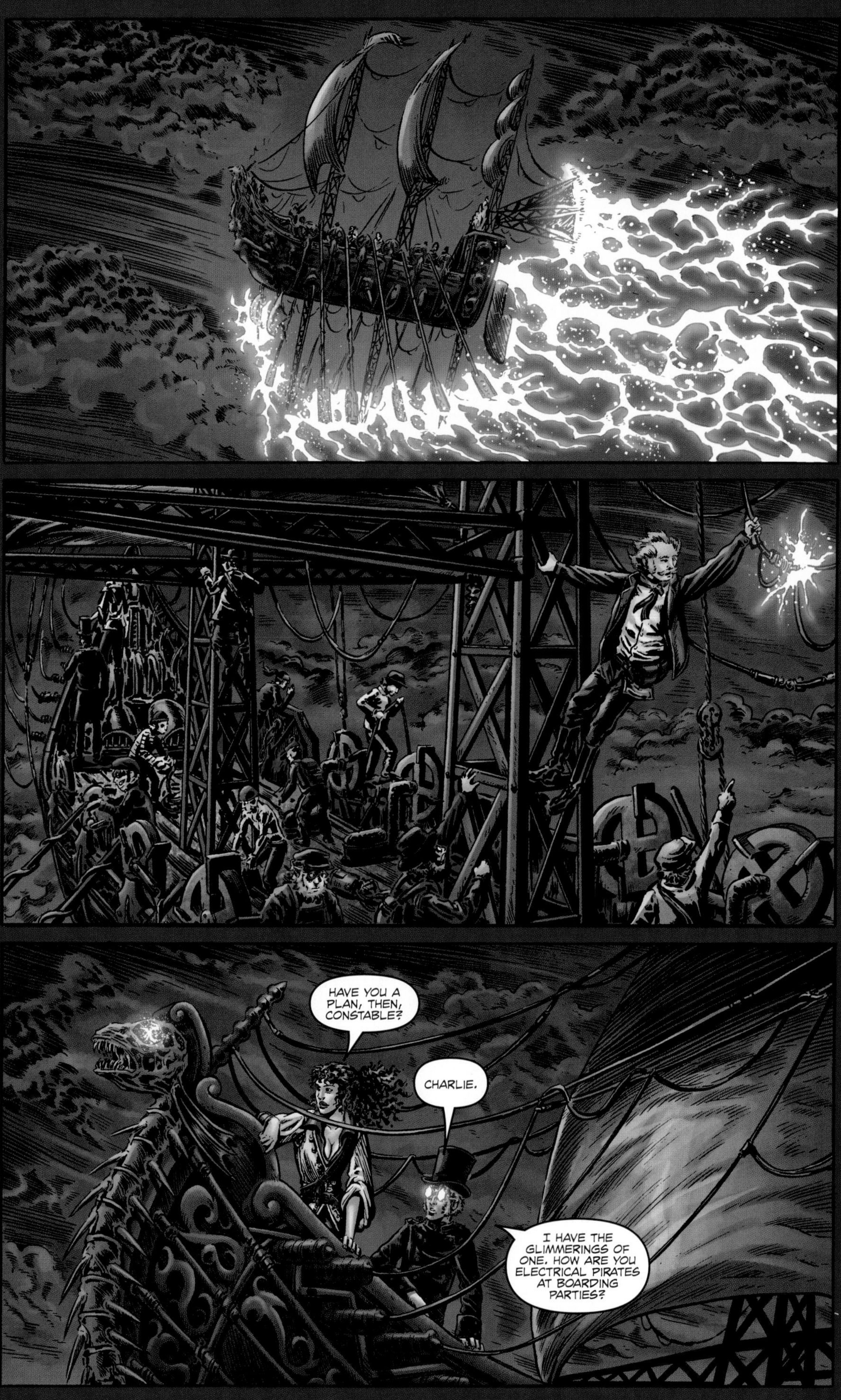
HAVE YOU A PLAN, THEN, CONSTABLE?
CHARLIE.
I HAVE THE GLIMMERINGS OF ONE. HOW ARE YOU ELECTRICAL PIRATES AT BOARDING PARTIES?

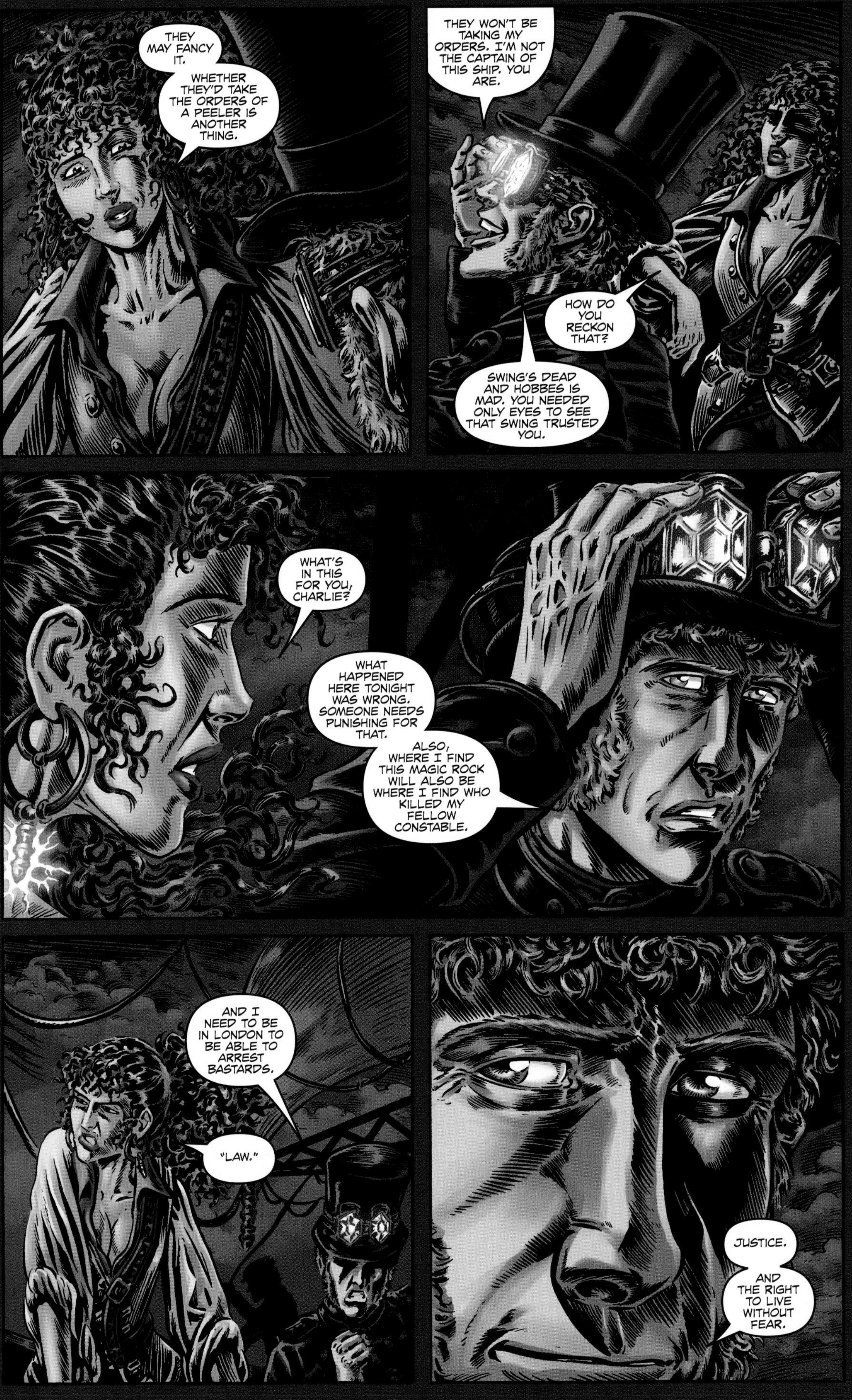
THEY MAY FANCY IT.
WHETHER THEY'D TAKE THE ORDERS OF A PEELER IS ANOTHER THING.
THEY WON'T BE TAKING MY ORDERS. I'M NOT THE CAPTAIN OF THIS SHIP. YOU ARE.
HOW DO YOU RECKON THAT?
SWING'S DEAD AND HOBBES IS MAD. YOU NEEDED ONLY EYES TO SEE THAT SWING TRUSTED YOU.
WHAT'S IN THIS FOR YOU, CHARLIE?
WHAT HAPPENED HERE TONIGHT WAS WRONG. SOMEONE NEEDS PUNISHING FOR THAT.
ALSO, WHERE I FIND THIS MAGIC ROCK WILL ALSO BE WHERE I FIND WHO KILLED MY FELLOW CONSTABLE.
AND I NEED TO BE IN LONDON TO BE ABLE TO ARREST BASTARDS.
"LAW."
JUSTICE.
AND THE RIGHT TO LIVE WITHOUT FEAR.

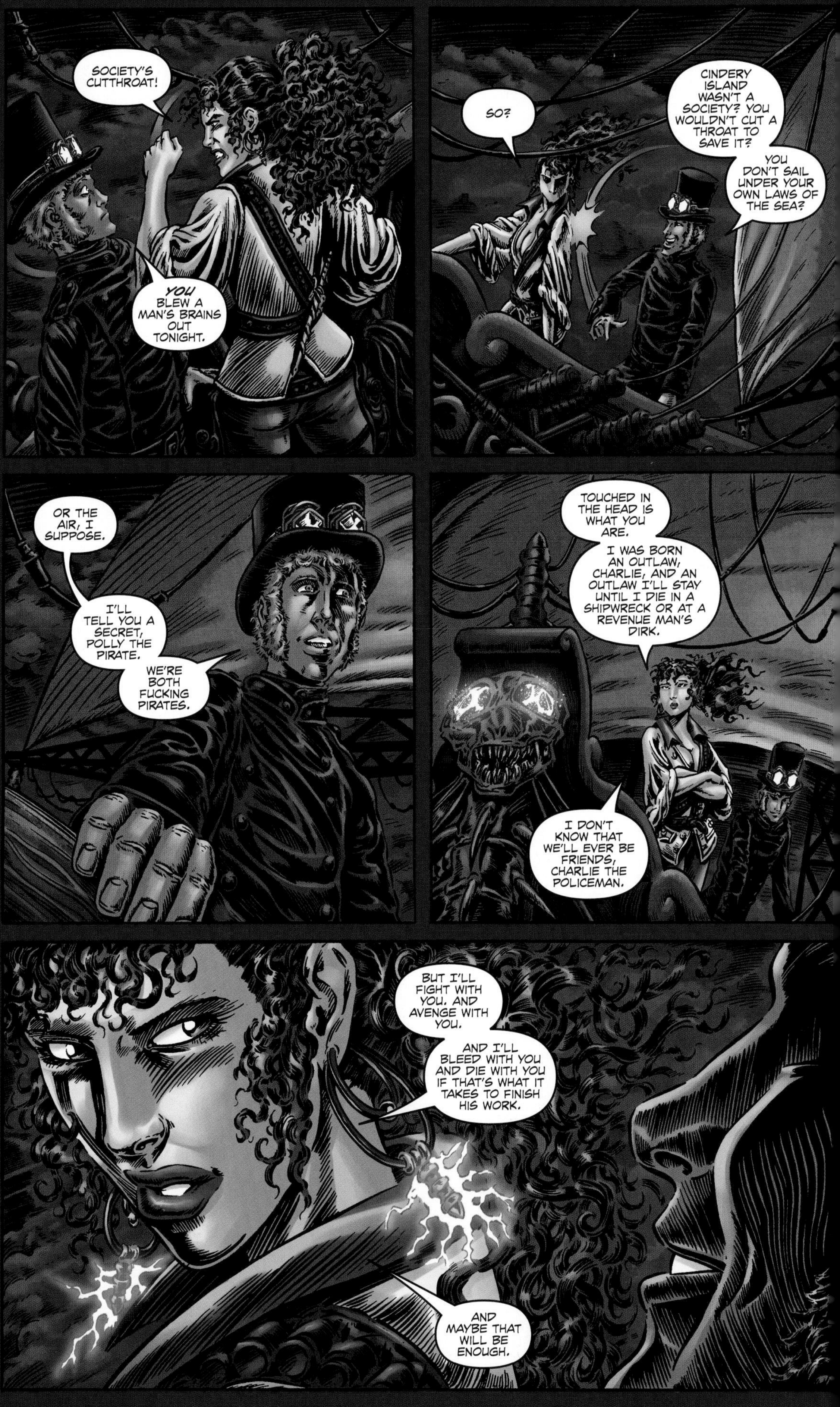
SOCIETY'S CUTTHROAT!
YOU BLEW A MAN'S BRAINS OUT TONIGHT.
SO?
CINDERY ISLAND WASN'T A SOCIETY? YOU WOULDN'T CUT A THROAT TO SAVE IT?
YOU DON'T SAIL UNDER YOUR OWN LAWS OF THE SEA?
OR THE AIR, I SUPPOSE.
I'LL TELL YOU A SECRET, POLLY THE PIRATE.
WE'RE BOTH FUCKING PIRATES.
TOUCHED IN THE HEAD IS WHAT YOU ARE.
I WAS BORN AN OUTLAW, CHARLIE, AND AN OUTLAW I'LL STAY UNTIL I DIE IN A SHIPWRECK OR AT A REVENUE MAN'S DIRK.
I DON'T KNOW THAT WE'LL EVER BE FRIENDS, CHARLIE THE POLICEMAN.
BUT I'LL FIGHT WITH YOU. AND AVENGE WITH YOU.
AND I'LL BLEED WITH YOU AND DIE WITH YOU IF THAT'S WHAT IT TAKES TO FINISH HIS WORK.
AND MAYBE THAT WILL BE ENOUGH.

The answering of the alchemical marriage I brokered. I am a man of philosophy, and pirates are brave in very specific and limited ways. Perhaps it did indeed take a policeman to conceive of taking the Club "mob-handed," as they say.

Perhaps I was merely a bad captain. The mad joy of cavorting as Swing was always tempered by the knowledge that I was wading out of my depth. And it is a certainty that it is the work of the sleepless doctor, not the fearless captain, that brings my voice to you now from the aether.

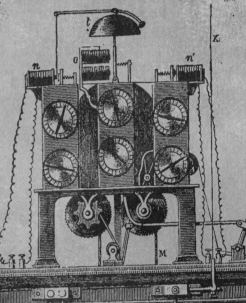

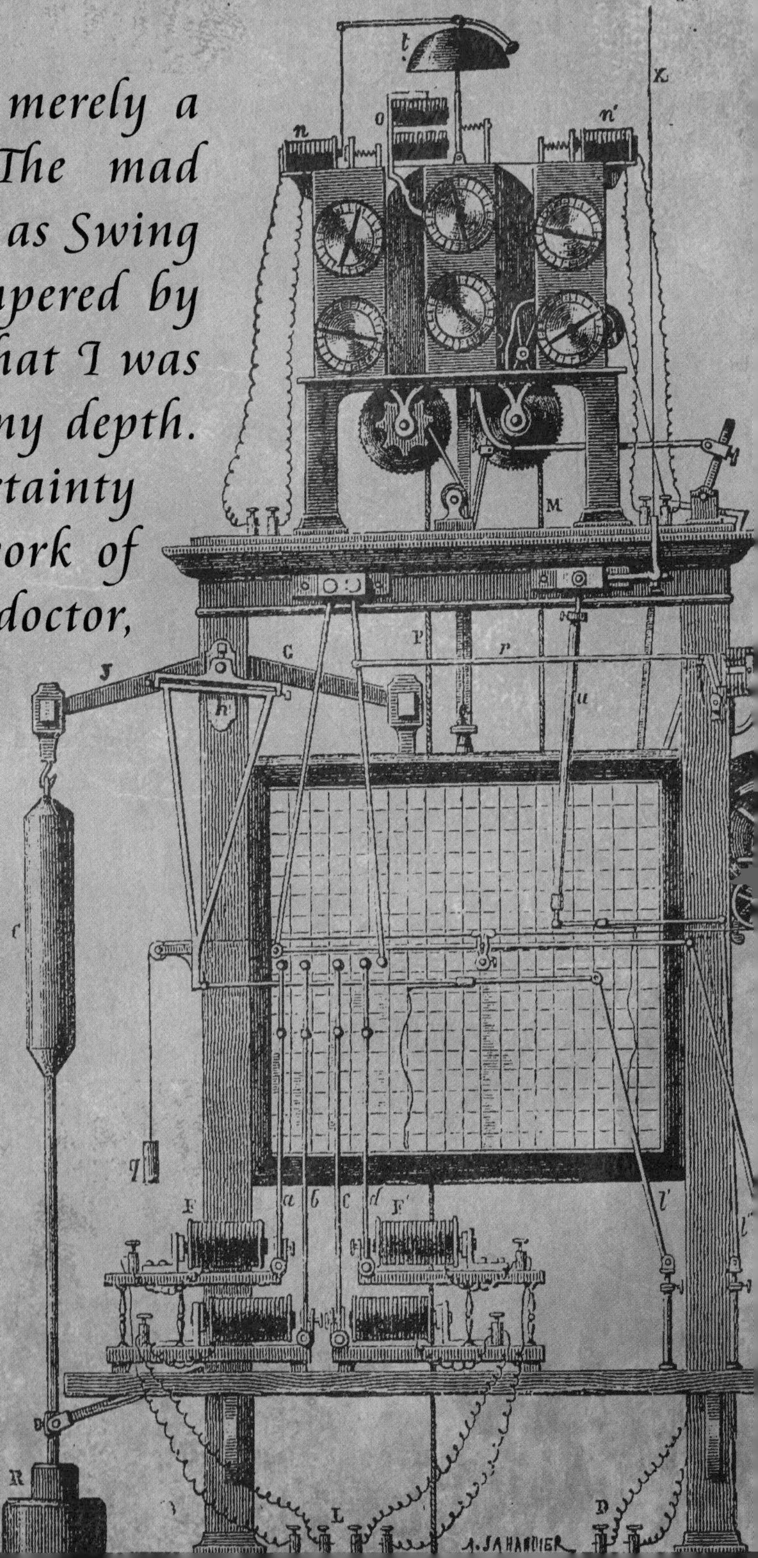

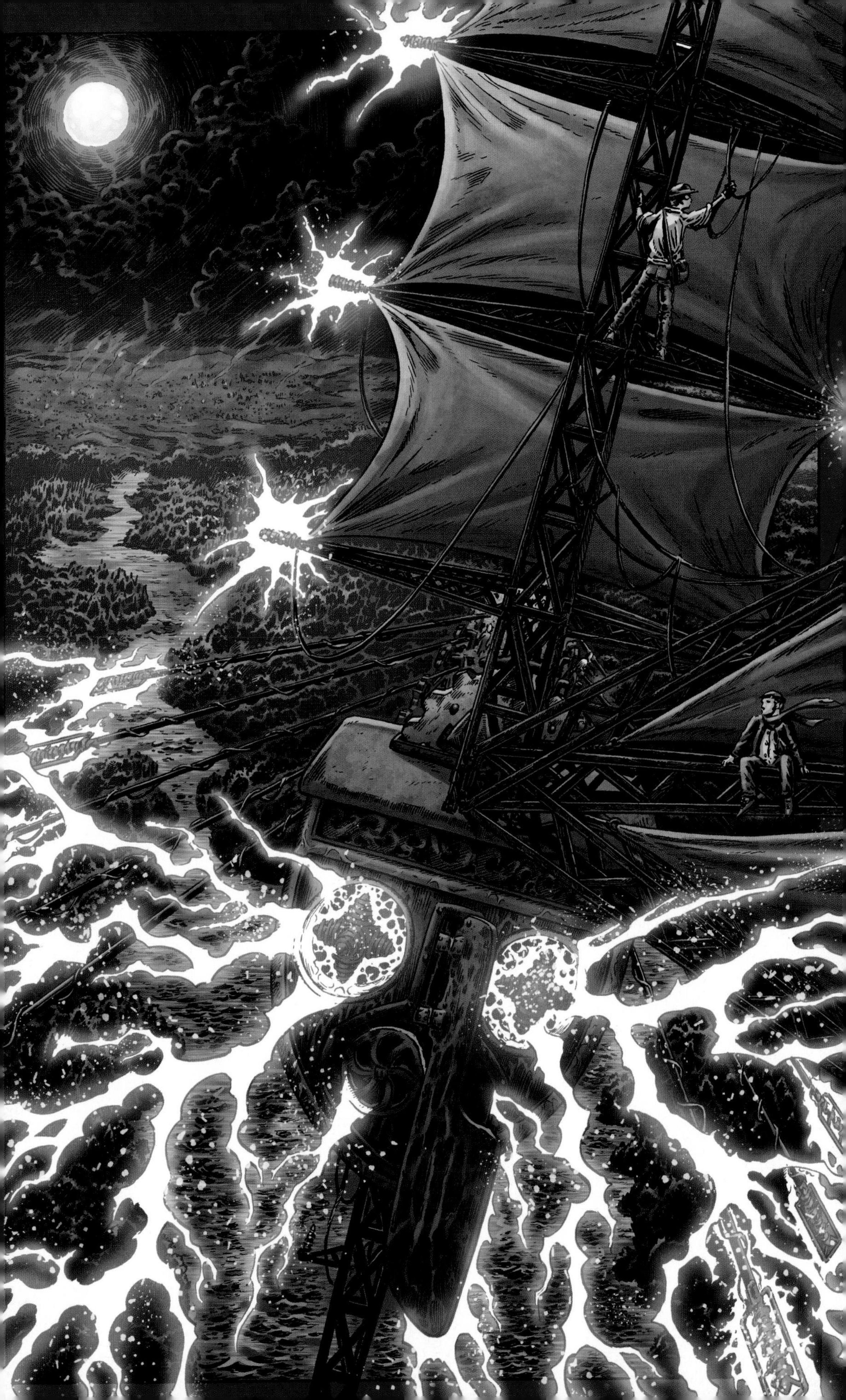

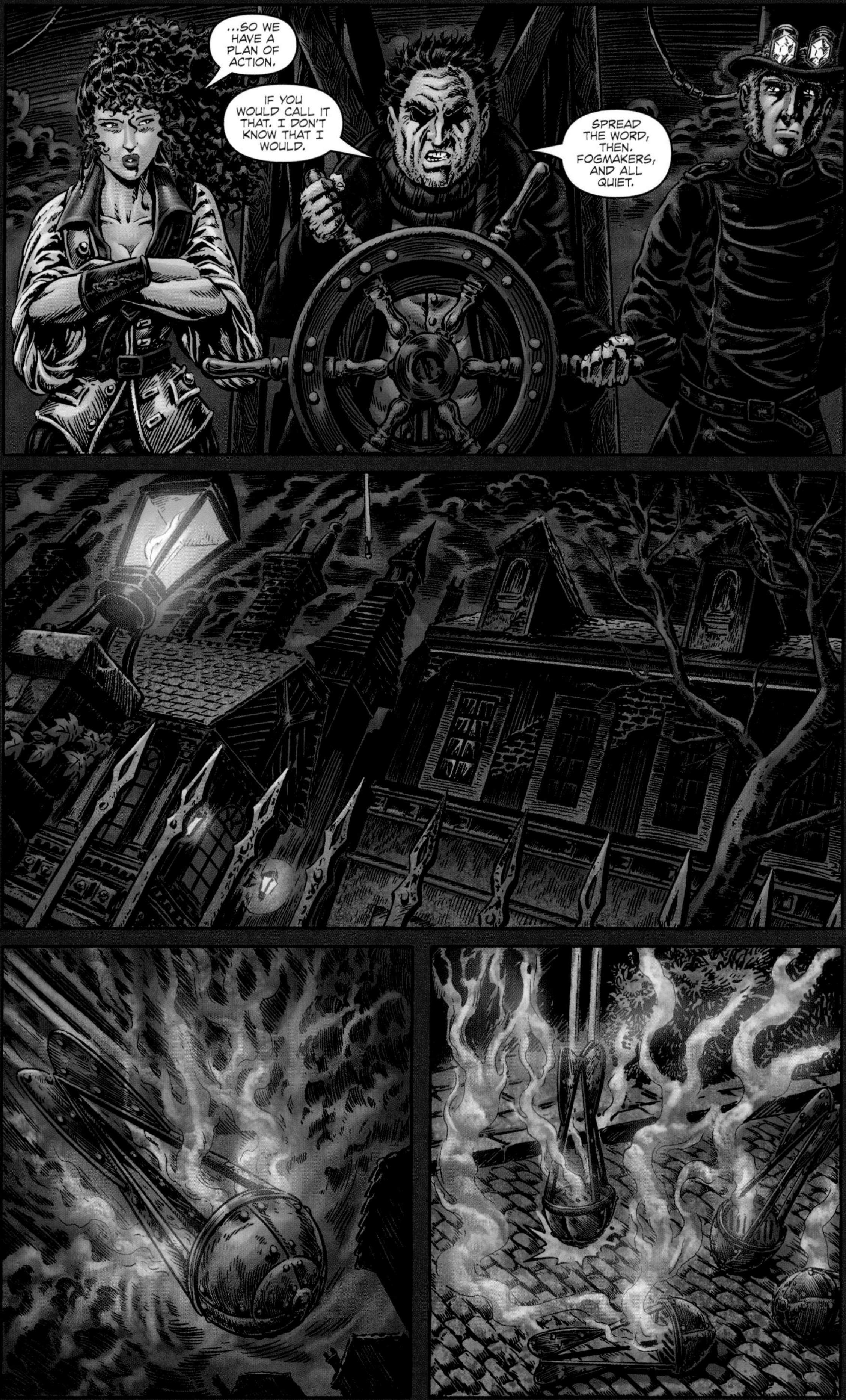
...SO WE HAVE A PLAN OF ACTION.
IF YOU WOULD CALL IT THAT. I DON'T KNOW THAT I WOULD.
SPREAD THE WORD, THEN. FOGMAKERS, AND ALL QUIET.

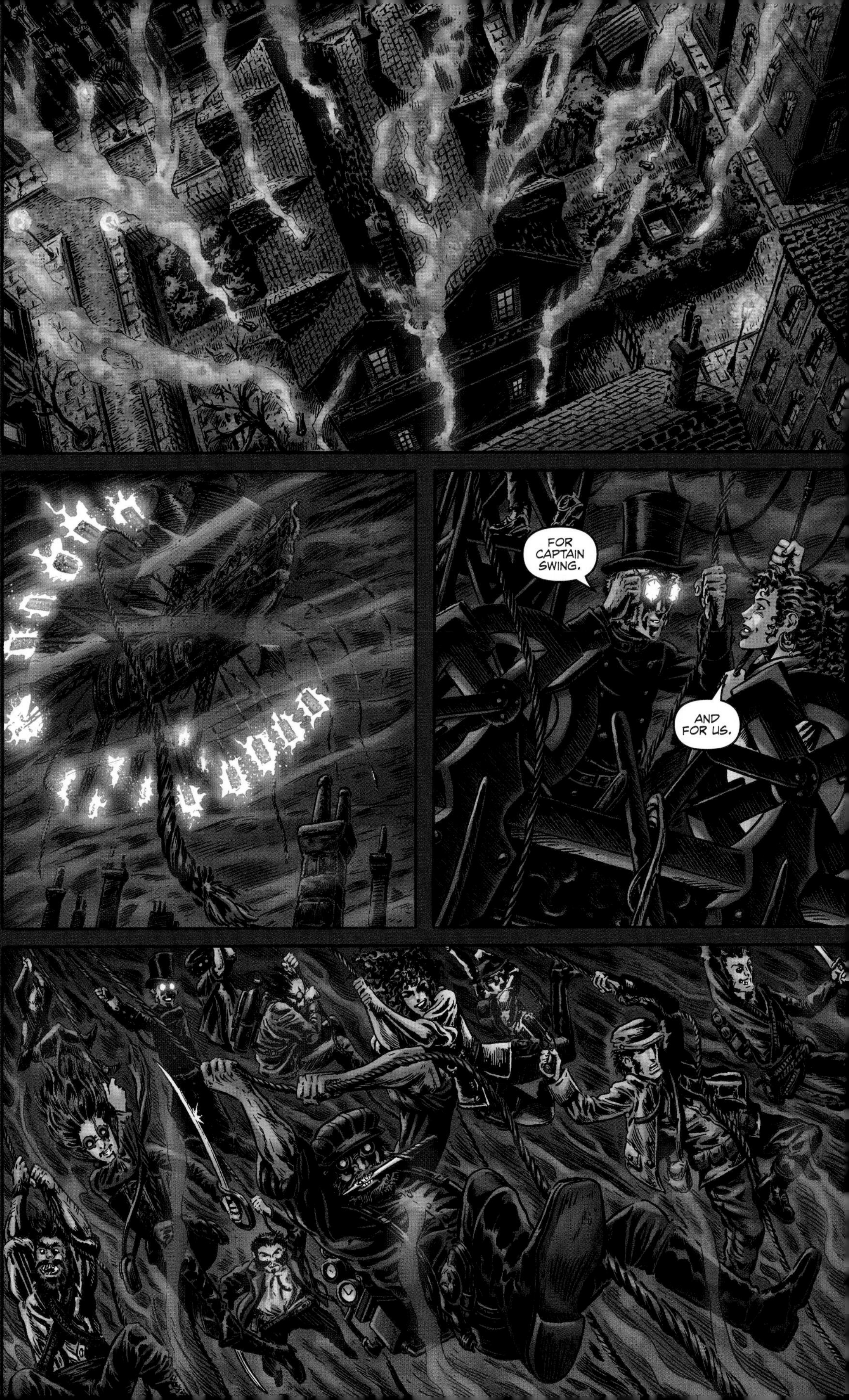
FOR CAPTAIN SWING.
AND FOR US.

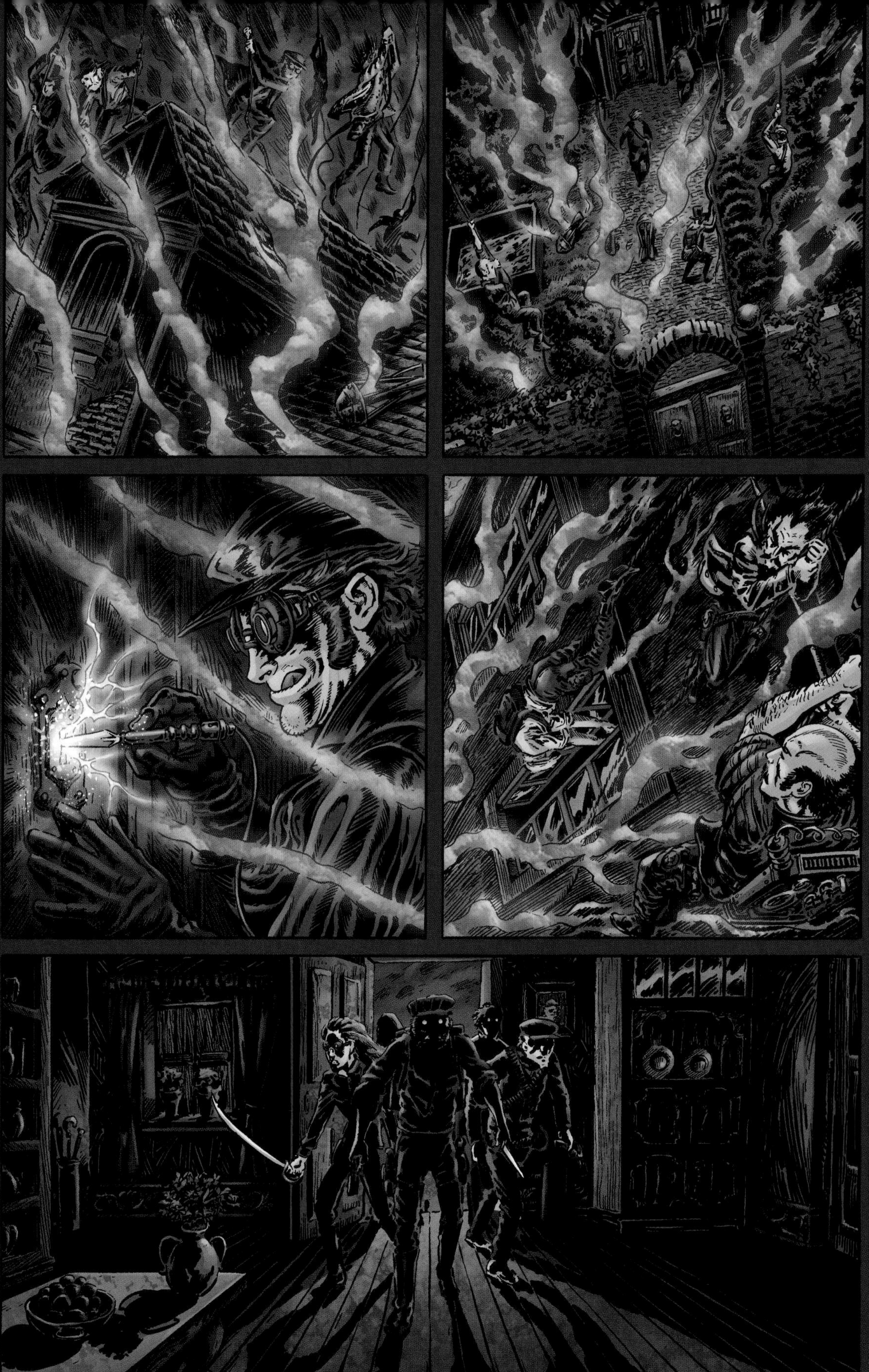

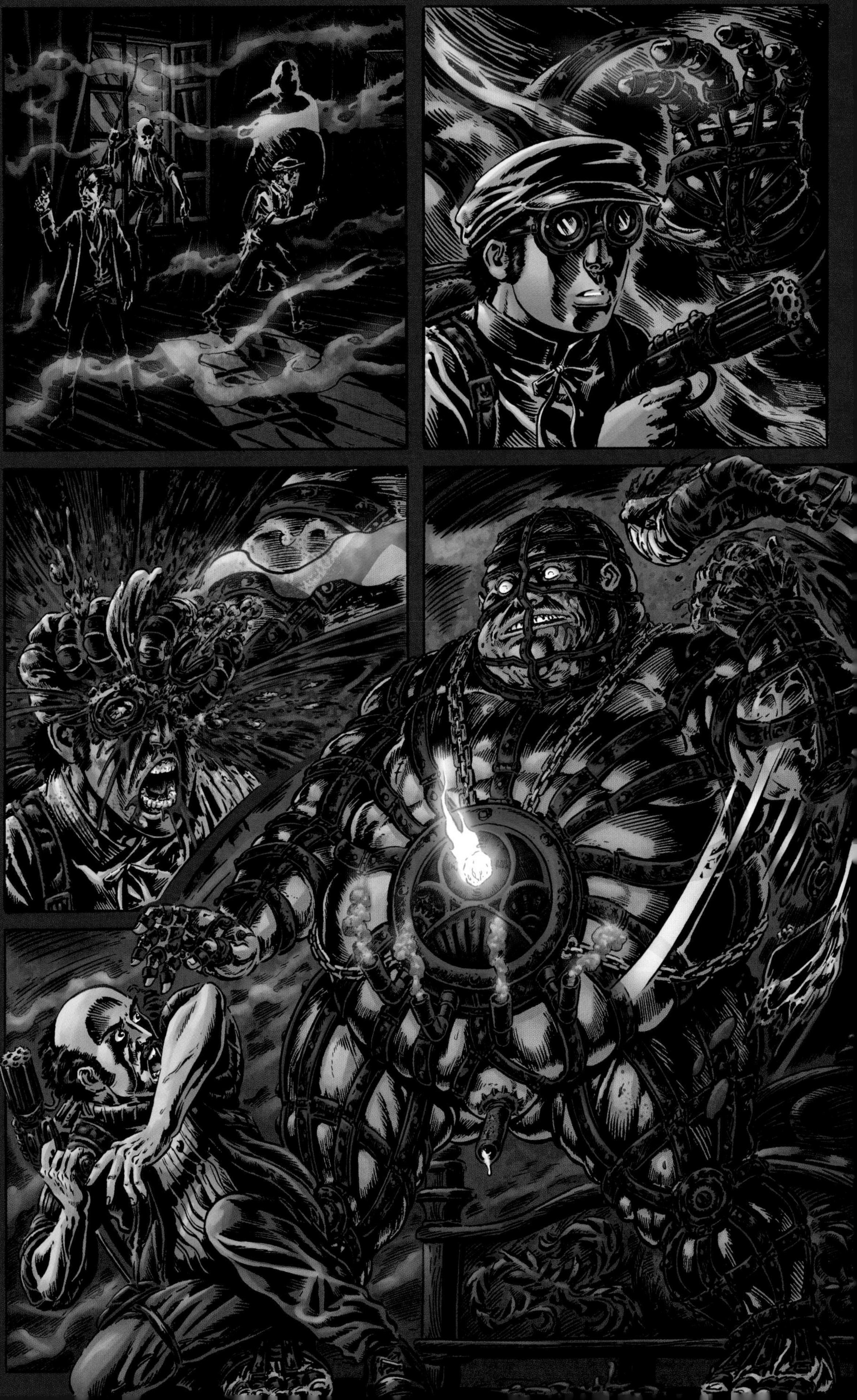

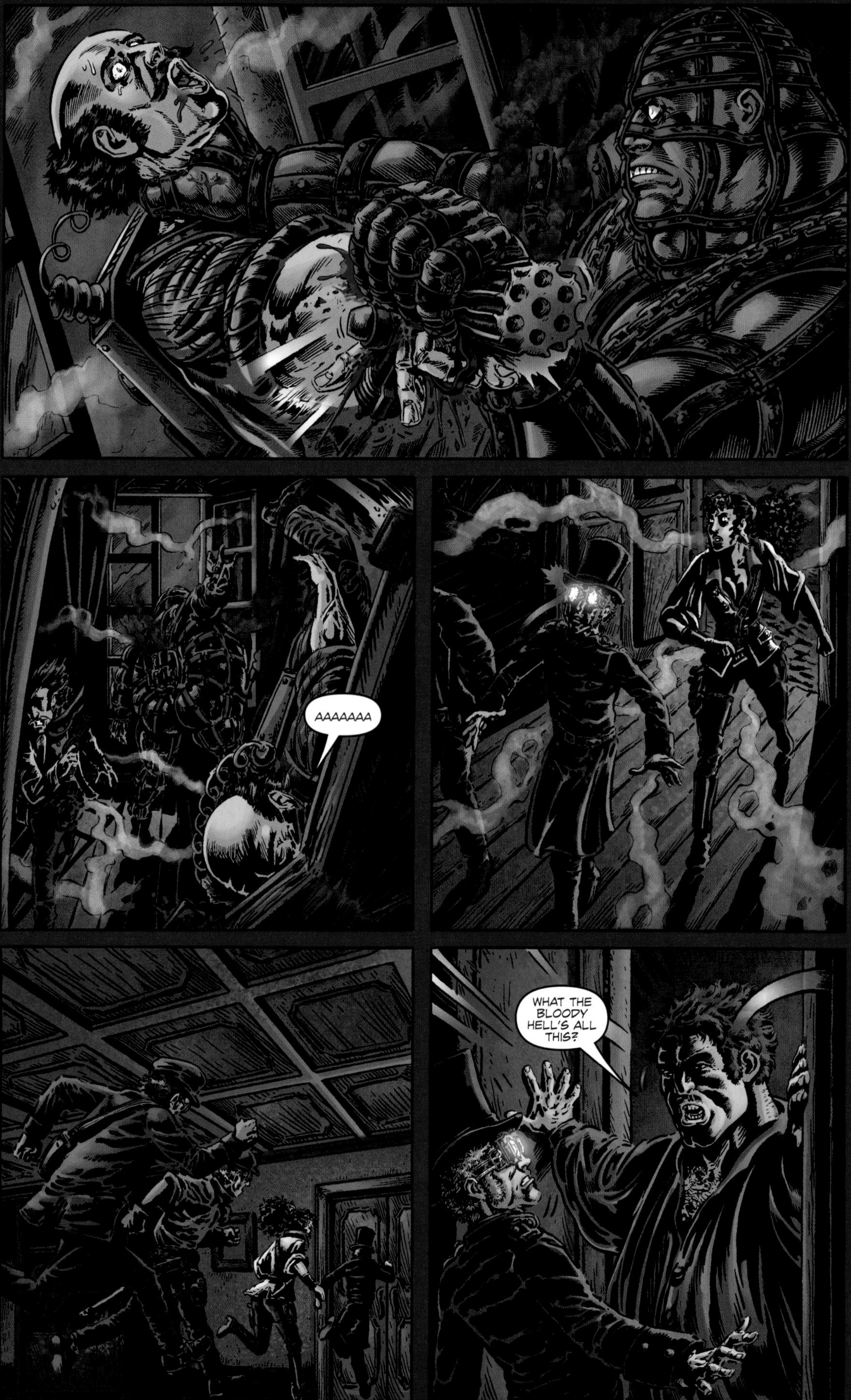
AAAAAAA
WHAT THE BLOODY HELL'S ALL THIS?

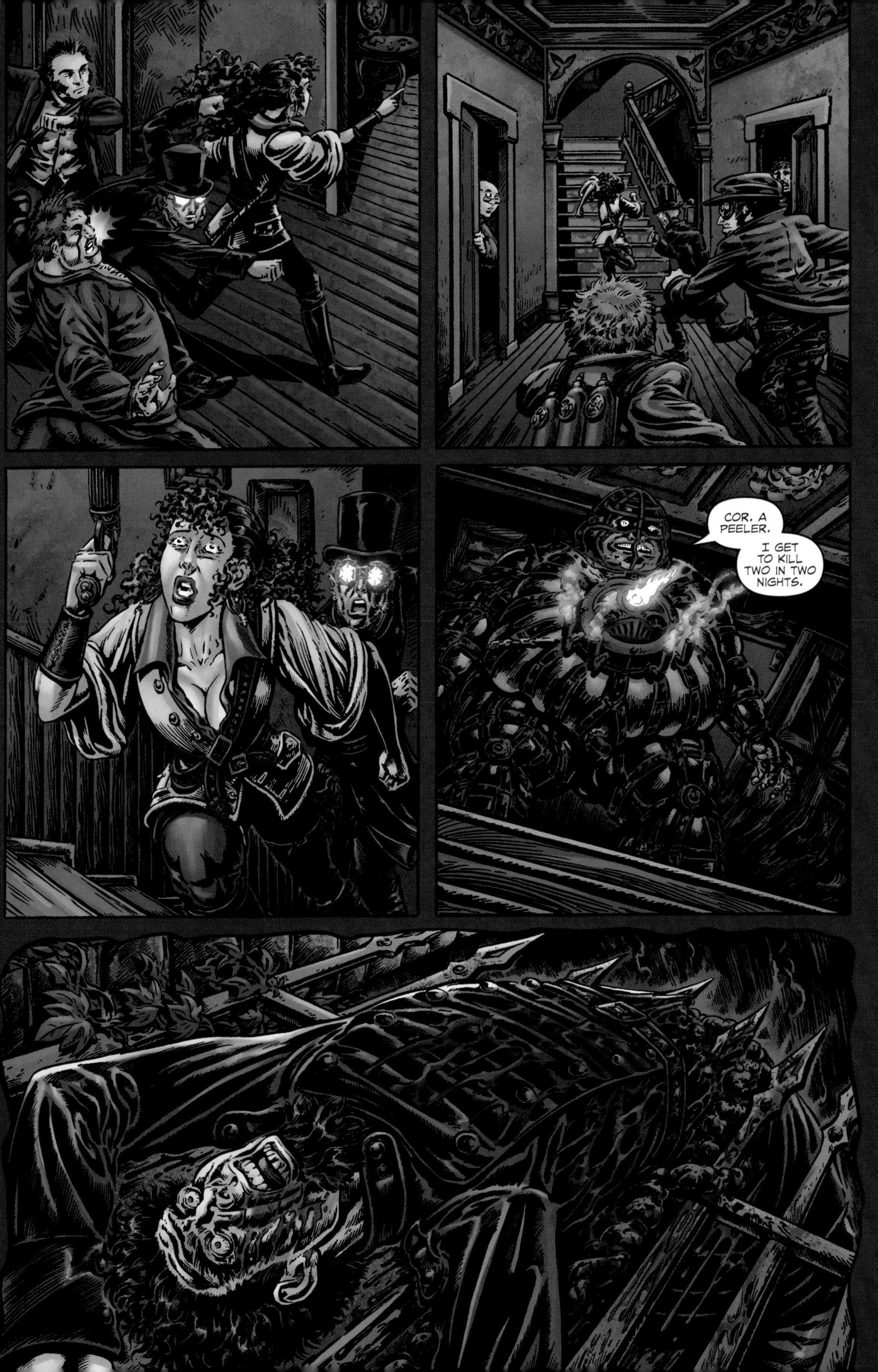

COR. A PEELER.
I GET TO KILL TWO IN TWO NIGHTS.

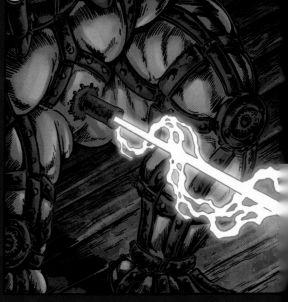

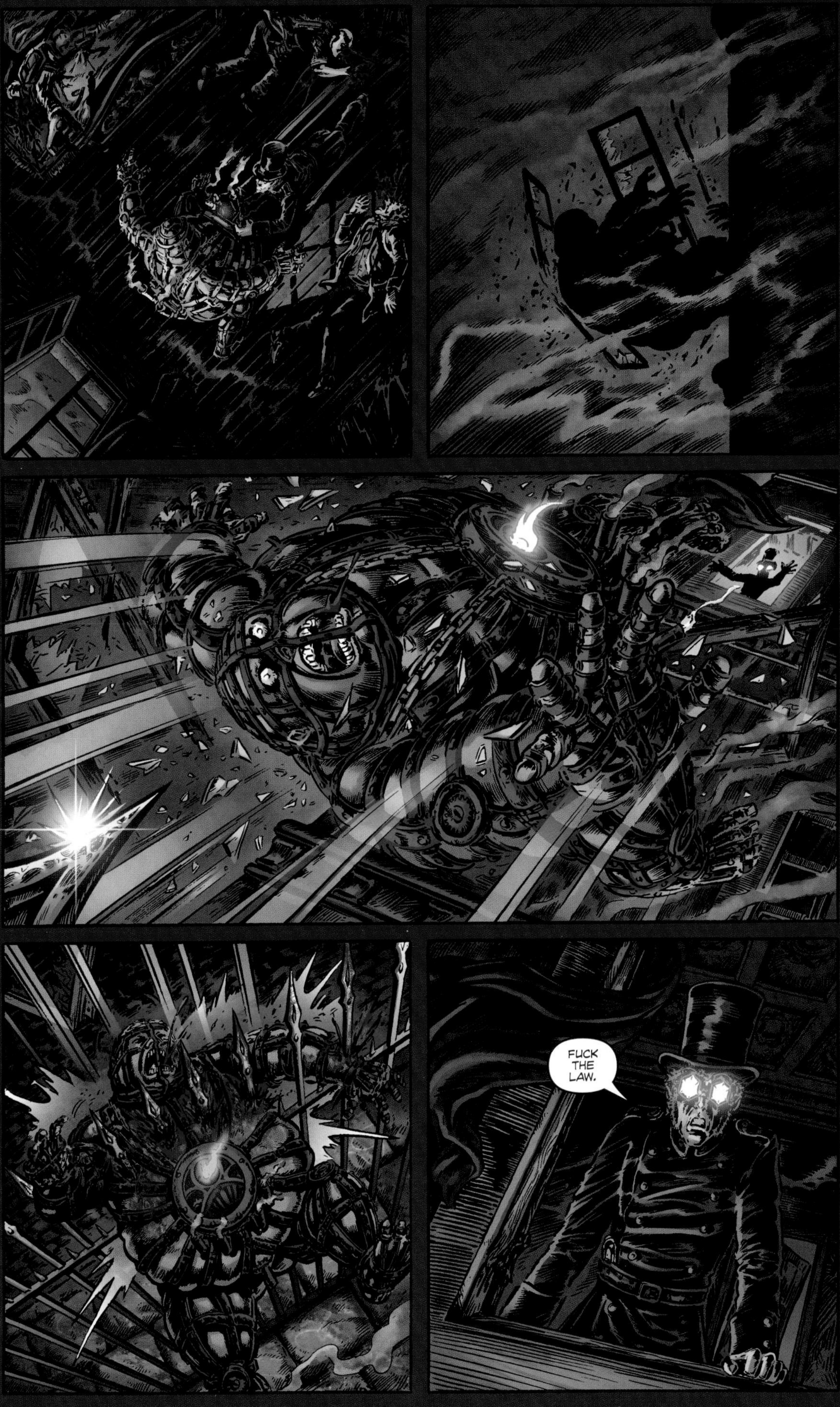
FUCK THE LAW.

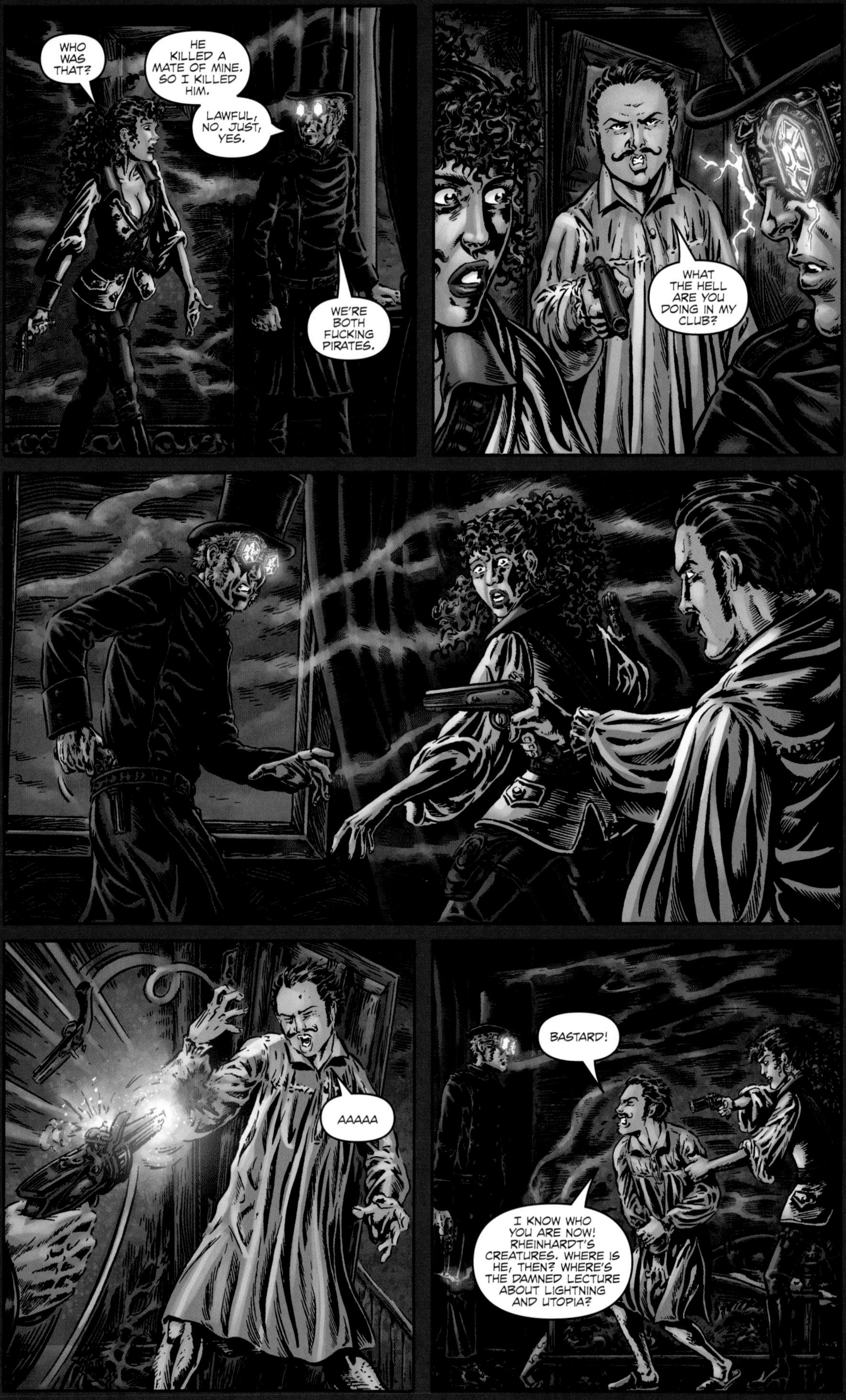
WHO WAS THAT?
HE KILLED A MATE OF MINE. SO I KILLED HIM.
LAWFUL, NO. JUST, YES.
WE'RE BOTH FUCKING PIRATES.
WHAT THE HELL ARE YOU DOING IN MY CLUB?
AAAAA
BASTARD!
I KNOW WHO YOU ARE NOW! RHEINHARDT'S CREATURES. WHERE IS HE, THEN? WHERE'S THE DAMNED LECTURE ABOUT LIGHTNING AND UTOPIA?

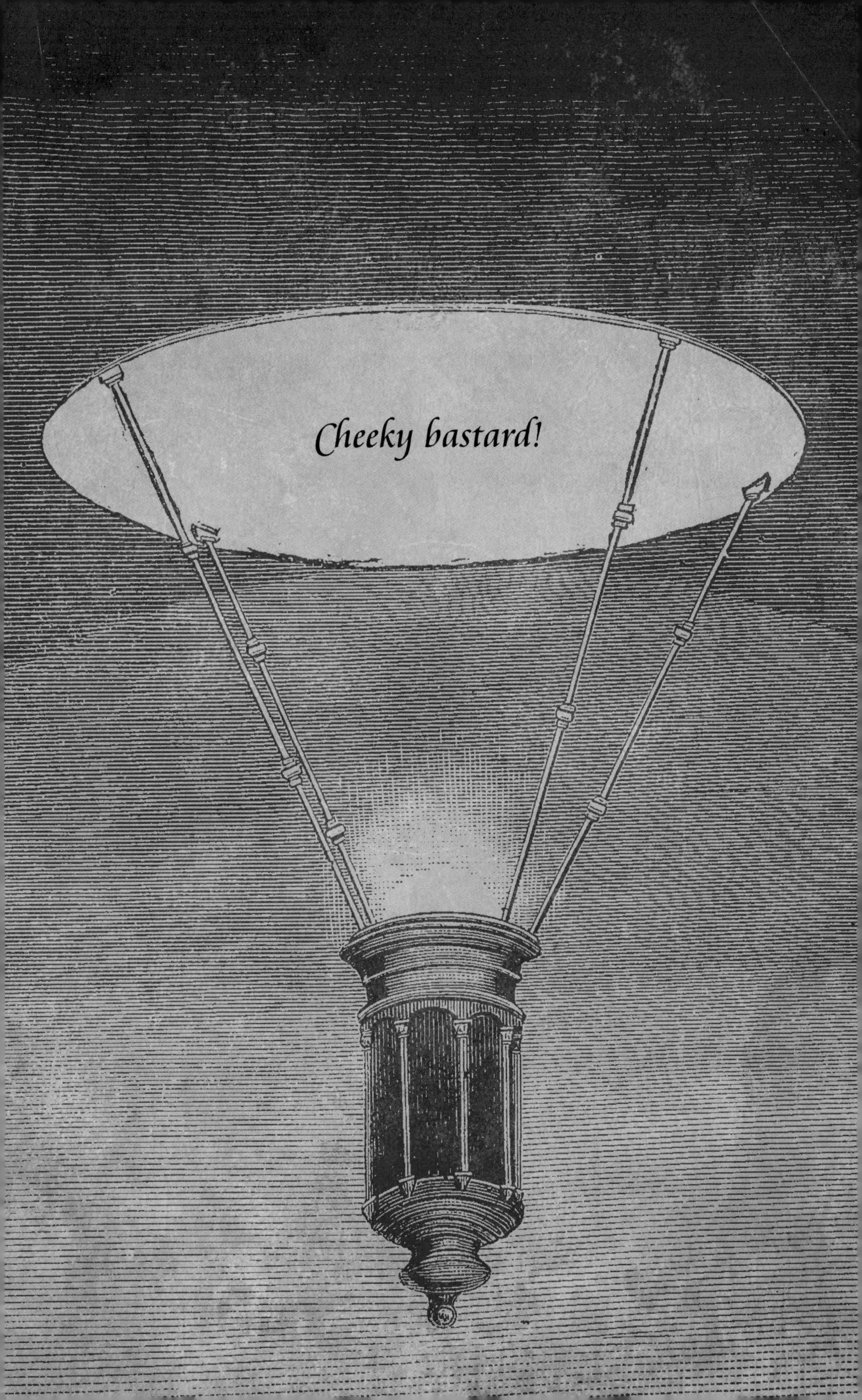
Cheeky bastard!

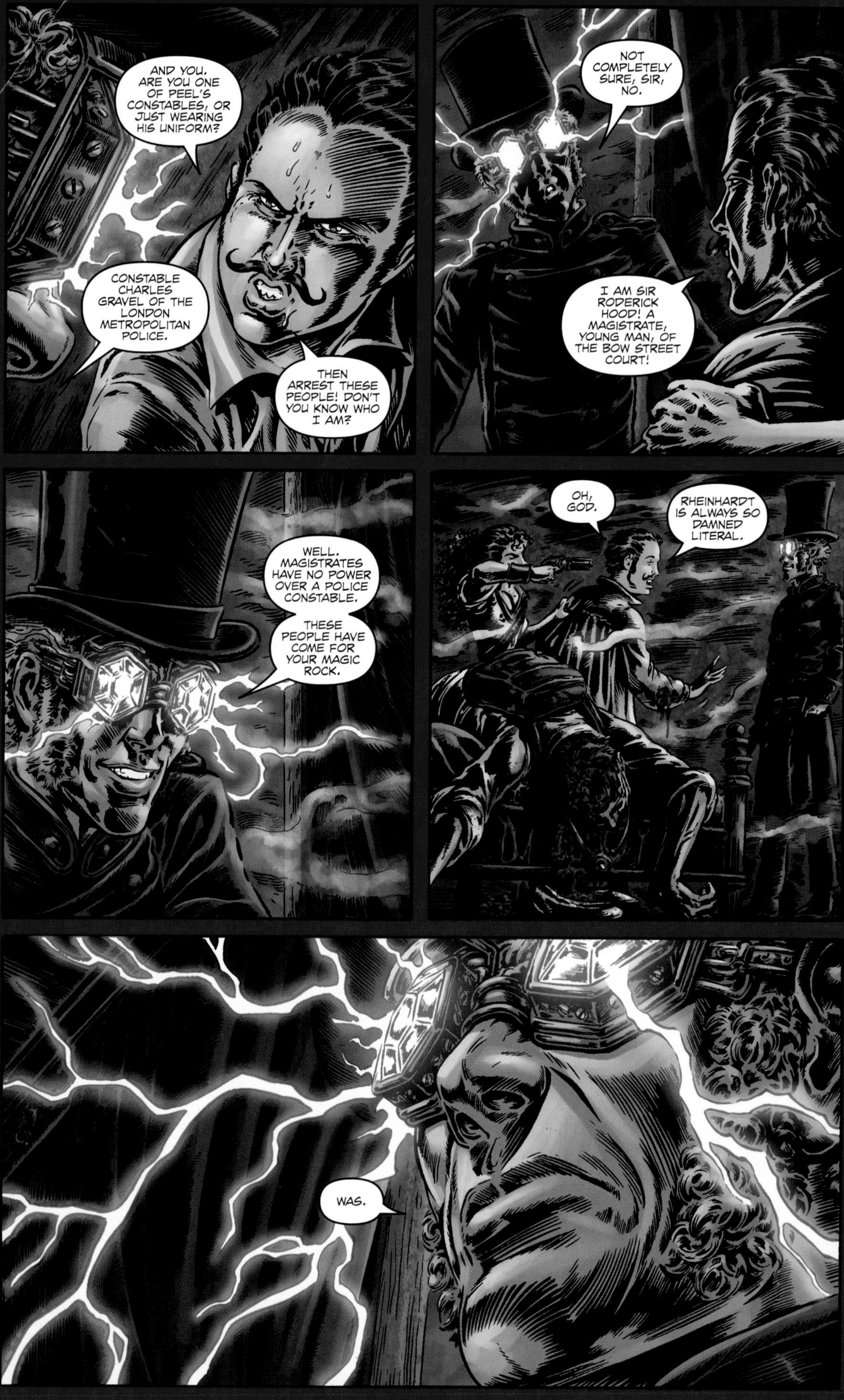
AND YOU. ARE YOU ONE OF PEEL'S CONSTABLES, OR JUST WEARING HIS UNIFORM?
CONSTABLE CHARLES GRAVEL OF THE LONDON METROPOLITAN POLICE.
THEN ARREST THESE PEOPLE! DON'T YOU KNOW WHO I AM?
NOT COMPLETELY SURE, SIR, NO.
I AM SIR RODERICK HOOD! A MAGISTRATE, YOUNG MAN, OF THE BOW STREET COURT!
WELL. MAGISTRATES HAVE NO POWER OVER A POLICE CONSTABLE.
THESE PEOPLE HAVE COME FOR YOUR MAGIC ROCK.
OH, GOD.
RHEINHARDT IS ALWAYS SO DAMNED LITERAL.
WAS.

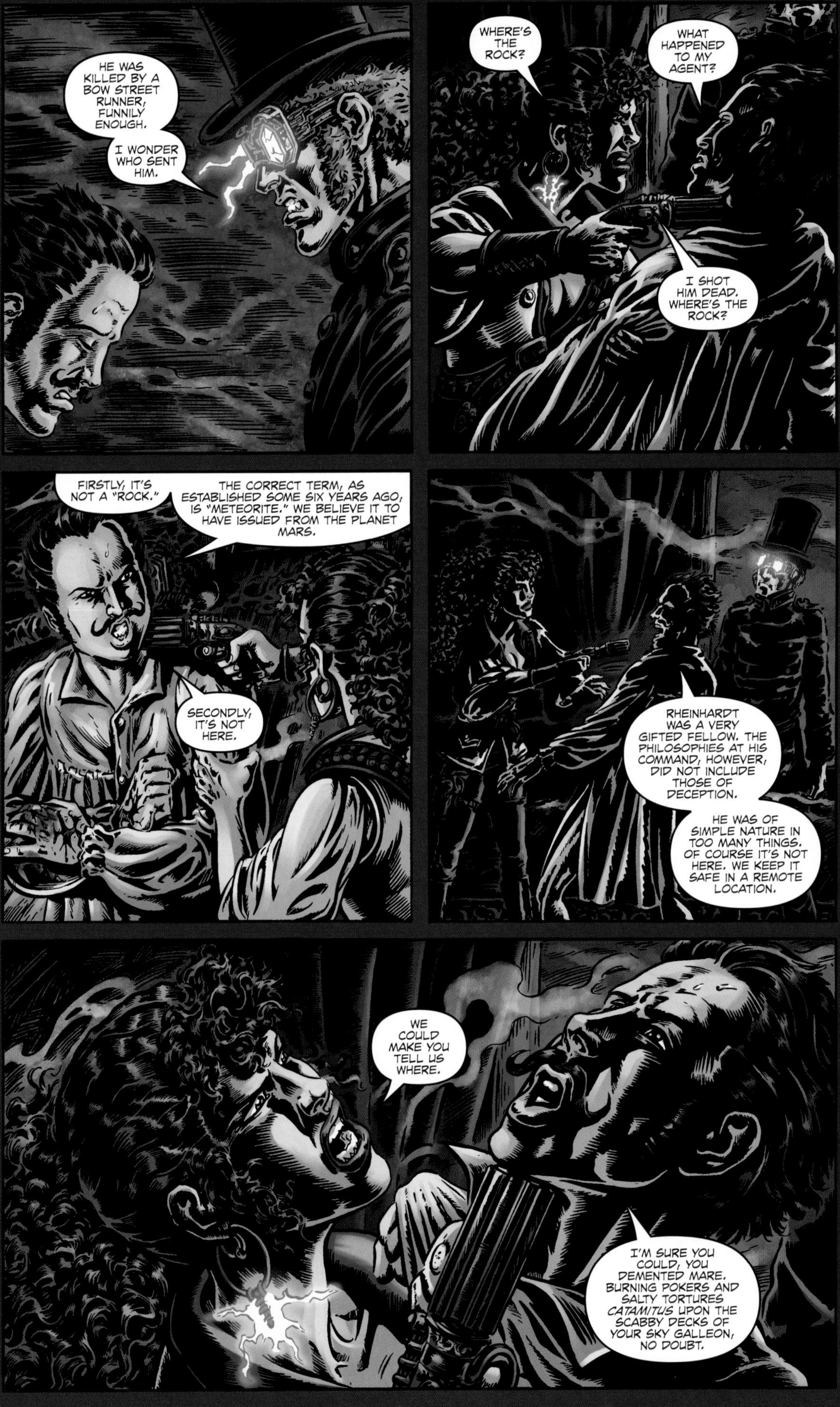
HE WAS KILLED BY A BOW STREET RUNNER, FUNNILY ENOUGH.
I WONDER WHO SENT HIM.
WHERE'S THE ROCK?
WHAT HAPPENED TO MY AGENT?
I SHOT HIM DEAD. WHERE'S THE ROCK?
FIRSTLY, IT'S NOT A "ROCK."
THE CORRECT TERM, AS ESTABLISHED SOME SIX YEARS AGO, IS "METEORITE." WE BELIEVE IT TO HAVE ISSUED FROM THE PLANET MARS.
SECONDLY, IT'S NOT HERE.
RHEINHARDT WAS A VERY GIFTED FELLOW. THE PHILOSOPHIES AT HIS COMMAND, HOWEVER, DID NOT INCLUDE THOSE OF DECEPTION.
HE WAS OF SIMPLE NATURE IN TOO MANY THINGS. OF COURSE IT'S NOT HERE. WE KEEP IT SAFE IN A REMOTE LOCATION.
WE COULD MAKE YOU TELL US WHERE.
I'M SURE YOU COULD, YOU DEMENTED MARE. BURNING POKERS AND SALTY TORTURES *CATAMITUS* UPON THE SCABBY DECKS OF YOUR SKY GALLEON, NO DOUBT.

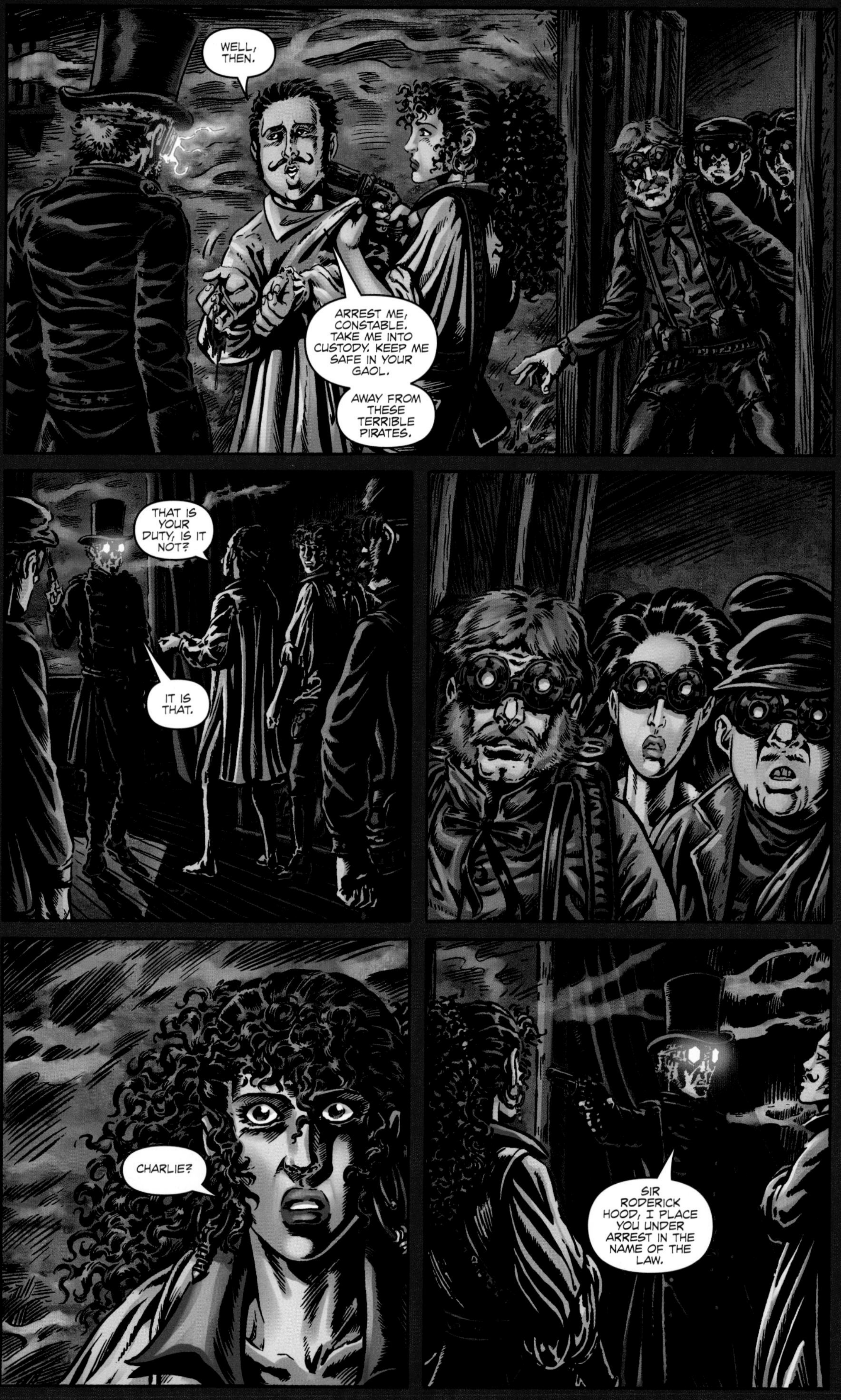
WELL, THEN.
ARREST ME, CONSTABLE. TAKE ME INTO CUSTODY. KEEP ME SAFE IN YOUR GAOL.
AWAY FROM THESE TERRIBLE PIRATES.
THAT IS YOUR DUTY, IS IT NOT?
IT IS THAT.
CHARLIE?
SIR RODERICK HOOD, I PLACE YOU UNDER ARREST IN THE NAME OF THE LAW.

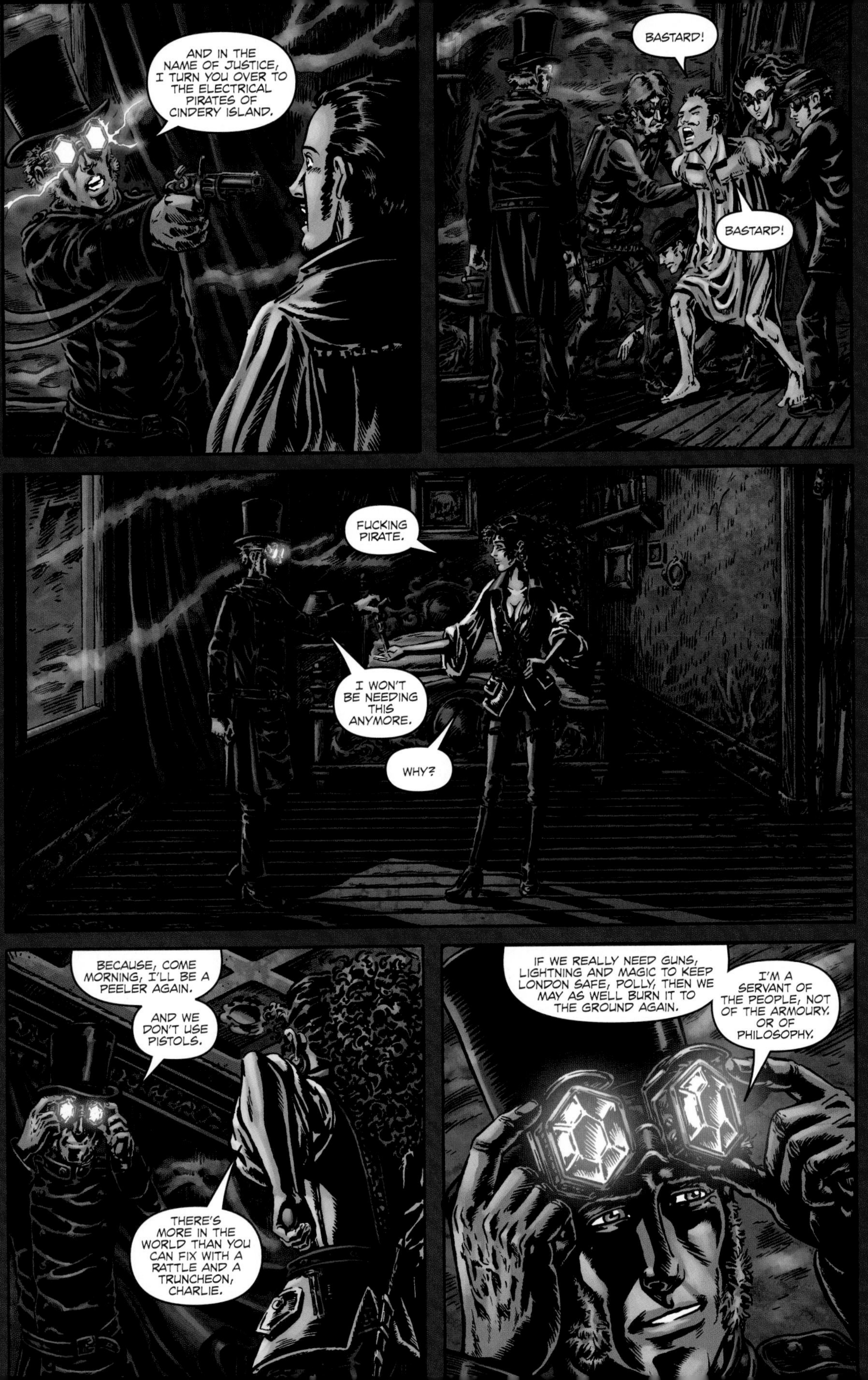
AND IN THE NAME OF JUSTICE, I TURN YOU OVER TO THE ELECTRICAL PIRATES OF CINDERY ISLAND.
BASTARD!
BASTARD!
FUCKING PIRATE.
I WON'T BE NEEDING THIS ANYMORE.
WHY?
BECAUSE, COME MORNING, I'LL BE A PEELER AGAIN.
AND WE DON'T USE PISTOLS.
THERE'S MORE IN THE WORLD THAN YOU CAN FIX WITH A RATTLE AND A TRUNCHEON, CHARLIE.
IF WE REALLY NEED GUNS, LIGHTNING AND MAGIC TO KEEP LONDON SAFE, POLLY, THEN WE MAY AS WELL BURN IT TO THE GROUND AGAIN.
I'M A SERVANT OF THE PEOPLE, NOT OF THE ARMOURY. OR OF PHILOSOPHY.

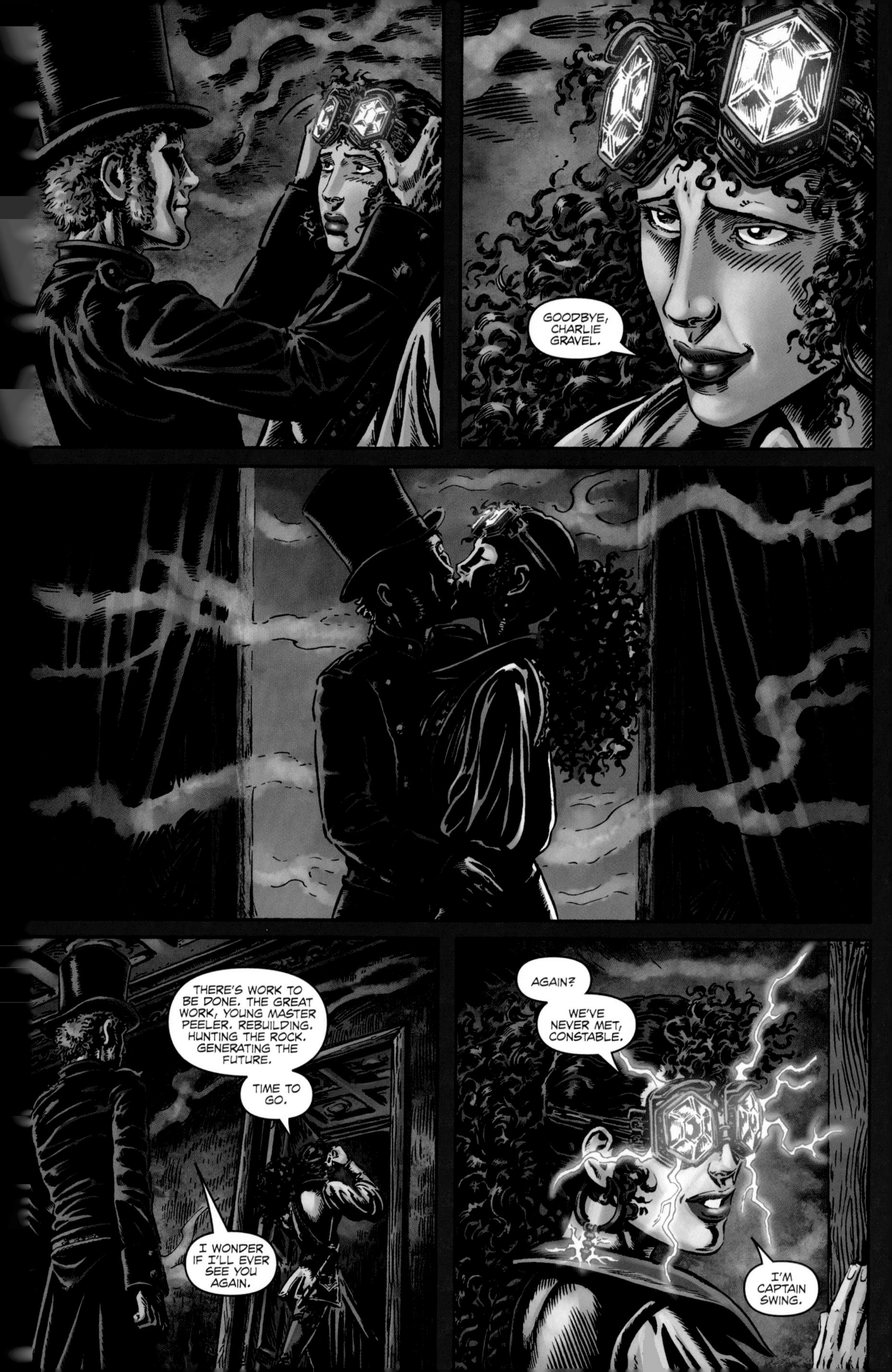
GOODBYE, CHARLIE GRAVEL.
THERE'S WORK TO BE DONE. THE GREAT WORK, YOUNG MASTER PEELER. REBUILDING. HUNTING THE ROCK. GENERATING THE FUTURE.
TIME TO GO.
I WONDER IF I'LL EVER SEE YOU AGAIN.
AGAIN?
WE'VE NEVER MET, CONSTABLE.
I'M CAPTAIN SWING.

Of Charlie Gravel and my dear Polly, I can say no more.

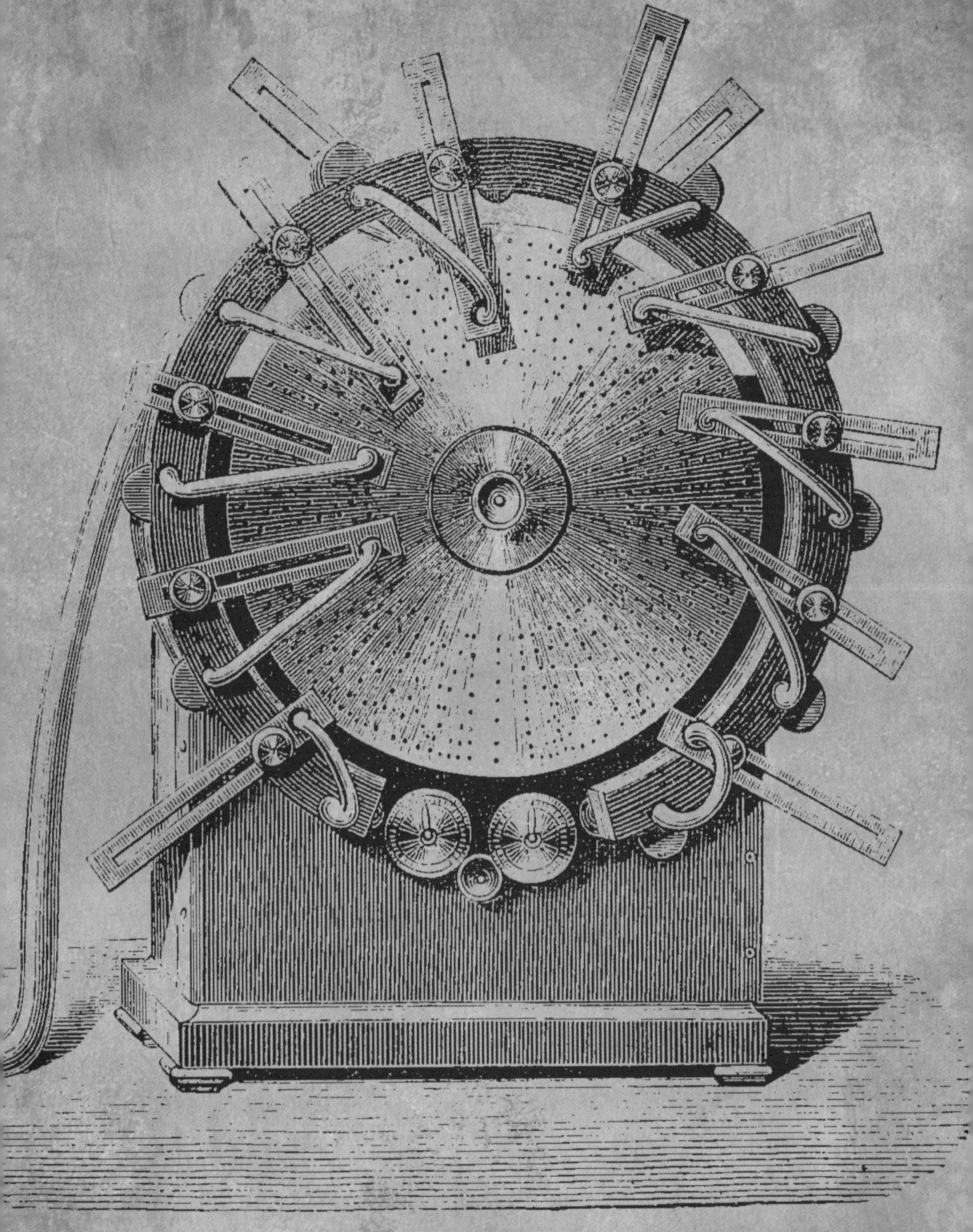

Save that this was not the end of either of their stories, and their lives to come were queerer than even an electrical pirate like myself might have imagined.

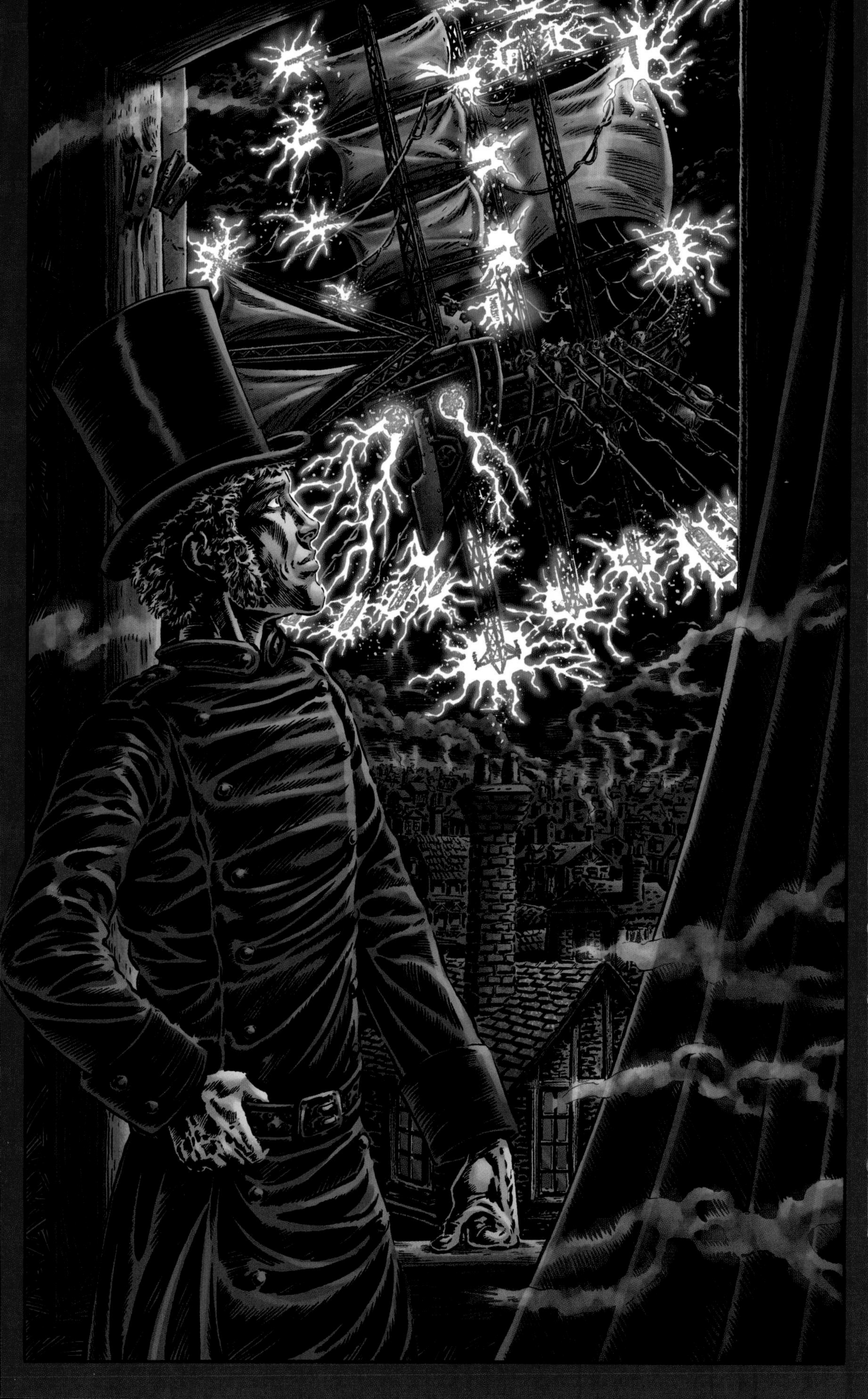

Later that year, there was a spate of riots by farm workers in the south of England who were reduced to starvation by the introduction of machinery that could do their jobs cheaply and tirelessly. They destroyed threshers, burned workhouses and sent manifestos of fiery intent to the landlords and magistrates. These letters were signed: "Captain Swing."

Constable Harry Lewis left the force in 1832, and became a journalist. When, in 1837, reports were made of a strange creature with glowing eyes who assaulted a businessman and then leapt to its escape over a ten-foot wall, there was only one name he could attach to the thing.

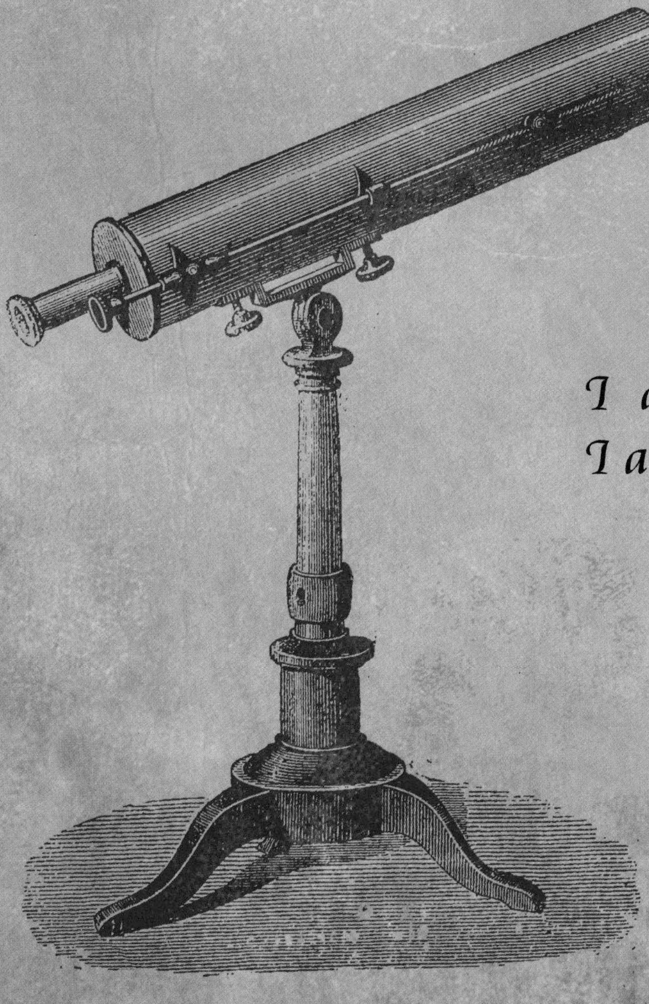

I am Captain Swing.
I am Spring-Heeled Jack.

And I will never die.

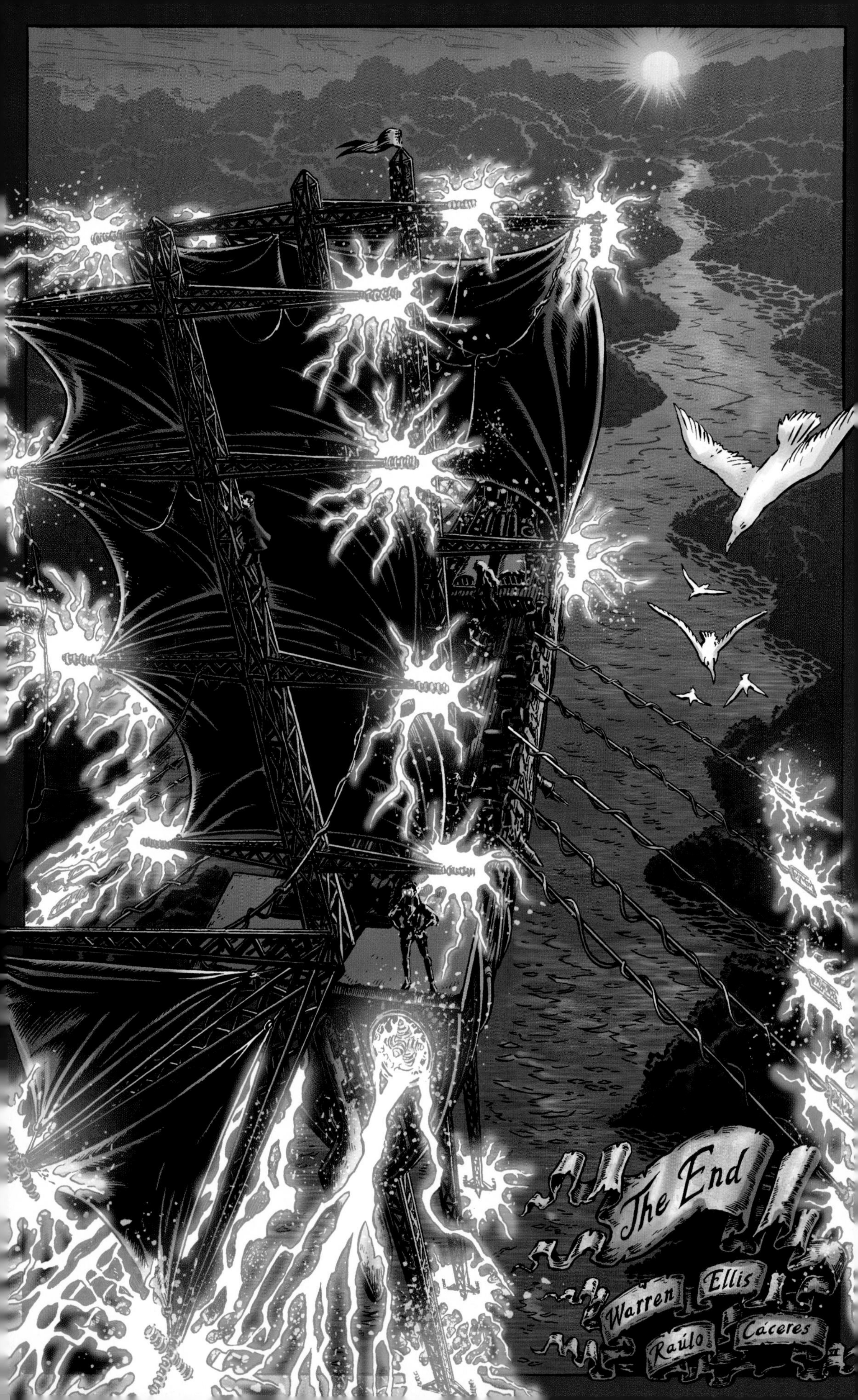
The End
Warren Ellis
Raúlo Cáceres

Captain Swing and the Electrical Pirates of Cindery Island .

Fin

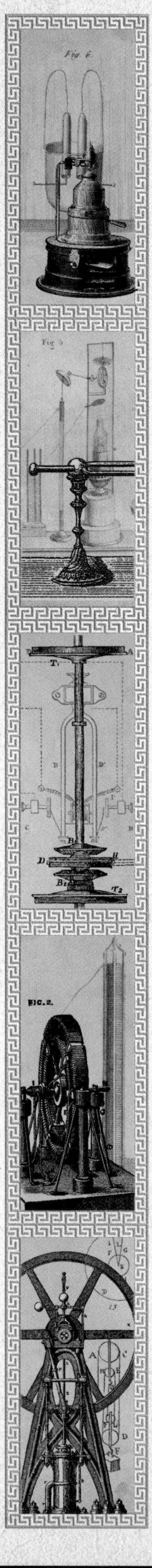

CAPTAIN SWING

and the ELECTRICAL PIRATES OF CINDERY ISLAND

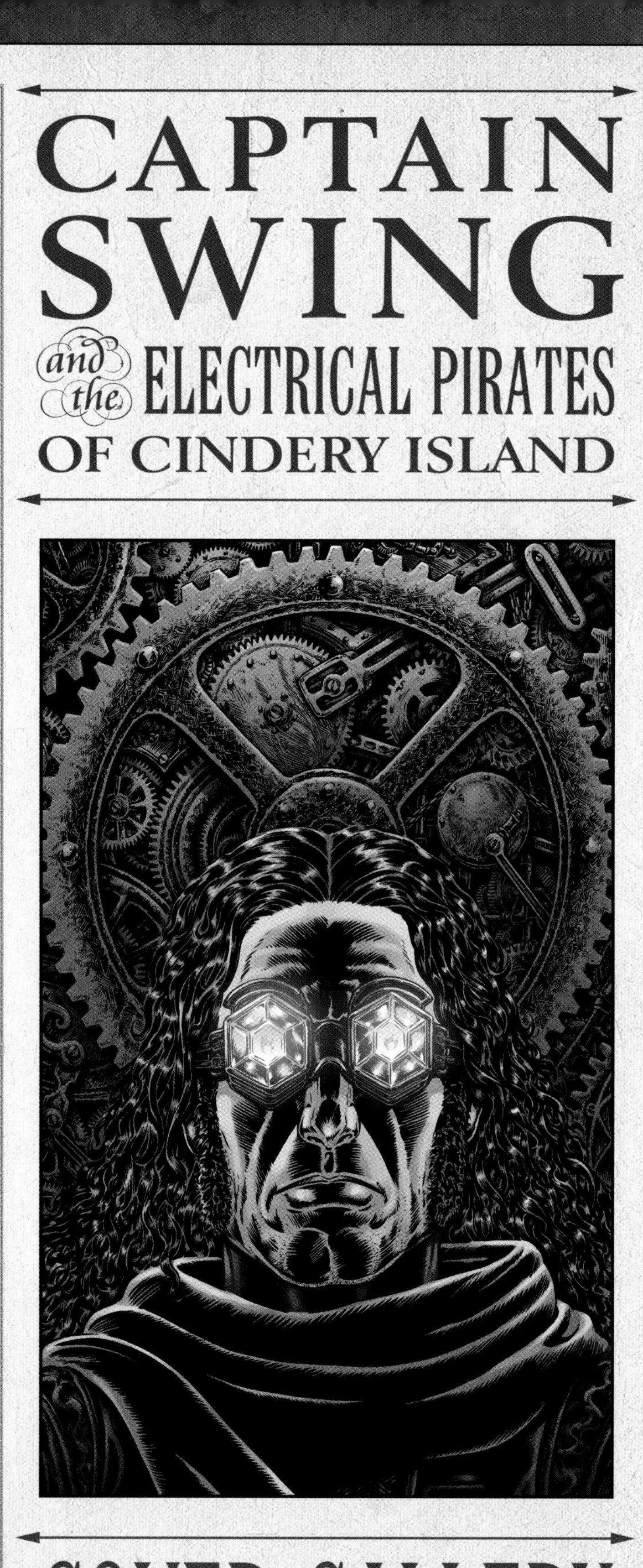

COVER GALLERY

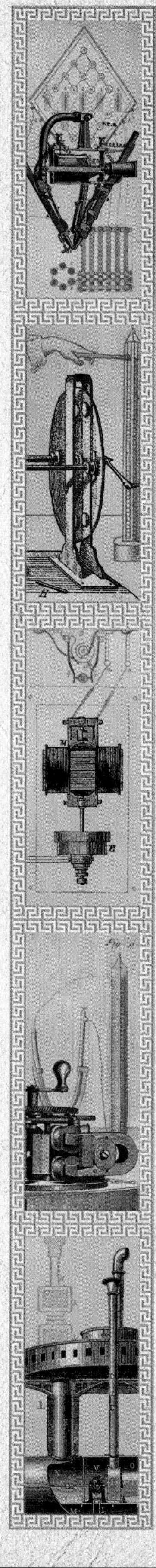

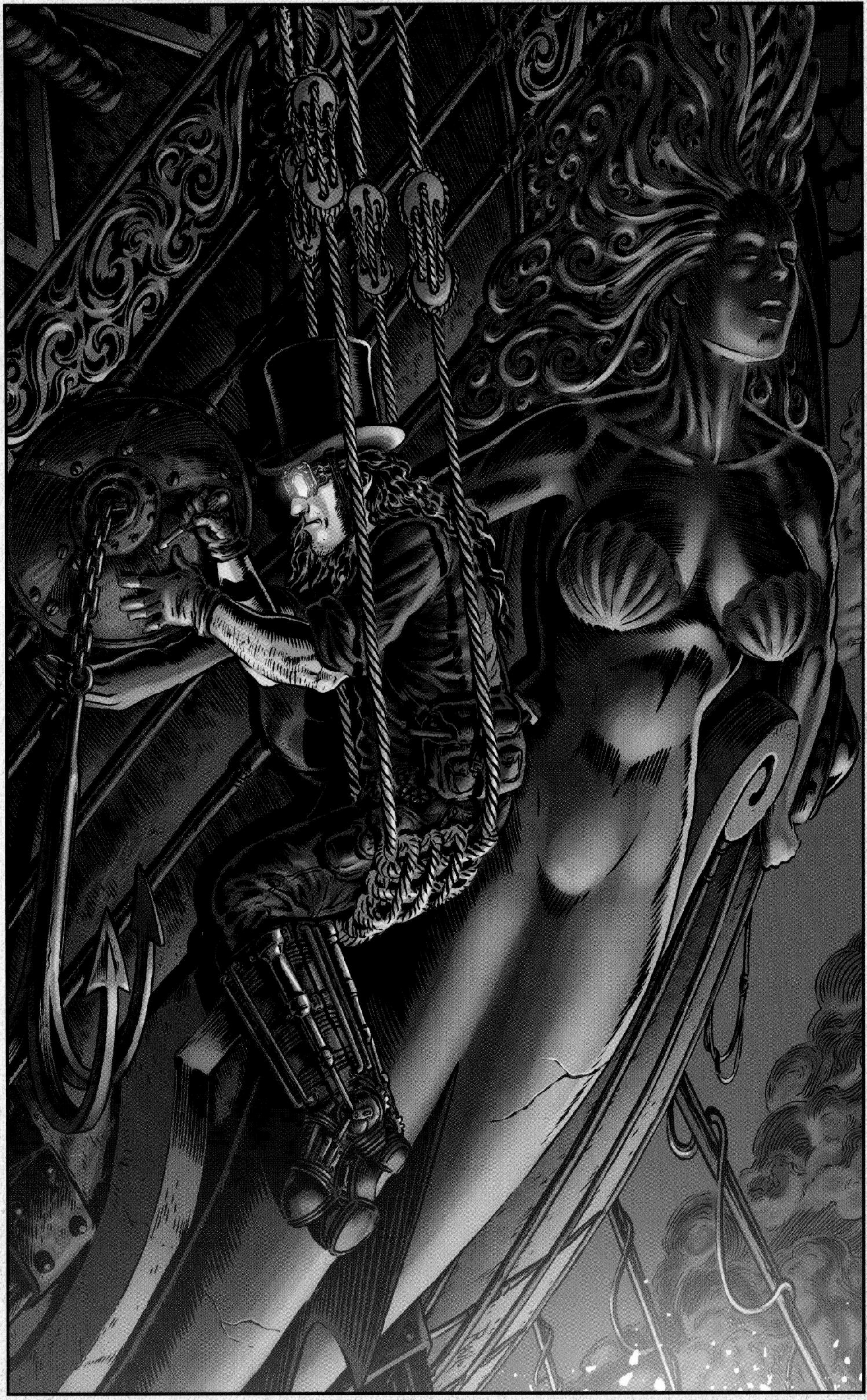

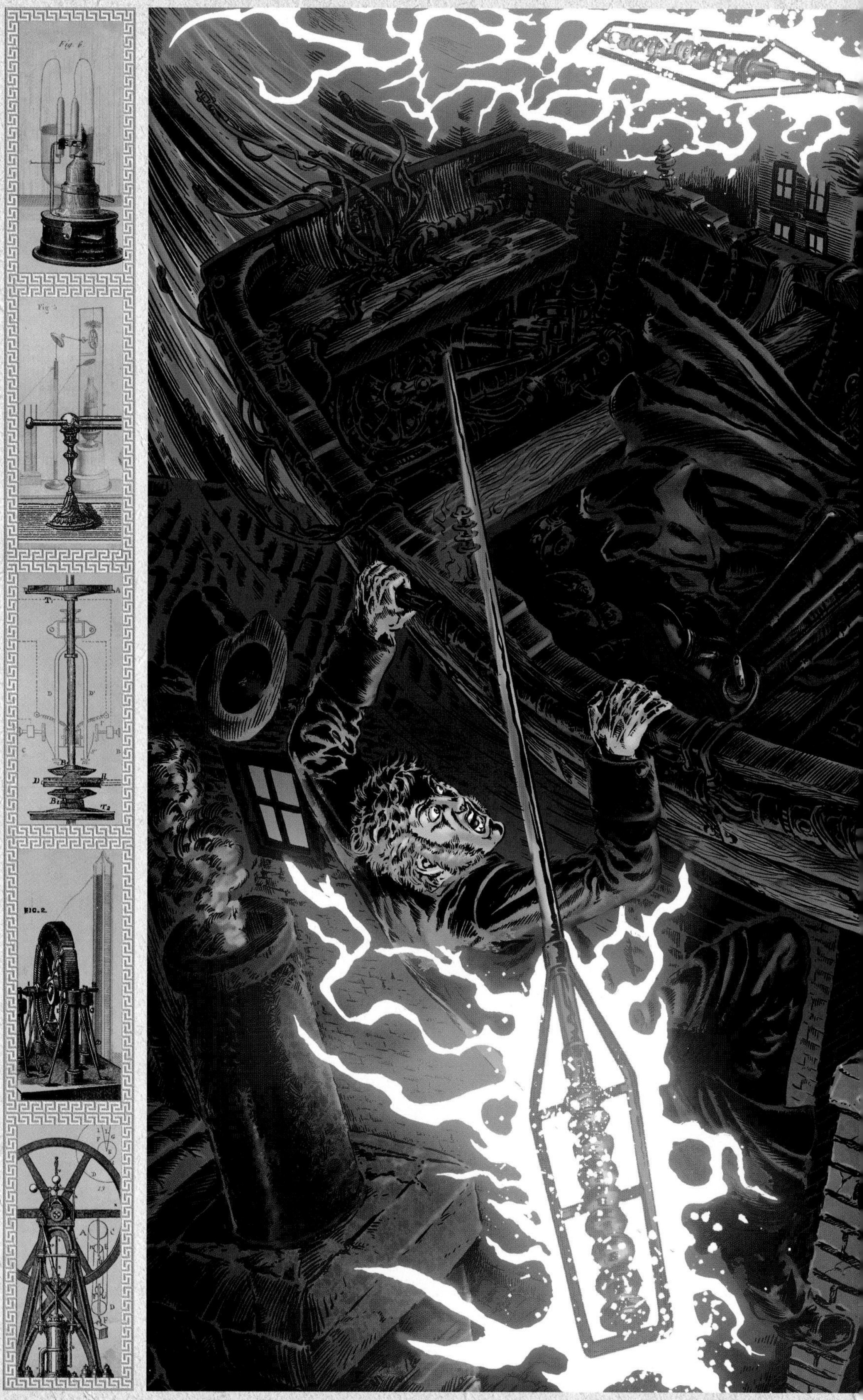
FIG. 2

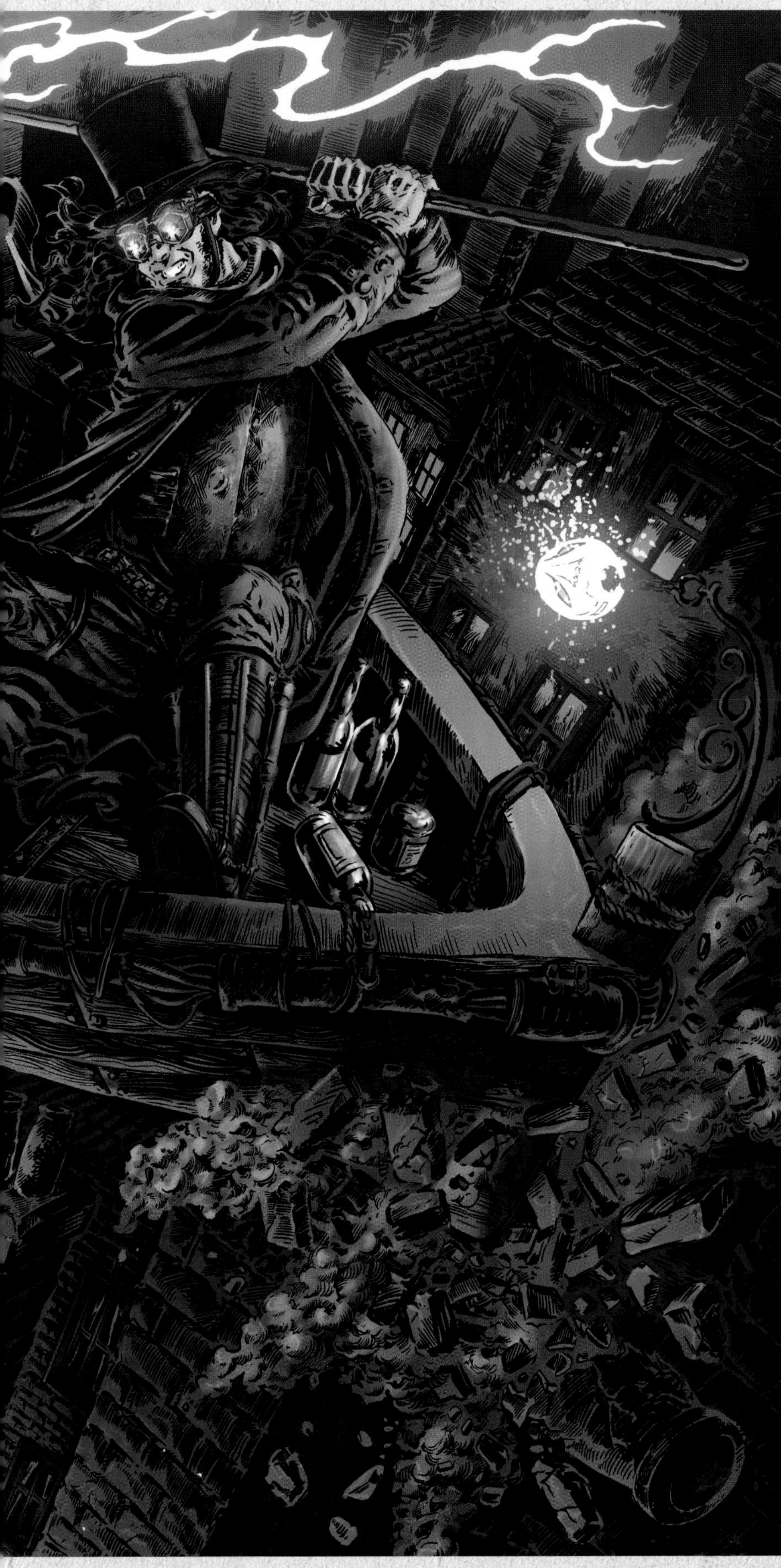

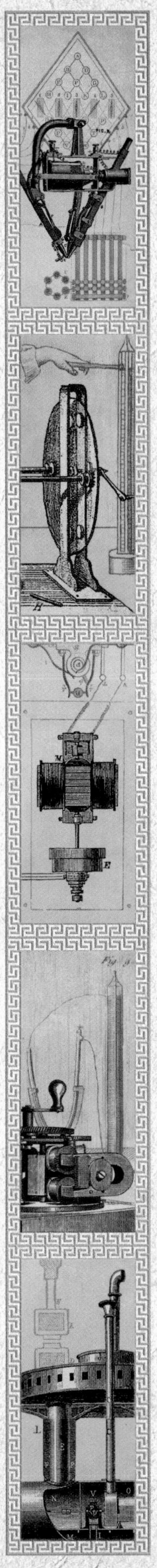

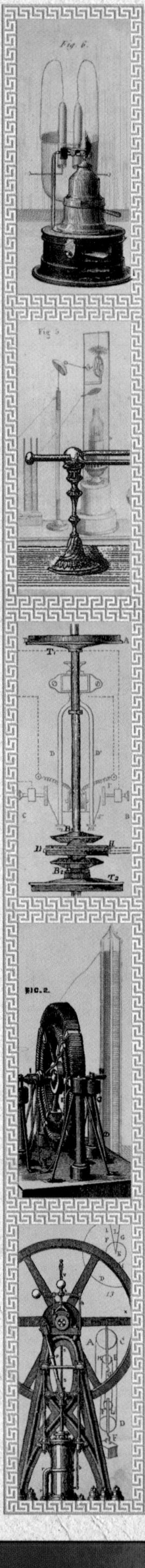
Fig 6.
Fig 5
FIG. 2.
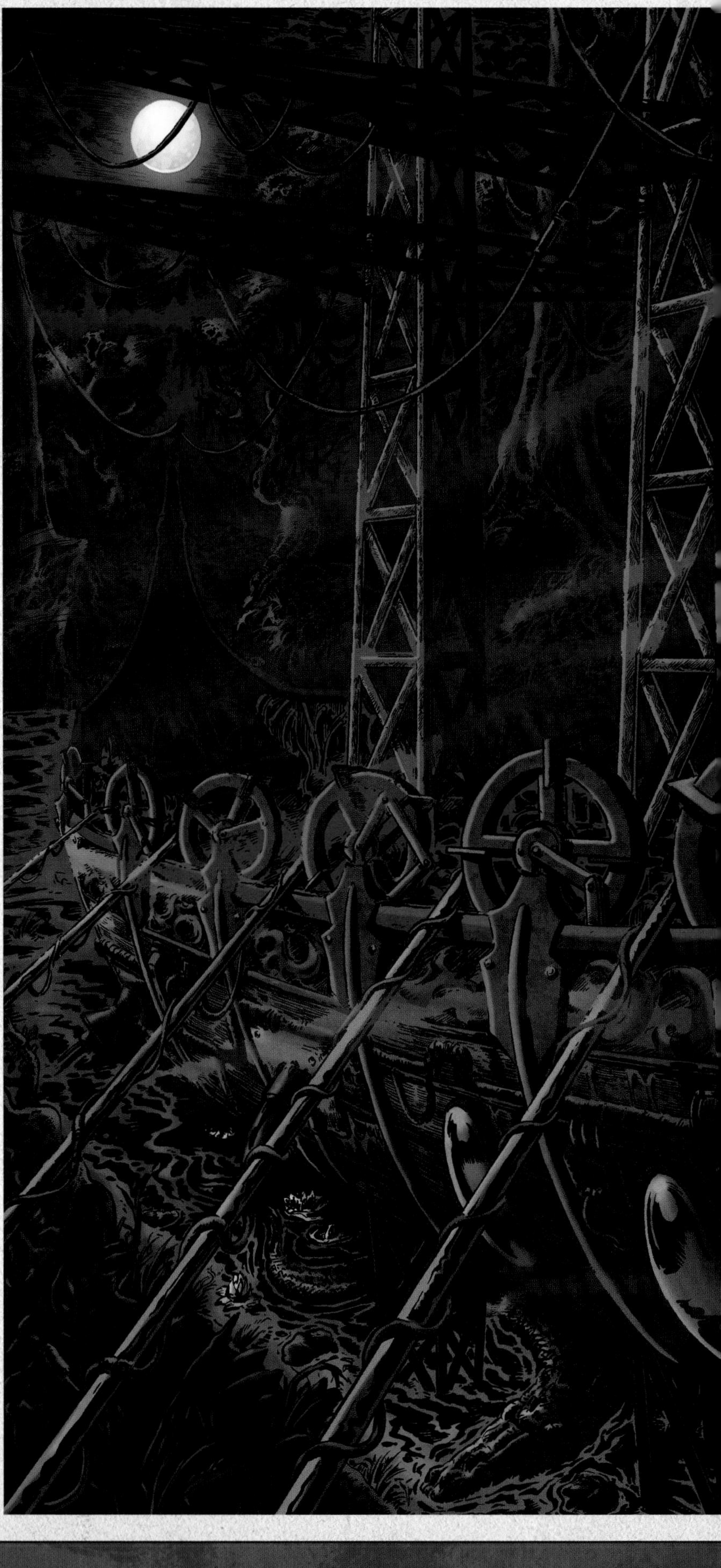

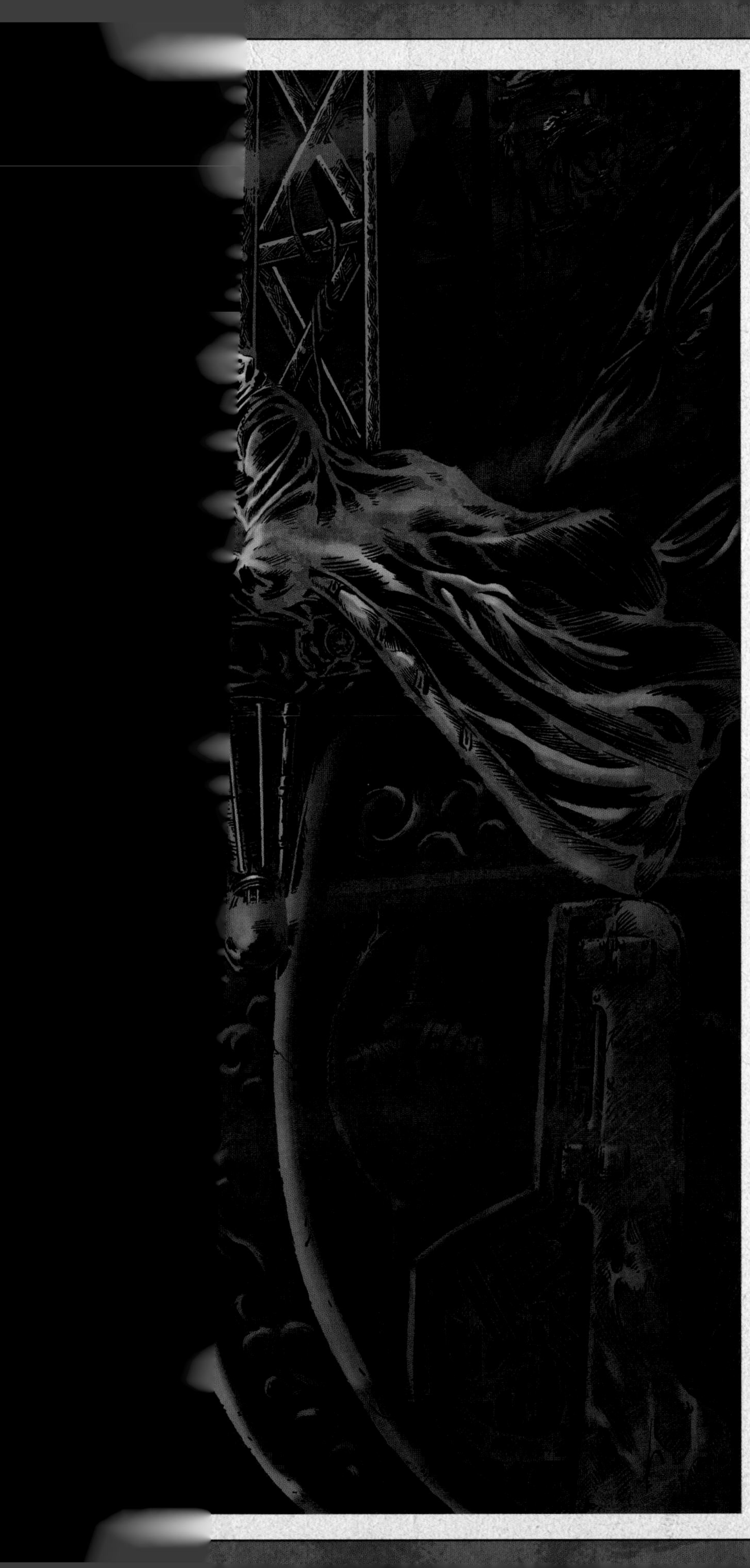
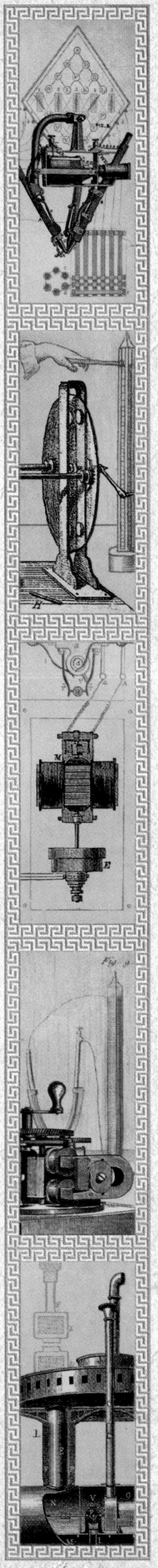

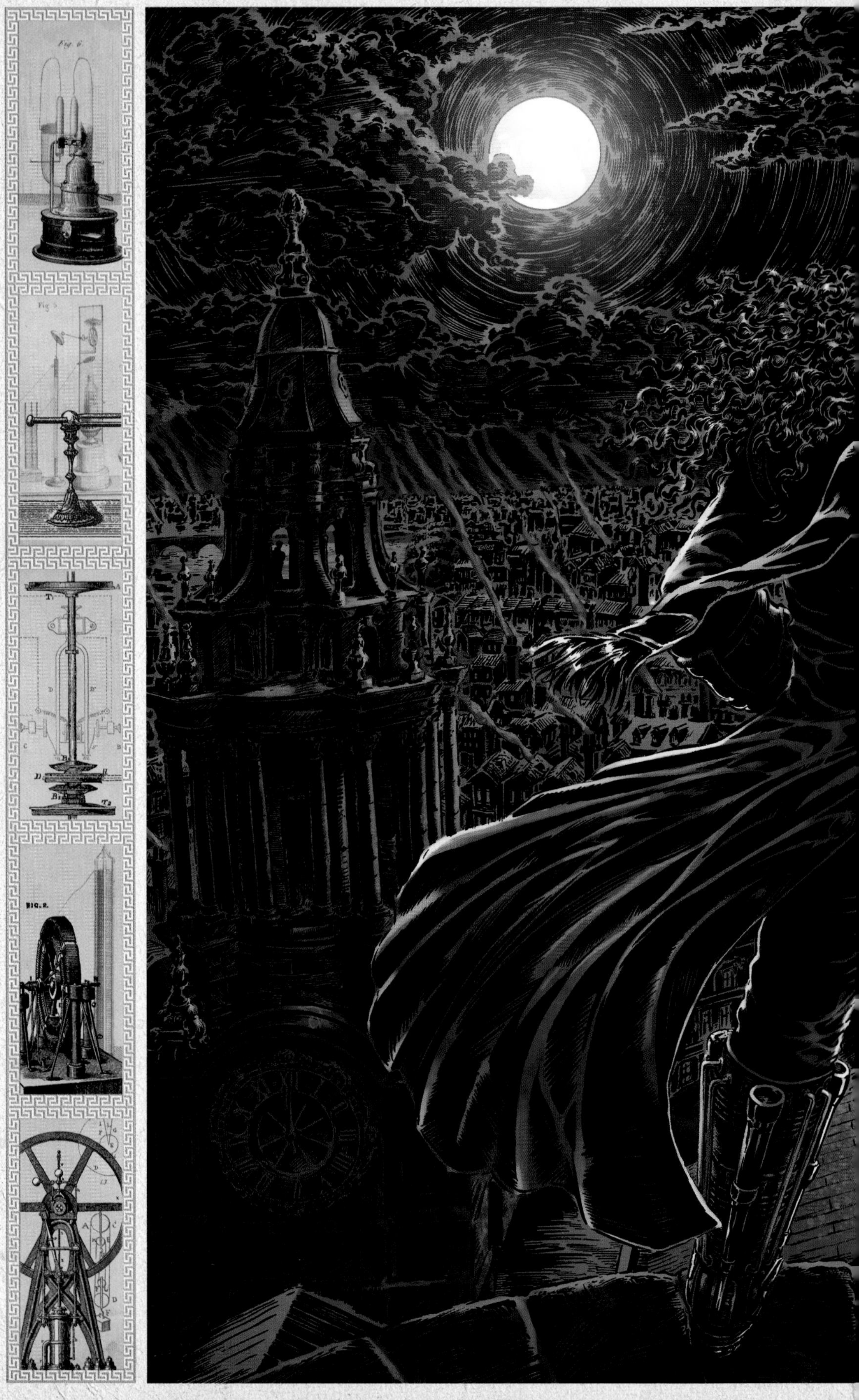

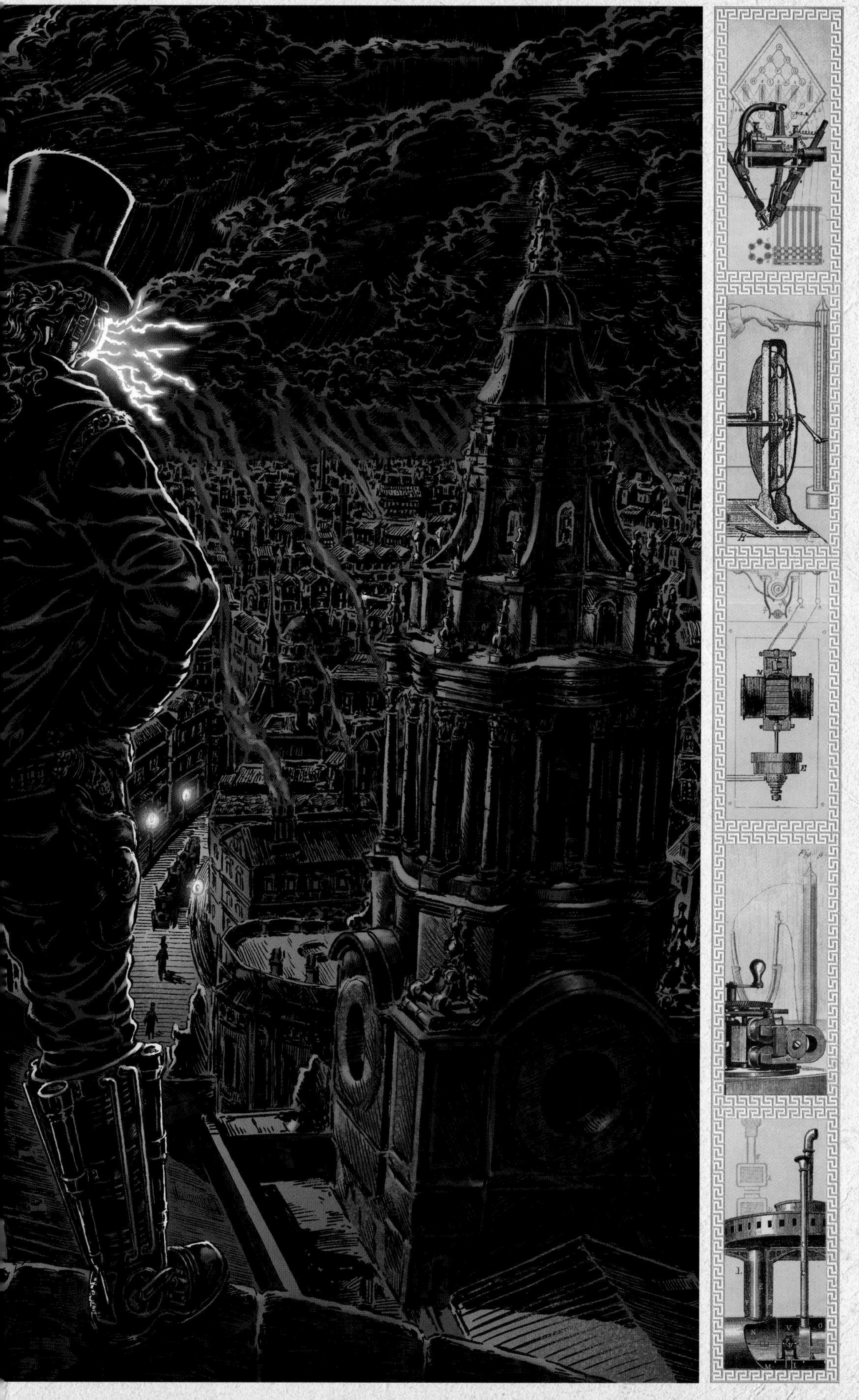

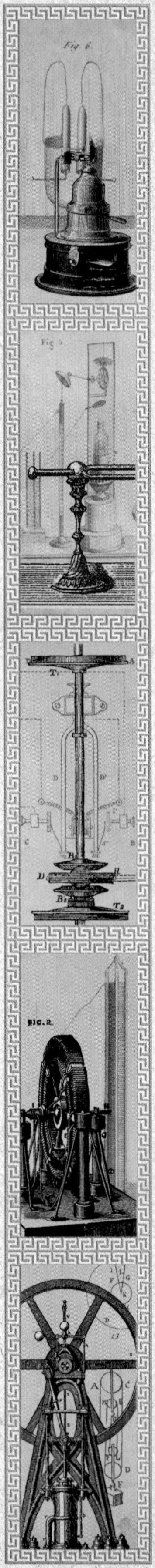

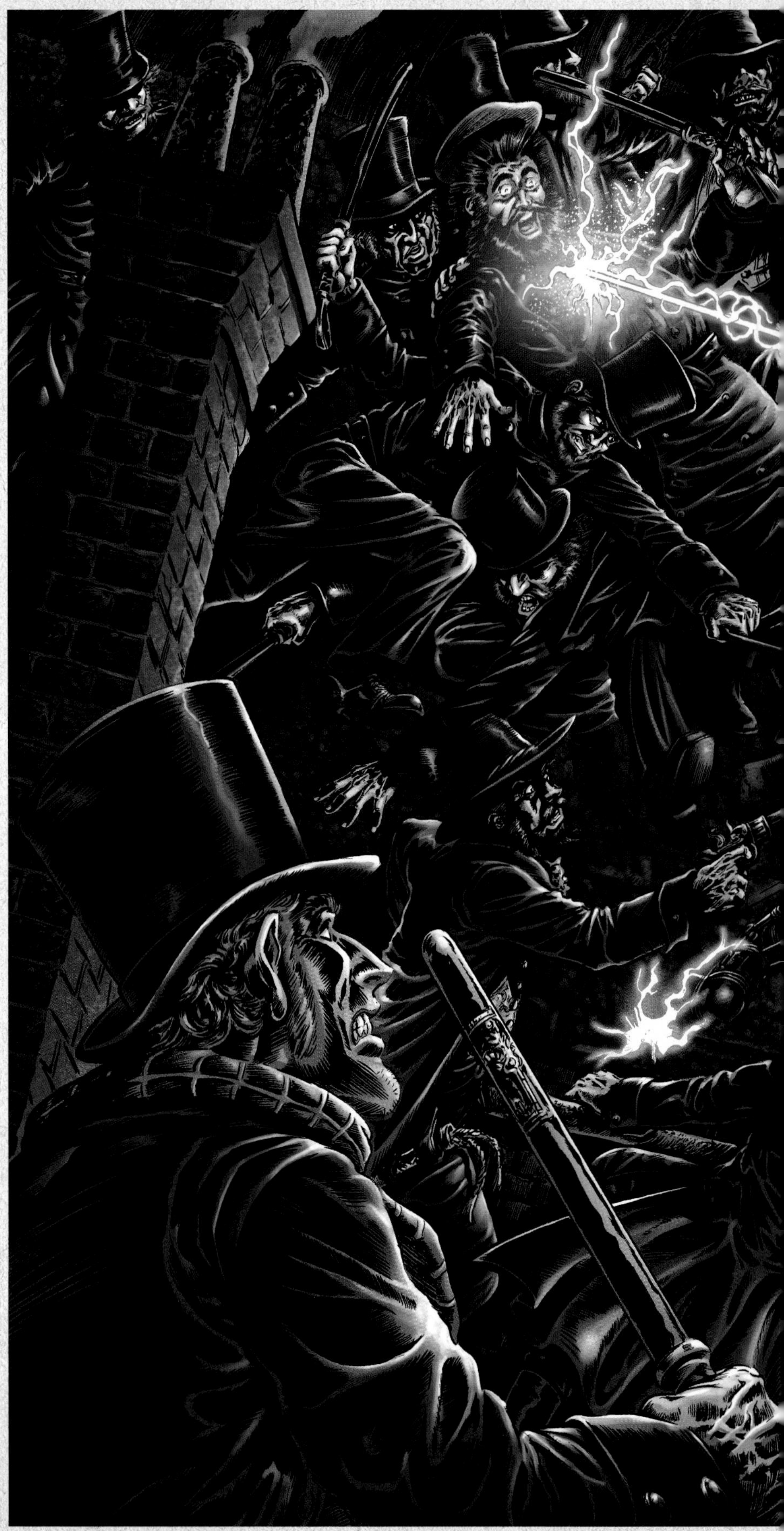

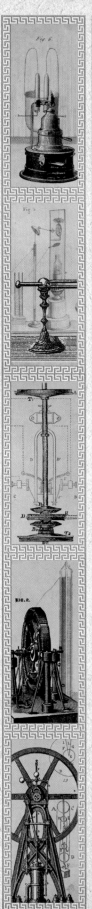

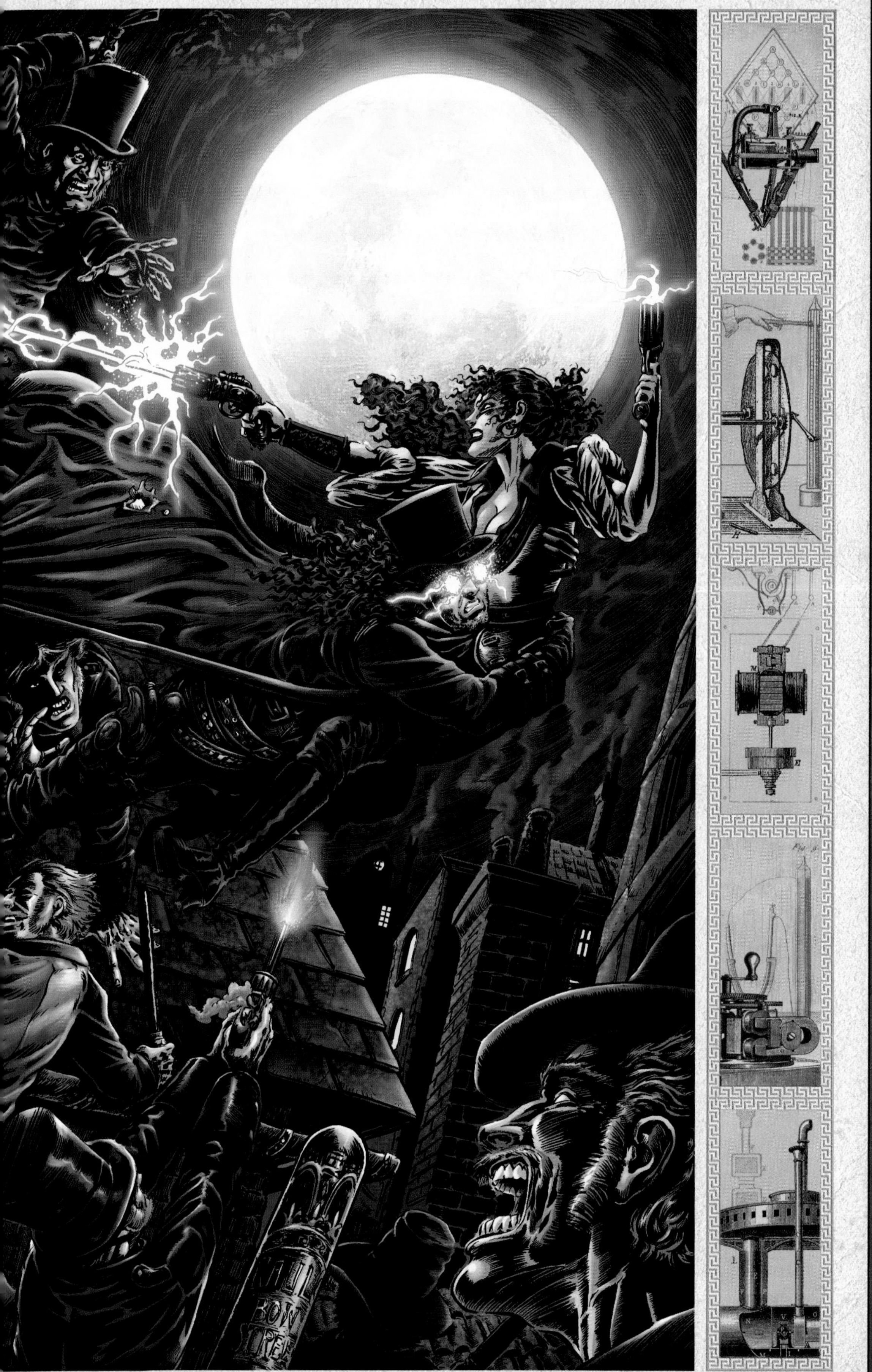